The Legacy of Billy Graham

The Legacy of Billy Graham

Critical Reflections on America's Greatest Evangelist

EDITED BY
MICHAEL G. LONG

Westminster John Knox Press
LOUISVILLE • LONDON

Scripture quotations from the New Revised Standard Version of the Bible are copyright © 1989 by the Division of Christian Education of the National Council of the Churches of Christ in the U.S.A. and are used by permission.

Book design by Sharon Adams
Cover design by designpointinc.com

First edition
Published by Westminster John Knox Press
Louisville, Kentucky

This book is printed on acid-free paper that meets the American National Standards Institute Z39.48 standard. ⊗

PRINTED IN THE UNITED STATES OF AMERICA

08 09 10 11 12 13 14 15 16 17 — 10 9 8 7 6 5 4 3 2 1

Library of Congress Cataloging-in-Publication Data

The legacy of Billy Graham : critical reflections on America's greatest evangelist / edited by Michael G. Long. — 1st ed.
    p. cm.
    ISBN 978-0-664-23138-5 (alk. paper)
  1. Graham, Billy, 1918—Influence.   2. United States—Church history.
3. Evangelists—United States—Biography.   I. Long, Michael G.
  BV3785.G69L44 2008
  269'.2092—dc22   2007031686

Contents

Acknowledgments

It takes courage to evaluate Billy Graham, especially because of his iconic status and age and health, and I am deeply grateful to the first-rank scholars who have dared to write critical chapters for this volume. Their professionalism has been extraordinary, their dedication exemplary, and their work exceptional. If it is true that gathering scholars for an edited volume can at times be like herding cats in a banquet room full of scattering mice, it is no less true that I have found immense pleasure in focusing these scholarly minds and generous hearts on a figure as compelling as Billy Graham.

Jack Keller of Westminster John Knox Press offered early enthusiasm for the book, and I am thankful for his quick reply to my initial inquiry and for his willingness to let me work with Jon Berquist, whose gifts and grace mark him as an editor among editors. My gratitude extends to Julie Tonini, whose professional conscientiousness kept us on track.

My friend Sharon Herr, who can see what I am blind to, proofread the manuscript with her characteristic care, treating the written words almost as lovingly as she reaches out to family, friends, and strangers.

Elizabethtown College, my home institution, granted me the space and time I needed to complete the task at hand, and few individuals have been as supportive of my work as Jeffery Long, the new chair of the religious studies department and a rising scholar in Hindu studies. A special word to the students in my classes on Christianity and politics, who have endured and encouraged my interest in Billy Graham: If I ever accept any offer of tenure that may come my way, I will do so largely because of your interest in the seminar room.

No one has meant more to me in the past decade than Karin, a true companion who makes it easy for me to be in love with her. Thanks for your warmth, Karin, and for being such an amazing mother to Jackson Griffith and Nathaniel Finn.

Our sons are always on the move, and they deserve my hugs and kisses for climbing on my lap and asking me to use the computer for galactic games, peek-a-boo with Elmo, or something, anything, other than a book on Billy Graham.

Contributors

Rufus Burrow Jr. is Indiana Professor of Christian Thought and Professor of Theological Social Ethics at Christian Theological Seminary. He is a leading authority on theological personalism and has recently authored *God and Human Dignity: The Personalism, Theology, and Ethics of Martin Luther King, Jr.*

Mark D. Chapman, Vice-Principal of Ripon College Cuddesdon, Oxford, is a world-renowned expert on church history and historical theology. He is also the acclaimed author of several books, including *Ernst Troeltsch and Liberal Theology: Religion and Cultural Synthesis in Wilhelmine Germany.*

John B. Cobb Jr. has held many positions, including Ingraham Professor of Theology at the Claremont School of Theology, Avery Professor at the Claremont Graduate School, and Visiting Professor at Vanderbilt, Harvard, and Chicago Divinity Schools. He has written many books on process theology and has recently coauthored *The American Empire and the Commonwealth of God: A Political, Economic, Religious Statement.*

Harvey Cox is Hollis Professor of Divinity at Harvard University. An American Baptist minister and prolific author, he has written extensively on religion, culture, and politics. His most recent book is *When Jesus Came to Harvard: Making Moral Choices Today.*

Gary Dorrien is Reinhold Niebuhr Professor of Social Ethics at Union Theological Seminary and Professor of Religion at Columbia University. He is the author of twelve books, including the critically acclaimed trilogy *The Making of American Liberal Theology*.

Heather Murray Elkins is Professor of Worship, Preaching, and the Arts at Drew Theological School and The Graduate Division of Religion at Drew University. Her most recent book is *The Holy Stuff of Life: Stories, Poems, and Prayers about Human Things*.

Leslie C. Griffin, the inaugural holder of the Larry and Joanne Doherty Chair in Legal Ethics at the University of Houston Law Center, has just authored *Law and Religion: Cases and Materials*.

Karen Lebacqz is the Robert Gordon Sproul Professor Emerita of Theological Ethics at the Pacific School of Religion. An expert in the ethics of stem cell research, she has authored or edited books in medical ethics, professional ethics, and Christian social ethics, including *Sexuality: A Reader*.

Thomas G. Long is Bandy Professor of Preaching at the Candler School of Theology at Emory University. His thirteen books include a second edition of *The Witness of Preaching*.

Ellen Ott Marshall, Associate Professor of Ethics at Claremont School of Theology, has written *Though the Fig Tree Does Not Blossom: Toward a Responsible Theology of Christian Hope*.

Steven P. Miller received a PhD in history from Vanderbilt University in 2006. His forthcoming book, tentatively titled *The Politics of Decency: Billy Graham, Evangelicalism, and the End of the Solid South*, will be published by the University of Pennsylvania Press.

Douglas Sturm is Professor Emeritus of Religion and Political Science at Bucknell University. He has authored several books on religion and politics, including *Belonging Together: Faith and Politics in a Relational World*.

Mark Lewis Taylor, the Maxwell M. Upson Professor of Theology and Culture at Princeton Theological Seminary, has recently written *Religion, Politics, and the Christian Right: Post-9/11 Powers and American Empire*.

J. Philip Wogaman is Professor Emeritus of Christian Social Ethics at Wesley Theological Seminary, a leader in several denominational and ecumenical organizations, and author of many books, including *Christian Perspectives on Politics*.

Introduction

Taking Billy Graham Seriously

MICHAEL G. LONG

"People forget that I am totally nonpartisan and that I do not take sides polit-ically." It was little more than a year into the Nixon presidency, Billy Graham was making another appearance on *The Dick Cavett Show*, and this time the audience members were deeply cynical. They were so cynical of Graham's claim to nonpartisanship that they laughed out loud. Cavett refused to join the chorus of guffaws, but he added his own characteristically wry commentary. "Yep," he said.[1]

Fast-forward thirty-five years to the 2005 New York crusade.

No one is laughing anymore, and no one is making wry comments—we are just surprised. After all those years of robustness—his strong chin cutting through the night air, his blue eyes gazing heavenward, his lean physique sym-bolizing the muscularity of evangelical Christianity—Billy Graham has finally become the "Lord's lion in winter."[2]

How shocked we are to see that the Billy Graham of the Nixon years—the defiant defender—has become an elderly man in need of a walker.

It seems disrespectful to criticize one who seems so frail, and the national media, hardened as they may be in this post-Watergate era, seem to bow their heads and pay homage to America's ailing evangelist. There are no hard ques-tions about his past, and the few times journalists do ask him about his damn-ing Nixon-era comments on Jews, they just sit back and give him all the time he needs to explain himself.[3] As Graham historian Steven Miller notes, the media have come to lionize this lion in winter.[4]

Perhaps Billy Graham deserves such respect. He has overcome so many things—the racism of the South where he was as a child, his virulent anti-communism, his intricate descriptions of heaven above, his unholy alliance with Nixon. And he has accomplished so much more—leading millions to faith and good works, traveling behind the Iron Curtain, helping Lyndon Johnson gain successful passage of antipoverty legislation, counseling Nixon to move beyond bitterness, pushing for nuclear treaties in the Reagan era, offering healing words to our broken hearts on September 11, 2001. If any lion in winter deserves our respect, surely it is Billy Graham.

Fast-forward again, this time to 2007.

As I put the finishing touches on this book, Billy Graham is still with us. He no longer preaches at crusades, and he receives regular medical treatment for swelling of the brain, not to mention numerous other ailments. There is a quietness that now surrounds Graham as he sits in his rocker atop the mountains of rural North Carolina—the type of serenity possessed by elderly politicians who have lived through one national crisis after another and who have resigned themselves, with all their acquired wisdom, to life far from the national stage they once commanded. For so many years a legend in the making, Billy Graham has finally become a legend of epic proportion—the elderly statesman of Protestant Christianity. Perhaps he is the last of the church fathers.

The serenity of Graham's latter days is all the more striking when we turn on our televisions and hear his fellow evangelists condemning Islam, blaming gays and lesbians for the terrorism we now face, and suggesting that God will harshly judge towns that refuse to include creationism in their school curriculum. By comparison, Graham seems so level-headed, so mainstream, so quiet. "He's not so bad when you look at everyone else who's out there now," said William Sloane Coffin Jr. after I had invited him, shortly before he died, to contribute to this book.

Graham's moderation—his diplomatic evangelicalism—might be part of the reason that Christian theologians have been reluctant to criticize him in recent years. Add in the factors of his age and personal growth, and the case against assessing his life and ministry seems all the more compelling.

But reluctance to criticize Billy Graham is not new. Not since Reinhold Niebuhr publicly lambasted the evangelist during the 1957 New York crusade has a leading Christian theologian granted significant critical attention to the ministry of Billy Graham. Radical Baptist Will Campbell joined other prophetic types in denouncing Graham's quietism during the Nixon and Vietnam eras, but this opposition came in the form of occasional counterpoints rather than as systematic assessments of strengths and weaknesses. After Niebuhr's articles, the most important critical work on Graham was a book written by religious historian William McLoughlin—and that was in 1960.

Graham's harshest critics have always been the Christian fundamentalists whose separatist ways he left far behind as he wove in and out of the corridors of worldly power. In their own sheltered ways, they continue to be loud. By contrast, Graham's most appreciative supporters have come from the evangelical community, and in their own well-publicized ways, they continue to speak loving words about their evangelist.

But since Niebuhr and McLoughlin, Christian theologians outside the fundamentalist and evangelical communities have largely dismissed Billy Graham as unworthy of critical engagement. They may be respectful of Graham, but many of these theologians consider him anachronistic—a leftover from premodern Christianity, an uneducated preacher who made good by slapping the backs of politicians, an Elmer Gantry with deep personal piety. Niebuhr set the tone for this dismissive wave of hand. An urban, educated snobbishness ran through his commentary on the evangelist, and many theologians have since inherited and embraced this type of snobbishness, even as the wider world lionizes him at this point in his life.

The lionizing, demonizing, and snobbishness are all unfortunate—and terribly unfair. Billy Graham deserves much better, and it is time that we take him seriously.

No Christian minister, after all, has been more influential in global politics, economics, and faith in the twentieth century, for good or ill, than Billy Graham. While theologians have been writing about and for themselves, Graham has been strategizing in the Oval Office, meeting with global business and labor leaders, and advising politicians during world conflicts, all the while preaching Christ crucified to hundreds of millions of individuals who know little if anything about Christian theology—postmodern, postcolonial, or postimperial. The cultural influence of Billy Graham simply has no equal as we head into this new century. To be sure, every now and then a Christian theologian or minister will make national news, but it is the name of Billy Graham that is seared in the hearts and minds of millions of women and men—powerful and lowly—across the entire globe.

The purpose of this book is to take Billy Graham seriously—to acknowledge his historical significance, finally, and embrace him as more than worthy of critical engagement by the brightest Christian thinkers of our day. Treating him as a serious figure, rather than as a mere caricature, will require exploring the strengths and weaknesses of his lifelong ministry, and as this book seeks to answer questions rarely asked—for example, Was Billy Graham right about theology and preaching, politics and economics, feminism and sex, war and peace, race and power?—it will set a tone that is both appreciative and critical. If there is anything clear about Billy Graham, it is that there are reasons galore for recognizing the immense value of his ministry and, at the same time, for refusing to grant him iconic status. Like all of us, Billy Graham is both saint and sinner, and if we are to treat him fairly and understand his legacy fully, we will refuse to lionize or demonize him.

Assessing his ministry is important not only for grasping his real legacy but also for moving into a future without Billy Graham to guide us as clearly as he has. Is there a better path than the one Graham has laid out for us as we begin to make our way through the twenty-first century? Many of the contributors to this book—progressive Christian theologians—think so, and while expressing appreciation for Graham, they will also encourage us to leave behind his faults and take up a Christianity that embraces critical biblical scholarship and opposes a faith, politics, or economics that is more easily aligned with the interests of the powerful than with the needs of those on society's margins.

There is no lionizing in the pages ahead, but neither are there dismissive laughs. Billy Graham deserves so much better—and so do we as we move into an uncertain future without his clarity.

NOTES

1. *The Dick Cavett Show*, May 5, 1970, ABC. The Nixon White House tracked and recorded some of Graham's television appearances. A copy of this show is referenced as WHCA 3704 at the National Archives in College Park (NARA).
2. "Billy Graham: Lord's Lion in Winter," *Newsweek* online interview with Jon Meacham, August 6, 2006, http://www.msnbc.msn.com/id/14206390/site/newsweek/?bctid=182654595.
3. Graham spoke of a "stranglehold" that he believed Jews had over the United States. "A lot of the Jews are great friends of mine," he added. "They swarm around me and are friendly to me, because they know that I'm friendly to Israel and so forth. But they don't know how I really feel about what they're doing to this country, and I have no power and no way to handle them. But I would stand up under proper circumstances" (White House Tape 662-4, February 1, 1972, NARA).
4. Steven P. Miller, "Billy Graham: Have Journalists Given Us an Accurate Picture?" *History News Network*, June 12, 2006, http://hnn.us/articles/25521.html.

Preaching and Theology

1

Preaching the Good News

THOMAS G. LONG

Assessing the religious and cultural impact of Billy Graham is, to a significant degree, a matter of measuring his impact as a preacher. For over sixty years, under tents and tabernacles, in stadiums and arenas, and on radio and television, Graham has been preaching, and in many ways the instrument of the sermon has been his single most palpable form of ministry, his most prominent and powerful means of public expression. Even his best-selling books and his syndicated newspaper columns are, in effect, retooled sermons. Unlike the apostle Paul, preaching his way through the Mediterranean world, Graham has been no founder of churches. Unlike Savonarola, who sailed on the power of his sermonic rhetoric into political power in Florence, Graham has never aspired to office. Unlike Billy Sunday, railing out against the saloons and the gin mills, Graham has not focused his ministry on a white-hot agenda of social reform. Graham has been an evangelist, a preacher to souls, pure and simple.

By the best estimates, Graham has preached to more people than any other preacher in history—more than 210 million people in over 185 countries. His sermons have been broadcast, recorded, archived, scrutinized, and held up as exemplars of the craft. Yet for all the ballyhoo about Graham being the quintessential American preacher, his sermons are, in fact, anomalies on the American preaching scene. Over the six decades of Graham's ministry, the American sermon has been fashioned and refashioned by such forces as neo-orthodoxy, narrative theology, the reforms of Vatican II, the therapeutic culture, liberation and feminist thought, and the electronic communication revolution, but

3

Graham's sermons have remained curiously untouched by any of this. To be sure, his cultural references have changed—from illustrations about Mickey Mantle to stories about Bono and Madonna—but his sermons, theologically and methodologically, have remained essentially the same from the Los Angeles revival of 1949 to the Flushing Meadows crusade of 2005, a still point in the moving homiletical universe.

THE ROOTS OF GRAHAM'S PREACHING

At age sixteen Billy Graham was dramatically changed—he would say "converted"—during a November 1934 Charlotte, North Carolina, revival conducted by the rough and ready itinerant Kentucky evangelist Mordecai Ham. A sensationalist and a provocateur, Ham, as he conducted revivals in southern hamlets, villages, and towns, often attracted crowds through carnival theatrics. His favorite technique was to inquire in each new place about the most notorious local sinners and atheists and then to issue pugnacious challenges to them by name from the pulpit. Ham was a vigorous, physical preacher, strutting across the stage and stirring up strong emotional responses, and it was not uncommon for his evangelistic services to be tinged with the threat of violence from those who were the targets of his sharp tongue.

Graham adopted as his own much of what he experienced in Ham's preaching, beginning with Ham's athletic style of delivery. Until illness and age subdued him, Graham was always a fiery and physically dramatic speaker, particularly in his earliest days as an evangelist. A reporter listening to him preach at a Houston revival in the 1950s observed that Graham "repeatedly banged his fists on the pulpit, clenched them in symbolic anguish against his temples, and swept the huge stadium with a punctuating forefinger."[1] Also commenting on his early style of delivery, William G. McLoughlin Jr. says of Graham, "As he retells the old Biblical stories of heroes, villains, and saints, he imitates their voices, assumes their postures, struts, gesticulates, crouches and sways to play each part."[2]

Graham's critics have sometimes ridiculed his hyperkinetic delivery as "Christian vaudeville,"[3] and, as he matured and became more prominent, Graham pulled back a bit on the histrionics. Though still a charismatic and physically active speaker, as he aged, he spoke with a more measured pace and more moderated use of his body. Some of this was no doubt due to the influence of his wife, Ruth, who, as a Presbyterian, never warmed to her husband's more frenetic sermons. "As an actor . . . I'm afraid he is pretty much a ham," she said. "When he starts that kind of acting sermon, I usually start to squirm. . . . Afterward, I'll say, 'Bill, Jesus didn't act out the gospel. He just preached it. I think that's all he has called you to do.'"[4]

Also, Graham has, throughout his career, preached a variation of the simple, even simplistic, twofold sin-and-redemption formula employed by Ham and by other "mass evangelists," such as the ex-baseball player turned evangelist Billy Sunday: first, present human sin in vivid, accusatory, and perhaps even lurid language, and second, summon the hearers, with equal passion, to open themselves to the rescuing, saving power of Jesus Christ. The night Graham heard Ham preach, his first words to the crowd were, "There's a great sinner in this place tonight." Graham later confided to his friend Grady Wilson, who was sitting beside him at the meeting, that he heard those words as if they had been addressed to him personally. "Mother's been telling him about me," Graham thought. Ham's direct appeal to a sinful and guilty self was what transformed Graham that cool, November night, and it is the approach Graham has sustained in his own preaching to this day.

Another characteristic of Ham's approach that has carried over into Graham's sermons is his antiecclesial bias, again a stock-in-trade theme for Billy Sunday and other revivalists. For Ham, participation in the church was at best irrelevant, and at worst antithetical, to a personal relationship to God through Christ, which could be established and maintained without the props of formal creed or communion. The teenaged Billy Graham who felt the effects of Ham's sweaty appeal was no wastrel or reprobate but a youth leader in a Charlotte, North Carolina, Presbyterian congregation. But those commitments would have been dismissed as spiritual static by Ham. Graham might well have heard remarks like these, typical of Ham's sermons:

> You say, "Why I've been a faithful Sunday School teacher. I've been a faithful member of this church. I've been loyal to the truth. I'm fundamental. I'm orthodox. I try to live right. I try to do the best I can. I don't know what else I can do." But that isn't acceptable to the Lord! That's what the "old man," Adam, is doing.[5]

By forming his own preaching after the pattern he observed in preachers like Mordecai Ham, Graham has placed himself firmly on the trajectory of emotional and personalistic American revival preaching arcing back at least to Charles G. Finney. As such, his preaching methods are curiously anachronistic. In the last half century, as American preaching has become highly creative and preachers all around him have experimented with everything from narrative to free-form structure to PowerPoint, Graham soldiers on with a preaching style shaped more by the communicational realities of the nineteenth century than the twenty-first. "The message I preach here is going to be the same. It hasn't changed," an eighty-six-year-old Graham said before his 2005 New York crusade. "Circumstances have changed. Problems have changed. But deep inside, man has not changed and the gospel hasn't changed."[6]

THE TYPICAL BILLY GRAHAM SERMON

The evangelistic sermon, of which Graham has been a noteworthy practitioner, cannot be fully captured in words on a page. It is, as Kenneth L. Woodward has described, "a genuine American performance art."[7] Graham himself liked to quote the eighteenth-century evangelist George Whitfield, who, when someone asked permission to print one of his sermons, said, "You may print it if you put in the thunder, the fire, and the lightning."[8]

Even so, the hundreds of manuscripts of Graham's sermons, preached over the many years of his ministry, do reveal much about the methods of his preaching. (Not all of Graham's sermons were actually penned by Graham; the claim that Graham has often used ghostwriters, who created sermons for him, carefully aping his style and vocabulary, is controversial but well documented.[9]) While not every sermon fits the pattern, many of Graham's sermons are arranged according to a four-part scheme. These parts are not so much sermon "points," to use the traditional vocabulary, as they are movements in a sermonic drama of personal redemption. They are as follows.

The Grave Crisis in Our Time

Sometimes this part of the sermon is prefaced by a brief reprise of the Scripture lesson on which the sermon is based, but this review of the text is essentially done in order to show that the passage calls us to think deeply about the human predicament and thus to allow Graham to segue into a presentation of the present moment as one of extraordinary crisis.

In describing the problems that bedevil humanity, Graham is usually newsworthy and often seriously hyperbolic. At the beginning of 1951, he preached, "Everyone seems to agree that a terrible catastrophe lies just ahead. . . . Selfishness seems to have gripped the entire human race. The worst that is in man is now manifesting itself."[10] By 1957, he was announcing, "Many students of world affairs believe that the world is plunging madly toward a third World War."[11] In 1961, pointing to communist threats in Europe, the Congo, and Southeast Asia, Graham quoted scientist James Orr, who warned, "The whole race is crumbling to destruction."[12] Graham agreed, adding, "Not only is the world itself facing its greatest crisis since our race appeared, but Christianity beholds giants rising out of the earth to contend with it, more powerful, more worldwide in the influence they are able to exert than any the church has known since the downfall of paganism fifteen hundred years ago."[13] Preaching at the Nixon White House in 1970, Graham declared that the affluences of society had created a great sense of alienation and emptiness and that "thousands are turning to drugs, thousands are even turning to suicide." He went on to claim, "Spiritual leanness haunts millions. The starvation of the human soul has reached alarming proportions."[14] In New York City in 2005, Graham told the Flushing Meadows crowd, "Tonight, I was interviewed by two of the national television people, and they both asked the same questions: 'What's wrong with our world? What's happening? Is there any answer to it?'"[15]

The evils change with the era—here communism, there nuclear war, now AIDS, then drugs—but the world inhabited by Billy Graham's sermons is forever on the brink of total ruination and disaster. He does not, like the classic street prophets of *New Yorker* cartoon fame, wear a sandwich board reading "The World Is Coming to an End," but it has been the opening salvo of his sermons for six decades. These are chronically "the worst of times," with hardly a glimmer of "the best of times," and were his sermons to end after this opening move, he would be merely a pulpiteering Chicken Little. But they do not end here, of course. They move on to a focus on the plight of the individual soul.

The Restless and Captive Soul

Homiletically, it is a rule of thumb that problems raised at the beginning of a sermon should be addressed somewhere in the body of the sermon. In short, preachers should not release snakes they cannot kill, or at least defang. But Graham consistently violates this rule. He describes an emergency, a world tottering on the brink of collapse, but not in order to sound a moral call to arms, to address social ills from the perspective of the gospel, or to summon his hearers to a globally.aware faith. He does not even urge them to rush into the desert to "flee from the wrath to come." Instead, he describes the shaking of the world's foundations simply as a backdrop for the real topic of the sermon: personal restlessness, brokenness, and alienation. For Graham, the full and only reason why the planet is in trouble is because it is populated by sinful individuals. He describes social gloom and makes dire pronouncements of catastrophe, not to set the church working for reconciliation, peace, or justice, but to claim that all anxiety about the plight of the world is but a mirror reflecting the true crisis of humanity: the bankruptcy of the individual soul.

In this second part of the sermon, Graham places his finger on the troubled inner spirit of his hearers, their loneliness, guilt, fear, and hunger for meaning. What he said in one of his 2005 New York sermons is characteristic of almost every Billy Graham sermon. Having raised the global issue of grinding poverty and hunger set amid the affluence of others, Graham then downsizes the problem to fit into the smaller space of the individual human heart:

> In Genesis, the Bible tells us that God made us in His image. We were meant to be like God! But sin intervened. We rebelled against God, and now there is another kind of poverty that plagues us—a poverty of the soul, where our longings are never satisfied, where our desires are never filled, where our hopes are unrealized and fears grow.
>
> Some of you tonight are in that situation. You have a girlfriend or a boyfriend who has left you, or you might have a death in your family, or you may have a habit you cannot control. You have tried to control it, but you've failed.[16]

Two characteristic marks of this second part of Graham's sermons are the citing of several biblical texts for authority, usually with the formulaic introduction "the Bible says," and the occasional swipe at "churchy" Christianity. Graham encourages his converts to become active in churches "where Christ is proclaimed," but church religion, in Graham's glossary, can too easily be about righteous appearances alone. God looks beneath the religious-looking surfaces to the true depths of the heart. "Now, take some of you people on Sunday morning," Graham told a Charlotte crusade in 1958. "You dress up and put a little halo on your head, and you go to church and look like a saint. . . . You get out of church, shake hands with the minister, go home, take the halo off, take your wings off, pick up your pitchfork, and the horns begin to grow again. No change has taken place."[17]

This naming of the hearers as troubled and restless, as sinners in full rebellion against God, who sees through their pretense to the truth about their lack of righteousness, sets up the third movement of the sermon: the divine remedy for sin.

God's Response and Invitation

In his early sermons, Graham had a very full theological understanding of how God responded to the dilemma of human sin, which essentially involved a substitutionary view of the atonement. Human beings can do nothing to address the problem of sin; only God can forgive sin and repair the broken spirit, and on the cross the sum of human sin was placed upon Jesus. What is left for the believer to do is to surrender. "I come to the cross," he preached,

> and I say, "Jesus is my Savior, and He is my own Savior. I am trusting in Him, and Him alone, for salvation. I am not trusting in anything or anybody but Christ. By faith, I surrender to Him."

... Now the moment you come to Christ by repentance and faith, God in a miraculous and glorious way, changes your life. He forgives all your past. He gives you a new nature. He gives you new values, and new motives, and a new direction in your life. He puts a smile on your face, and a spring in your step, and joy in your soul.[18]

Presented in such bare terms, as Graham was wont to do, this process of redemption came perilously close to being a quasi-mathematical transaction. The believer changes his attitude toward God, and God responds by changing the divine attitude toward the believer, which in turn allows the believer to change his inner values and attitude toward the whole of life. In Graham's later sermons, though, the clumsy tit-for-tat machinery has largely given way to a more intimate, loving understanding of God's role in the drama of salvation. Although the theological details are fuzzy and not worked through, in Graham's most recent sermons, the God who demands satisfaction for sin fades, and the God who loves and embraces the brokenhearted sinner is emphasized. "I read somewhere that what young people want and need from older people first of all is to be loved," Graham told the last New York crusade, "and the Bible says God loves you. God loves *you*! God loves everyone here tonight."[19]

Get Up Out of Your Seat and Come to Christ

All of Graham's public crusade sermons are aimed at a single telos: the conversion of individual hearers. Graham does not mince words at the end of his sermons; like the good salesman he has always been, he tries to close the deal. In Charlotte in 1958, he concluded his sermon with words he would repeat, in one form or another, thousands of times, all the way to the very last service in New York in 2005:

> I'm going to ask you to get up out of your seat, hundreds of you, right now. Get up out of your seat, and come and stand right here. And say tonight, "I want Christ. I am ready to pay the price. I am ready to renounce my sins. I'm ready to receive Him as Lord and Master and Savior. I'm ready to follow and serve Him. I don't care what it costs. I'm ready by God's grace to pay the price."[20]

And get up out of their seats, they do. Nearly three million people over the last sixty years have walked forward at the end of Graham's sermons.[21] When one compares this amazing track record of effectiveness with the actual substance of the preaching, with the plausibility of Graham's simple formula in a world of increasing complexity, one wonders, why?

THE PUZZLE OF GRAHAM'S PREACHING

The enigma of Billy Graham's preaching is that it produces such dramatic results when, honesty compels us to say, most of his sermons fail almost every imaginable test of quality—theological, ethical, homiletical, and aesthetic. Graham has never claimed to be an excellent or deep preacher, and, technically at least, he is right to avoid claiming these titles. Structurally, Graham's sermons are rhetorical dinosaurs full of canned illustrations, suspect logic, sometimes wild misstatements of fact, simplistic ideas, and nigh-fundamentalist theology. Yet over the years, millions have made a decision to follow Christ in response to his preaching. To be sure, many of those people sooner or later slipped back into their old life patterns (one of the most frequent criticisms of Graham and his evangelistic techniques has to do with his poor "staying power" statistics), but others of his "converts" have genuinely grown and matured as Christians. Some of them have even achieved a much greater complexity and depth in their faith than Graham has achieved himself, and they consider their initiation into the Christian community via a Graham crusade to be a kind of "breech birth." For some people, hearing Graham preach is a bit like going to an old school chiropractor; you may not appreciate all of his theories, but you walk a little straighter after the visit.

Criticisms of Graham are easy to produce since he makes himself into a large target. In the 1950s, Reinhold Niebuhr famously and publicly scolded Graham in a series of essays and articles for being pietistic, moralistic, and individualistic. Niebuhr was especially bothered by the flow of Graham's typical sermons, an issue I identified earlier—a homiletical tendency to describe large social issues and problems and then, in reductionistic fashion, to suggest that the solution to them is personal salvation alone. As a case in point, Niebuhr cited a Graham sermon on the "Seven Deadly Sins" in which Graham had discussed America's "economy of abundance." Niebuhr zeros in for the kill: "But having dealt with this sin of a whole culture, he irrelevantly presents Christian salvation as a kind of magic panacea, with the assurance that the 'blood of Jesus Christ' can save us from this sin, too. There is nothing here about the temptations to which even the most devoted Christians are subject in a very wealthy nation."[22]

Niebuhr was right, of course, and while Graham was fully aware of the great theologian's criticisms, and took them seriously, there is little evidence that he took them to heart. Despite the much heralded social gestures, such as racially integrating his crusades, Graham never really walked the aisle at Niebuhr's crusade, never turned his preaching over to a broader, more socially alert understanding of the gospel. He has remained a "hot gospeler" to this day, insisting that every human problem, when seen for what it truly is, falls before the remedy of personal forgiveness and that every human being has but one compelling spiritual need—individual submission to Christ. According to Graham, even the Buddha at the end of his life was "still searching for truth"— the truth that is is Jesus Christ.[23]

To Niebuhr's general critique of the theological and social analytical depth of Graham's sermons, we can add a few more demurrers:

Plausibility. In some ways it is ironic that Graham's preaching career has been such a long one. John the Baptist–type preachers, who thunder that "even now the ax is laid to the root of the tree," generally exit the scene after a few sweaty sermons. Either the ax falls or it doesn't. But Graham has been announcing the urgent crisis of a world coming apart at the seams for years. Through nearly a dozen presidential administrations and countless social and cultural changes and permutations, Graham continues to claim that never before in the history of the human race have we faced a moment so full of dread and urgency. As William McLoughlin said, "Ten years of crisis is the limit of human endurance, and Billy Graham has now had his ten years."[24]

But McLoughlin made that remark in 1960, and Graham still stands in the pulpit almost half a century later, dressed for combat, his trumpet sounding the battle alarm. Only in America, perhaps, a culture without a strong sense of historical memory, a culture in which tragedies like the events of September 11, 2001, are forever seen out of social and historical context and as perpetual signs of the crisis that can ever strike without warning, could a preacher shout like an air raid siren for nearly seventy years and still be taken seriously.

Biblical exegesis. In a 1999 online chat, a young pastor asked Graham for advice about ministry that he could "use the rest of his life." Graham replied, in part, that "a young minister must know the Bible and preach from the Bible. I believe," he added, "that God uses what we call expository preaching—which means that you explain paragraph by paragraph, chapter by chapter to the congregation what God said."[25]

Strangely, though, very few of Graham's sermons display anything like the methods and results of expository preaching, which he so solidly advocates. In fact, most do not show evidence of significant interpretation of the biblical text at all. To be sure, Graham has plenty of biblical references in his sermon, and occasionally some pieces of Bible-encyclopedia-type data will appear sprinkled into the material, but as for wrestling with the ambiguities of the text, as for clinging to the text as a major source of the sermons' intellectual and theological content, this is mostly absent from Graham's preaching. What gives content and shape to Graham's preaching is the die-cut sin-to-salvation theological template that dominates almost every sermon. Indeed, biblical texts are used mainly as proof texts, as illustrations of and warrants for a theological paradigm of rebellion-redemption already in place. For the most part, every text, whether psalm or parable or prophetic oracle, is pounded into the square hole of Graham's prefabricated sermon design.

Years ago, when his friend and fellow evangelist Charles Templeton challenged Graham's simplistic use of the Bible and posed some hard questions about the flat and literalistic way he uses Scripture, Graham was at first at a loss for words. Finally he replied to Templeton's dismay: "Chuck, look, I haven't a good enough mind to settle these questions. The finest minds in the world have looked and come down on both sides. I don't have the time, the inclination, or the set of mind to pursue them. I found that if I say 'The Bible says' and 'God says,' I get results. I have decided that I am not going to wrestle with these questions any longer."[26]

Ambivalence toward culture. There runs through the entire corpus of Graham's sermons a profoundly divided mind about the place and value of culture. On the one hand, Graham possesses all of the native suspicions of a white southern farm boy about the ruling elites of finance, education, and media. "The higher the civilization," he observes, "the higher the suicide rate."[27] He plays to working-class prejudices by frequently depicting people who have achieved status and celebrity, people who have attended the best schools and who bring down the big salaries but who are wretched nonetheless. He preached, "I go to some colleges where there are no rules. Everything is permissive, and you find the most miserable-looking, unhappy people."[28] In Graham's sermons, people have fortune, power, education, and fame, but they remain restless and unhappy, ignorant about what gives true meaning in life. In one sermon, Graham reports being invited to address eight hundred scientists at a convention. After doing a bit of "aw shucks" about "being like a fish out of water because I know very little about science," Graham gets to the point and reverses the cultural tables. When it comes to the human equation, it was the scientists who were clueless. "Science needs the help of the church," one of the convention leaders confided in Graham.[29]

On the other hand, Graham is himself a member of the celebrity class, and his sermons are salted with references to playing golf with Eisenhower, conversing with Karl Barth, and hosting rock stars in his home. Graham works both sides of the street, at one and the same time flattering his listeners' desire to believe that egghead Harvard graduates automatically know less about life than the average working Joe and vicariously satisfying their desire to ride in limousines, converse with movie stars, and tee up a golf ball at Augusta National.

William Franklin "Billy" Graham Jr., known around the world as one of Christendom's greatest preachers, would, based on his usual level of sermon exegesis, structure, theology, and language, perhaps struggle to get a grade of C in an intellectually demanding seminary preaching course. But for Graham and his hearers, the eventfulness of their encounter has never been about the technical quality of his sermons. Theologically, Billy Graham may well stand as a prominent representative of a truth that applies to all Christian preachers: the words of sermons may well be weak, shallow, and misguided, but they can also be taken by God's Spirit to accomplish more than their intrinsic worth would allow. Many preachers would understand Graham's experience that the act of preaching seems to him like "wrestling with the devil," who does everything to make a mockery of the event of proclamation, including magnifying the flaws of preacher and sermon. When the sermon is over, Graham has said, "some sort of physical energy goes out of me and I feel terribly weak. I'm depleted."[30] Even the best sermons, as Karl Barth reminded us, involve an embarrassing presumption on the part of frail human speakers to try and capture divine lightning in a bottle made of mere words. If the Spirit does not choose to speak in and through the sermon, preaching becomes a laughable, vain, and foolish activity indeed. Better to get a job putting cherries on cupcakes.

There is yet one more thing to be said about Graham's sermons, namely, their efficacy as iconic and ritual events. Graham is not exactly a typical postmodern celebrity, famous basically for being famous, but his celebrity status is now a key to the power of his preaching. It hasn't hurt him through the years that he has the clean good looks and the soothing voice and the confident calm of the boy you wish lived next door. It also has not hurt him that he is humble and self-effacing, that he admits he possesses little in the way of fancy knowledge and that he hasn't the foggiest notion how a computer works. For millions of people with ordinary lives and modest ambitions and hopes, Billy Graham is one of them. They do not so much listen to the content of his messages; they participate in the event of Billy Graham. They are, for a moment, Billy Graham, and he is, himself, the message. He believes, really believes, in the innocent and righteous faith of their childhood, and, having seemingly kept himself free from scandal and impropriety, he embodies the pure, honest life we once believed we could live. Through him, we hobnob with royalty, visit exotic places, and dine with Fortune 500 CEOs. What could seem like shameless name-dropping in his sermons is, to his hearers, only a gracious invitation to go where Billy has gone and to meet those whom he has met. If occasionally some opportunist like Nixon uses him for nefarious political purposes, well, it's just a sign of Billy's innocent trust of all people. The Rev. Dr. Graham is loved and welcomed all over the world, but to us, he's just "Billy," our Billy.

And then our Billy gets up on the rostrum, folds his hands in prayer, and preaches. We know what he is going to say. He says it every time, in one way or another. He is going to say that he knows how lonely and disappointed and sad we are, knows that life has not turned out as we had hoped. But he is also going to give us a chance to start over, to wipe the slate clean and start afresh.

In his book *The Redemptive Self: Stories Americans Live By*, Dan P. McAdams makes the case that Americans, especially the most generative citizens among us, both live by and tell stories of redemption, religious and secular. Down in our philosophical and civic religious souls, he argues, we are optimistically persuaded "that we will be delivered from our pain and suffering no matter what, that we will overcome in the long run, that we will rise from the depths of the present, that things will get better and that we will eventually grow and find fulfillment in the world."[31]

That's our story, and we're sticking to it. But life gets so complicated and weighed down and messed up and sad that it is sometimes hard to hold on to this story and even harder to live it out. We are, as Paul Simon once sang, "slip-sliding away." And then there is Billy Graham, standing there under the klieg lights, full of confidence and faith and righteousness, his strong and mellow voice reassuring us that our story of redemption is true and that personal renewal is within our grasp.

Years ago, Graham was scheduled to preach at the Citadel, the famous South Carolina military academy. As he walked across the campus with the school's president, General Mark Clark, a cadet approached Graham and said, "Mr. Graham, you're not going to let us down, are you?" Graham asked him what he meant, and he answered, "You are going to tell us how to be converted, aren't you?"[32]

This is an interesting and revealing exchange. It was not as if the cadet was seeking information. His very question shows that he knew what to expect from a Billy Graham sermon. He was not a religious seeker asking for the secret of conversion to the truth; he was an insider hoping that Graham would fulfill his expectations by sticking to the script. The cadet was like a child at bedtime asking for an old and familiar book to be read, ready to be comforted by the expected rhythms and the beloved story. At no time was this more evident than in the climactic 2005 New York crusade. Graham's sermons were versions of the same sermons he has preached throughout his career; in fact, some of the material he preached in 2005 he had preached in New York in 1957. But this time Graham made his way to the pulpit using a walker. His voice was softer, and his age and illness sometimes caused him to stumble over words and to lose his focus momentarily. The sermons were shorter, almost schematic diagrams of the sermons of old. But the thousands who had come listened to him in rapt silence. They were doing more than hearing a Billy Graham sermon; they were participating in a Billy Graham event.

What did Graham think about what the Citadel cadet told him? "I went into that chapel service with that on my mind and my heart," Graham says. Of course. Sermon after sermon, year after year, decade after decade, he always has.

NOTES

1. *Houston Post*, June 2, 1952, 1, cited in William G. McLoughlin Jr., *Billy Graham: Revivalist in a Secular Age* (New York: Ronald Press, 1960), 124.
2. McLoughlin, *Billy Graham*, 125.
3. Nancy Gibbs and Richard N. Ostling, "God's Billy Pulpit," *Time*, November 15, 1993, http://www.time.com/time/magazine/article/0,9171,979573,00.html.
4. Quoted in Stanley High, *Billy Graham* (New York: McGraw-Hill, 1956), 86, and cited in James E. Kilgore, *Billy Graham the Preacher* (New York: Exposition Press, 1968), 23–24.
5. Mordecai Ham, "What Do You Offer God?" http://sermons.christiansunite.com/Mordecai_Ham.shtml. Billy Sunday often preached the same antiecclesial message. In one of his sermons he said, "There are lots of men who will be true in all these things, and false to Jesus Christ. They will go to church and partake of the communion, then will line up in front of some bar and tell smutty stories. True in business, true to lodge, true in society, true in the home, but a perjurer in the sight of God. If you are such a man you are a backslider—a backslider, sir, and a liar" (Billy Sunday, "Backsliding," http://www.billysunday.org/sermons/backsliding.html).
6. Quoted in Andy Newman, "For an Ailing Graham, a Crusade with a Little Less Fire," *New York Times*, June 22, 2005, B2.
7. Kenneth L. Woodward, "A Voice in a Crowded Wilderness," *New York Times*, June 26, 2005, D13.
8. Billy Graham, *The Challenge: Sermons from Madison Square Garden* (Garden City, NY: Doubleday, 1969), ix–x.
9. See Michael G. Long, *Billy Graham and the Beloved Community* (New York: Palgrave Macmillan, 2006), 227–32.
10. Billy Graham, "Whither Bound?" in *America's Hour of Decision* (Wheaton, IL: Van Kampen Press, 1951), 139.
11. Billy Graham, "The Signs of the Times," a sermon on *The Hour of Decision* (Minneapolis: Billy Graham Evangelistic Association, 1957), n.p.
12. Billy Graham, *Prepare for the Storm* (Minneapolis: Billy Graham Evangelistic Association, 1961), 2.
13. Ibid., 3.
14. Billy Graham, "God's Answer to Man's Dilemma," in *White House Sermons*, ed. Ben Hibbs (New York: Harper & Row, 1972), 137–38.
15. Billy Graham, "You Must Be Born Again," in *Living in God's Love: The New York Crusade* (New York: G. P. Putnam's Sons, 2005), 50.
16. Billy Graham, "The Rich Young Ruler," in *Living in God's Love*, 79–81.
17. Billy Graham, "Conversion," Billy Graham Archives, http://www.wheaton.edu/bgc/archives/docs/bg-charlotte/1003.html.
18. Ibid.
19. Graham, "Rich Young Ruler," 83.
20. Billy Graham, "Rich Young Ruler," Billy Graham Archives, http://www.wheaton.edu/bgc/archives/docs/bg-charlotte/1002.html.
21. Gibbs and Ostling, "God's Billy Pulpit."
22. Reinhold Niebuhr, "Literalism, Individualism, and Billy Graham," *Christian Century*, May 23, 1956, 641.

23. In one of his sermons in the 2005 New York crusade, Graham said, "You know, Buddha said at the end of his life, 'I'm still searching for truth.' Jesus said, 'I am the truth.'" See Graham, "Rich Young Ruler," in *Living in God's Love*, 86.
24. McLoughlin, *Billy Graham*, 231.
25. Online chat with Billy Graham, http://www.time.com/time/community/transcripts/199/070699grahamtime100.html.
26. As quoted in William Martin, *A Prophet with Honor*, and cited in Gibbs and Ostling, "God's Billy Pulpit."
27. Billy Graham, "Two Sets of Eyes," in *Challenge*, 129.
28. Billy Graham, "The Giants You Face," in *Challenge*, 143.
29. Billy Graham, "The Second Coming of Christ," Billy Graham Archives, http://www.wheaton.edu/bgc/archives/docs/bg-charlotte/1005.html.
30. Quoted in Gibbs and Ostling, "God's Billy Pulpit."
31. Dan P. McAdams, *The Redemptive Self: Stories Americans Live By* (Oxford: Oxford University Press, 2006), 4.
32. Graham, "Conversion."

2

The Tangible Evangelism of Billy Graham

Heather Murray Elkins

WHEN SEEING IS BELIEVING

I'm in my early teens when I attend a Billy Graham crusade in Tucson, Arizona. This encounter with the world's most well-known evangelist leaves a first impression that's sure to be permanent. I'm aware of the cool night air, the music, the electricity of his voice, the stars visible at the edges of the stadium lights of the University of Arizona. The sheer size of the gathering impresses me, since I'm not a football fan and have never seen that many bodies in one space at one time.

The assured voice coming out of the midst of the blond southern whirlwind keeps prodding us with the sharp edges of our failures, our weaknesses, our doubts. We're "come-shorters" and we're guilty of sins that are "not the big ones, but the little, common, everyday sins that lead to the cross."

Then comes the security meltdown. "You've been confirmed, received Communion, the ordinances, but have you really received him?" Was I sure of Christ? Was Christ sure of me? I watch the preacher pace the length of the platform, calling us to make a decision that would remove all doubt.

One is rarely sure of anything as a teenager. I have hope, but not an unassailable conviction of my eternal salvation. I covertly study the faces of the adults around me. I'm sitting separately from my family because we'd arrived late and had to separate to get seats. The strangers around me seem to be listening intently but don't seem emotionally stirred up. They're just listening, hard.

The sermon comes to a quick end. The preacher concludes with a call to come forward, to commit our lives to Christ. He repeats the call several times and then falls silent, waiting. There's a long moment before the classic crusade hymn begins, "Just as I Am." I wonder what he will do if nobody moves. The music starts, but no one around me seems to be getting up.

Then I catch the first sign of movement. A figure seated right behind the home team's goal line steps down from the bleachers and out onto the field. He's a soldier. He marches nearly the length of the field, alone, as we watch in utter silence, spellbound by his single-minded action.

The war in Vietnam is making headlines, with skirmishes on the front lines of campuses as well as jungles. We sit and watch him march. God and country and Billy Graham fuse into an icon, a symbol that's visible, tangible, audible. I wonder for a moment whether this gesture has been staged, but then the groundswell sweeps most of us out of our seats and down to the field.

We're all soldiers for Christ.

I have chosen the term "tangible evangelism" in this chapter to describe the work of Billy Graham in order to underscore the physical, social, and political bodies that his ministry involves. These are carefully nurtured structures for the public expression of faith on a local and global level. Think of what is physically and politically required for the transformation of a civic place into holy ground—the recruitment of 2,500-member choirs, the coordination with mayors and councils to establish citywide bus services, the ecumenical prayer breakfasts with pastors and laity, ranging from grocery clerks to members of Congress. The collective impact of the ecumenical network builds for months in preparation for each crusade.

There is also the Billy Graham Evangelistic Association's truly evangelical use of technology: radio, selected use of television, journals, global travel, newspapers, mailing campaigns, printed educational materials for every age level, films, virtual presence via satellites, user-friendly Web sites, and (first, last, and always) music. The BGEA's Web sites allow a viewer to click into a prayer support group in almost every country in the world. At the heart of this outreach is a man on a mission for God who has become famous for an altar call that includes directions on how to come to Christ—physically, spiritually, literally.

Graham's own definition of an evangelist puts the primary attention on language, on the tradition of *declaring* the gospel of Jesus Christ. This is a particular form of proclamation by a person with a special calling and skill to address a particular audience: "a person who has been called and especially equipped by God to declare the Good News to those who have not yet accepted it, with the goal of challenging them to turn to Christ in repentance and faith and to follow Him in obedience to His will."[1]

The support structures for this calling and equipping, as well as Graham's preaching itself, have impacted the social, political, and spiritual identity of a nation for over fifty years. It is impossible to separate these powerful associations. Beyond the opening illustration, one example of this complex relationship can be seen in the history of the name of his public preaching events. Graham used the term "campaign" until 1950, when he changed the term to "crusade."[2] This was an attempt to distance his work from some of his more opportunistic predecessors who had manipulated feelings and finances in ways Graham found offensive. The old term also described the process by which politicians come to power.

Crusade, yes. Campaign, no. That choice remained unchanged until after September 11, 2001, when an attempt was made to put some distance between the rhetoric of President Bush and an evangelist. Many American Muslims as well as other religious leaders were appalled at President Bush's call for a "crusade" against Islamic terrorists. The word appeared to legitimate Christian violence against Muslims, and its use exposed the ugly face of the American anti-Semitism that ironically coexists in the same cultural ethos as the Christian premillennial understanding of Christ's second coming.

In an attempt to stem this contagious controversy, BGEA decided to use the term "missions." The rhetorical change was of short duration, and the familiar term "crusades" was back in place by the time the war in Iraq was declared.[3] (Even though Graham's son, Franklin, uses the term "festivals" for his gatherings, he is very public in his support of a greater U.S. military response to Islamic fundamentalism. His support appears as a Christian call to arms in a war that many conservatives believe is holy.)

American fundamentalism has certainly been nourished by Graham's neo-evangelical leadership. Still, for many Americans of a wide range of faith traditions he remains an international leader worthy of respect, if for no other reason than he has consistently practiced what he preaches when it comes to the Ten Commandments. Worthy of respect, yes, but that doesn't deflect the critical analysis of the ways that this evangelist has tangibly altered the political consciousness of American life.

One can make a compelling argument that a significant portion of the population of this nation and this evangelist discovered their identity together, coming of age and finding a global voice in the same time span. Graham began practicing his student sermons by preaching to stumps in rural Florida and eventually graduated to a worldwide revival operation involving 210 million people in 186 different countries. In the same fifty years, the United States moved from being a leading nation to seeing itself as more than a nation—as a (self-named) *superpower* or, as more recently described, an *empire*.

But both Graham and the United States are now entering a time of limitation. International perception of U.S. power is shifting with the winds of war in Iraq, and the last Billy Graham crusade is now a matter of record. The crusader and the country face a sense of mortality. One appears to be more at peace than the other.

THE MAN IS THE MEDIUM, THE MESSAGE,
AND THE MESSENGER

Ask Billy Graham how he has done all that he has done, and he answers, "God." Colleagues close to him assure the insistent press and persistent preachers that Graham does not know why people come forward when he invites them. He steadfastly believes that this is the work of the Holy Spirit. His calling, his gift, his ministry is to invite, so he invites. The simplicity of the answer underestimates the well-managed organization that supports this culture of conversion. It is clearly the case, however, that the man, Billy Graham, is the medium, the message, and the messenger.

If we use one of the classical definitions of preaching to explain his influence on the public, it is *ethos* that makes Billy Graham who he is, the most famous evangelist in the world. *Ethos* is "the worthiness of the speaker, rather than *logos*, reason, or *pathos*, the capacity to stir emotion."[4] Thousands came to hear his final crusade for the simple reason that he was a good man who was famous for helping people to be good.

If an upcoming generation loses sight of his stature as an internationally known spiritual leader and asks, "Billy who?" as once this generation said, "Moody who?" then the televised segments and video streams will continue to circulate evidence of his spiritual stature and personal friendships with world leaders and international faith communities. This mediating or marketing of the virtual Graham enhances the possibility of manipulation, however. The ethical constraints and commitments that Graham placed on his ministry, such as fiscal responsibility, ecumenical support of local ministries, and a consistent witness for religious tolerance can be erased by reframing his work into ministries indifferent or hostile to those concerns.

Ethos requires a living presence. The public sense of this preacher's moral character was not created in a vacuum, or through virtual reality. An astonishing network of personal relationships provides the ties that bind Graham to nearly every country in the world. It is Graham's character, his public and private self, that convinces his responsible critics that he is a good man, a man with a dangerously innocent sense of power perhaps, but a good man. Of note, however, is a *Daily Worker* quote about Billy Graham, "He speaks with an arrogant humility which is terrifying."[5] It is this ethos of a true servant of Christ who loves and is loved by the world that serves as the foundation of his mission, as well as his personal friendship with every president since Truman, a claim not without irony, given the diversity of character and characters who have occupied the Oval Office.

Graham's evangelical ethos matches Phillips Brooks's definition of preaching as "truth through personality."[6] This perception of truth through personality created an iconic presence of Graham as *the* American Christian, although he is not a great preacher, as Graham himself admits. His call to conversion is as much about being an American as it is about being a Christian. As he repeated in many settings, "This is a defining act, you coming out from the crowd as the individual you are. It helps you become a better citizen."[7] It does not take much encouragement after watching several of his classic crusades on television to think that if the American eagle could speak, its voice would sound like Billy Graham. His voice carries a natural authority enhanced by his conviction that he has been charged with a sense of urgency as well as agency.

John Broadus (1827–1895), professor of homiletics and the first Southern Baptist to give the Beecher Lectures at Yale, describes this charismatic combination of authority and simplicity in *A Treatise on the Preparation and Delivery of Sermons*. It was the authoritative book for Southern Baptist preachers for more than half a century. Graham would have read this text and certainly understood why this combination of authority and simplicity makes an effective communicator in a postmodern age of spin doctors and sound bites. Broadus writes:

> Now the things which ought *most* to be thought of by the preacher, are piety and knowledge, and the blessing of God. . . . In all speaking, especially in preaching, naturalness, genuineness, even though awkward, is really more effective for all the highest ends, than the most elegant artificiality.[8]

Another key to the way that Graham's evangelism mobilized a civic identity for his listeners is the importance he placed on the free will of the individual, and by association, society. Graham's Arminianism is a significant part of his evangelical identity as a preacher. A century before Billy Graham issued his first invitation, Charles Finney (1792–1875) described the core imperative of evangelical preaching in "How to Preach the Gospel." This theological understanding of the agency of the preacher undergirds Graham's practice:

> In the conversion of a sinner, it is true that God gives the truth efficiency to turn the sinner to God. He is an active, voluntary, powerful agent in changing the mind. But he is not the only agent. The one that brings the truth to his notice is also an agent. We are apt to speak of ministers and other men as only *instruments* in converting sinners. This is not exactly correct. Man is something more than an instrument.

Truth is the mere unconscious instrument. But man is more; he is a voluntary, responsible agent in the business.[9]

Graham's style of evangelization is the embodiment of this understanding of an individual as a voluntary, responsible agent, a citizen in the realm of God and the state. Much of his work on race relations and religious tolerance came from his conviction that individuals who were right with God would carry those redeemed relationships into their businesses, their homes, and their neighborhoods. He refused to hold a crusade in cities that practiced segregation, and he often named the need for better housing and schools in cities as part of the Christian response to the gospel of Christ. The following is from a 1957 sermon in Madison Square Garden:

You become a witness for Christ in your bearing, your better housing, your racial relations. Christ calls you to him and then sends you back into the world.

Lenin once said that "a communist is a dead man on furlough."

You bear that cross. You die to yourself to become the right kind of father/mother/daughter/son. This is what faithfulness in the church means.

You are redeemed. You are blood-bought people in this world for Christ.

Was Billy Graham right? Yes, if that theological alignment is primarily defined by the conviction that preaching the gospel and a public confession of faith in Christ is a matter of life and death. Finney provides a vivid example of this in his story of a man who has wandered dangerously close to the edge of the Niagara Falls. He is literally backing over the edge when someone sees what's happening and shouts, "Stop!"

Not only does the preacher cry, *Stop*, but through the living voice of the preacher the Spirit cries, *Stop*. The preacher cries, "Turn ye, why will ye die." The Spirit pours the expostulation home with such power, that the sinner turns.[10]

This is descriptive of Graham's sense of self as an evangelist, a lifesaver shouting for thousands to turn so they will not die. He offers the promise that if they respond to the living voice of the preacher as the voice of the Spirit, all doubt about their salvation can be removed. It was not just a promise of safety that he preached. In many of the early radio broadcasts and then televised crusades, Graham intentionally created for his audiences a sense of being in real danger. He reminded his hearers in Minneapolis that "in ten years, one out of every four of you in this great crowd will be dead. Are you ready for your last days?"

This is the question that haunts the 1960s generation. Graham cites the threat of nuclear war, raising it like a threatening cloud, naming their inchoate fear. The raised voice, the articulate hands raised to plead for or point to the sinner, and the rapid strides back and forth across the platform are his well-practiced forms of shouting "Stop." It is often unclear to the contemporary viewer of these classic crusades why the good news requires so much shouting.

Graham has grown quieter and gentler in his rescue-mission preaching in recent years. This is for theological as well as psychological reasons. "While earlier a great deal of anger was detected in his manner, he now realizes that the preacher's attitude toward rebellious sinners should be the compassion of the God who became incarnate in order to deliver them from sin."[11] This transition can be found in individual sermons throughout his ministry: the justice of a God who is outraged by our willfulness and a compassionate God who keeps calling prodigal sons and daughters to come home.

The balance has shifted more to the compassionate voice as Graham has aged, but the two have always been interwoven in his preaching. This is from one of his classic crusade sermons:

> God loves you. I beg of you tonight, not to turn your back, don't crucify him again. The sin of rejecting love is the greatest sin. [His voice slows and softens here.] You know what it's like to have your love rejected. Then you reject love, and you turn it down, but when you turn down the pardon of God, you reject the love of God. There is no other way except by the way of the cross. [His voice lifts in volume and his right hand gestures directly at the audience.] Are you sure your sins are forgiven? There is no other way except by the way of the cross. There was no other way. [His right hand raises and comes down sharply on the Bible he is holding.]

Whether he is shouting or consoling, the voice carries authority. Some ascribe this to the southern comfort of his speech, others to the world-famous names that he casually drops into his sermons; for still others it is the fame of the man himself. But for Graham and a significant portion of his audience, it's the first-person use of Scripture under the inspiration of the Holy Spirit: "The Bible says . . ." This expression collapses the distinction between preacher and text. The man becomes the word.

THE BIBLE SAYS . . .

Graham's doctrine of biblical inspiration is translated into a daily discipline of biblical study and prayer. He is famous for wearing out the Bibles that he carries everywhere he goes, and one of the hallmarks of his services is the sight of hundreds of hands turning the pages of Bibles that Graham requests they bring to every service. This hands-on approach to the text is modeled by the man himself. He carries a Bible through his services, lifts it high, and holds it open, with its soft leather edges curling over his fingers as he reads. The erect spine and the convicting first-person voice create an impression that the man has been transfigured into the book. This isn't the spoken word, but the word speaking.

Preaching as an embodied word that encounters us is outlined in H. H. Farmer's *The Servant of the Word*. This homiletic approach is understood to involve a primary exercise of will on the part of the preacher and the hearer. There must be an articulated claim of the gospel, which creates shared meaning between the word, the hearer, and the preacher, who is nothing more and nothing less than a servant of the word.[12]

This is proclamation that assumes the biblical authority of, not the spoken word, but the Speaking Word. *The Bible says. . .* This is an oral truth claim that surpasses textual interpretations and can become a powerful and intentional dislocation of sacred texts as texts. The authority of the Word is centered in the first-person word; the evangelist is the Evangel incarnated, and every text starts and ends with John 3:16.

This form of first person speaking—*The Bible says . . .*—does not come without struggle for knowledge; Graham talks about the locked doors of some scriptural texts whose mystery is God's self. He also exercises a freedom of interpretation that distances him from fundamentalism, particularly in his public use of a wide variety of biblical translations, resisting the claim of the King James Version as the very language of God.

He also directs his hearers to the daily carrying, reading, and studying of Scripture. But his interpretive approach is primarily oral, and the way he fuses passages together tends to displace the textual authority of biblical scholars and sometimes the text itself. He does take seriously the condition of biblical illiteracy in many of his listeners, and he uses stripped-down narrative lines in his sermons. What the Bible says is the old, old story of salvation found in John 3:16.

Yet if his humility and willingness to open himself to Scripture as the word of God are removed from this relationship, idolatry can result. As John Cobb puts it, "I am convinced that the Bible is not the proper object of faith. Such faith is a form of idolatry, that is, of making a god out of a creature. For those who have such faith, it is an obstacle to a full Christian experience and life. It is a form of bondage instead of Christian freedom. For those who suppose that this faith is required of every Christian, it is an obstacle to identifying themselves as Christians at all."[13]

The paradox of Graham's relationship to Scripture and Christ as the Word of God can be illustrated by the crucifixion scene of the Isenheim Altarpiece, one of Karl Barth's favorite paintings. In this painting now identified as the work of Mathis Neithardt, not Grunewald, John the Baptist is holding the book of Isaiah as he gestures toward the dying Christ. Written over his head are the words "He must increase. I must decrease." Generations of homileti-cians have named this image as the embodiment of faithful preaching, but it also expresses the dilemma of this world-famous preacher. No matter how steadfastly Graham points toward Christ, the eyes of the world stray to the man who's holding the book.

HOLY SPACE AND CIVIC PLACE

The City of Angels was the site of the first major success of the Graham orga-nization to convert civic space to holy ground through a crusade. In 1949 the city of angels, movie stars, cops, gangsters, and thousands of "the churched" saw the rebirth of a great American Awakening through every form of media that made the city famous. This was the first full-scale use of Graham's care-ful research into public areas and major cities as sites for reclamation, as set-tings for crusades that sought to transform them into New Jerusalems. Graham offered pastors and civic leaders a vision of themselves as leading cit-izens of "cities set upon a hill," using the language of the Puritan preachers. These crusades were conversions of space as well as people.

Graham prepared for each crusade by ordering and reading local newspa-pers weeks before he arrived. The physical environment of each place was fac-tored into his intensive preparation for the particularities of each city, each gathering. His ability to discern what each place needed as signs of familiarity and signals of recognition determined the volume and pace of his voice as well as what he wore.

When he was right, he was very right. Witness the account of his last cru-sade, known as the Thirty-Day Miracle and held in Flushing Meadows in Queens. Arthur Bailey, the crusade associate of the BGEA who had major oversight of this crusade, said:

> As we considered the possibility of Flushing Meadows, we were informed that 130 languages were represented in that area. We could not travel to every place in the world, but at Corona Park Mr. Graham would be speaking to the world. If you hold a meeting in Manhattan, you have a more media-based dynamic. If you hold a meeting in Queens, you have an international, people-oriented dynamic.[14]

The Los Angeles pentecostal outpouring had been literally prayed into existence, as hundreds of new prayer groups had been formed for the sole pur-pose of praying for the crusade. Many pastors, initially skeptical or outright resistant, found themselves swept up in this boundary-crossing evangelism that formed and reformed often segregated congregations into an ecumenical body of Christ. No matter how temporary this ecclesial partnership might prove to be, countless Christians were called, trained, and empowered to speak and act in the public sphere for something they believed to be true. This public witness training took place in record numbers across the country and around the world. This is the basic training for citizenship in the kingdom of Christ as well as in the "one nation, under God," and pastors and congregational leaders have leading roles in this dual citizenship.

Graham has consistently demonstrated a sensitivity and recognition of the essential loneliness and increasing social marginalization of individual congregational leaders, both lay and clergy, and the appeal of creating renewable civic relationships. As Rev. Robert J. Johannson, pastoral chairman of the 2005 NY Crusade Committee, describes it, "No one else has that kind of clout. We, who have been marginalized in the media, have been put on their radar because of the Graham meeting. For that, it was worth all the effort. The Graham crusade took us who were marginalized and said: 'Hey, we are here all the time. Come see what we are doing.'"[15]

This public coming "to voice" of a previously silent majority requires that normal social pressures be ignored. Graham's sermons provide the motivational key that encourages his hearers to ignore social conditioning that might keep them in their seats and away from the cameras. "Pilate was a coward. Many of you are afraid to give your life to Christ. Afraid that some sneering business acquaintance, some school friend will make fun of you. And, like Pilate, you crucify Christ afresh."

This is daring his hearers to break their paralysis, their silence, their fear of public action. He calls them to get up, to come forward, to exercise their freedom of will. "Choose to live a clean, wholesome life for Christ. They will respect you for living for Christ." This particular challenge may have been effective in motivating men to move, a call to muscular Christianity that the Promise Keepers utilized much later, but it is within the basic definition of an evangelist as any person (woman, child, or man) who has been called and equipped by God to witness to those who have not yet accepted a truth claim.

There are clear directions for how audience members are to transform their conscious thought, their act of will, into action. This is tangible evangelism, an embodied call to make an individual response surrounded by so many others that there is literally a river of humanity flowing forward to be altered (or "altared"). Graham is not instructing them on how to break their moral paralysis with intellectual arguments. He challenges them to turn to Christ in repentance and faith. To follow Christ is understood to be measurable in a verbal action (confessing sin and then confessing Christ) followed by physical action (coming forward). Those who do come are cautioned against wanting to "feel differently." This is not a matter of feeling but of will, the will to turn a private decision into a public action that has eternal consequences.

ENTERING HEAVEN

The sermon is coming to a close. The invitation to come to Christ and secure one's entrance into heaven is given. The time for public witness has come. In words that have been repeated hundreds of times in cities around the world, Graham says:

> Here's how we're going to do it. I'm going to ask you to come. It's a long way, but Jesus went a long way for you. I don't know who you are, or what you are; you can come forward. Your friends and relatives, they'll wait on you. Don't you turn away. You come. Come; get up out of your seat just as you are, you may not understand it all; you'll never understand it all. There's plenty of time. You come. Your friends and relatives, they'll wait on you. Don't you turn away. You come. Come; get up out of your seat. There's plenty of time. You come.

Graham ends his invitation, then falls silent. He bows his head, cupping his chin in his hand, reflecting or praying. He then quietly watches, as ten, twenty, and then hundreds of people begin to move, a steady stream of men, women, teenagers, even children.

One sermon and an invitation to Christ is physically given to thousands of citizens in one place as well as electronically delivered to one hundred million people in forty-eight languages. What happens now? "Read the literature. Go to church next Sunday." Graham gives these direct instructions as the choir finishes its final verse. He invites all those who are standing in front of the platform to join him in prayer, to repeat after him:

> Dear Lord Jesus, I know that I am a sinner and need Your forgiveness. I believe that You died for my sins. I want to turn from my sins. I now invite You to come into my heart and life. I want to trust and follow You as Lord and Savior. In Jesus' name. Amen.

The prayer they are taught to say has remained unchanged for almost half a century. It is found on the Web sites, and it is what you will hear if you call the number on the television screen. This is evangelism by the book. Use training materials and volunteers to teach new and old disciples how to pray, to recruit, train, send out thousands of the baptized to knock on the doors of strangers. Teach ordinary Christians to speak clearly about their conviction, and ask for a public demonstration of faith by taking action in a very public place.

This training has all the potential for voter registration and public rallies. The extraordinary success of these crusades provided the added assurance to the participants that this was not only the Christian way of acting but also the American way of expressing citizenship. Each city itself would be given a voice and a vision for Christ. The question is, was this voice, this vision, only a reflex action, or was it a sustainable civic and religious relationship?

If these widespread crusades were not translated directly into political campaigns for socially progressive congregations who were involved in public health and housing, racial justice, and the economic isolation of the poor, why not? Did these congregations or pastors participate in the planning of the crusades? Did conservative congregations follow up more effectively on the inherently evangelical pattern of simple direct address to individuals and/or the virtual community created with a sophisticated use of public media?

In the final analysis of Graham's evangelical influence, does the question of class or theology matter most? Were liberal and progressive churches not constitutionally able to sustain a socially active ministry of the working poor instead of a service ministry to the poor poor? Conservative churches kept their distance from public political confrontations until well-funded think tanks, such as the Institute for Religion and Democracy, or religious figures with national political aspirations, such as Pat Robertson, began to call for the conversion of the American voter in matters of church and state. This equipping of voluntary, responsible agents in the citizenship in the realm of God and the state as crusaders for a Christian nation was a natural extension of Graham's work.

THE MAKING OF A PRESIDENT

Graham's personal relationship with every American president from Truman to George W. Bush is the stuff of postmodern myth and global legend. It began, however, with a misstep. Truman gave the evangelist a cautious and brief interview at the urging of a congressman. Armed conflict in Korea had broken out just weeks earlier, so Graham urged Truman to declare a national day of prayer, much in the tradition of early colonial preachers' advice to presidents. The meeting concluded with a private moment of prayer that became a public icon as Graham and his associates reenacted the kneeling postures for photographers outside the Oval Office. This public blurring of private access backfired, and he was banned from the White House.[16]

Having learned a hard lesson, Graham regained the confidence of succeeding leaders. He made reference to his friendship with and easy access to world leaders in his sermons, but he revealed very few intimate details. This access to world leaders often provided his primary sermon illustrations and heightened the powerful first-person identification of the speaker with the word itself: *The Bible says . . .*

This is the power of performative language: words that do what they say. Certainly the story of Nixon consulting with Graham on New Year's Day in 1968 carries that message. As Nixon struggled with whether or not to run for president, Graham repeated his earlier prediction, "Dick, I think it is your destiny to be president." That we even have an account of this conversation underscores the presidential influence that Graham possessed.[17]

His spiritual, political, and cultural influence on American presidents is most clearly evident in George W. Bush's account of his own conversion, a direct result of hearing and talking with Graham in 1985. Graham had been invited to a weekend with George H. W. Bush's family to preach and talk informally with family members. Here is the president's version of this event:

> He didn't lecture or admonish; he shared warmth and concern. Billy Graham didn't make you feel guilty; he made you feel loved. Over the course of that weekend, Reverend Graham planted a mustard seed in my soul, a seed that grew over the next year. He led me to the path and I began walking. It was the beginning of a change in my life.[18]

Here is a twenty-first-century parable at work. The loving, nonjudgmental evangelist is invited into the home of a loving father who is seeking ways to help his wayward son "come to himself" and return to his rightful place. This is the parable of Jesus still known by heart in a postbiblical culture. This is the potent story of a reformed alcoholic prodigal son that will generate public approval, not condemnation. Converted by Billy Graham himself, the prodigal returns to his father's house and assumes the robe of authority, and the ring that rules.

There is certainly a similarity in the religious voice of the converter and the converted. Inspiration is directly delivered; there is no mediatory presence required. According to their own accounts, each man communicates directly, personally with God (for Graham, it is Jesus, through the work of the Holy Spirit).

One major critical difference, however, is the marked humility with which Graham confesses past mistakes in judgment, even if, as the *Daily Worker* observed, "He speaks with an arrogant humility which is terrifying." There is a noticeable lack of any kind of humility in the public voice of George W. Bush. He often speaks with a simplistic arrogance that can be terrorizing. He never publicly admits that there might be an ontological distinction between what he wants and what God wills. It is here that Billy Graham steadfastly struggles to maintain his integrity, his ethos, by resisting the temptation to blur that distinction.

CHRISTMAS WITH BILLY GRAHAM

If you tuned in to the Billy Graham Christmas television special that aired nationwide December 2–10, 2006, you would have received a 1979 Christmas greeting from Billy Graham, as well as his most recent address as part of his son's festival in Baltimore. Viewers could also join the festival via the Web before and after Christmas. The tradition of soul- and body-stirring music performed by internationally recognized soloists continued, with Christmas music videos from Paul Baloche, Erin O'Donnell, and Grammy Award–winner Michael W. Smith.

In addition to the preaching and the music, there were two testimonies, one from a father whose son was killed in Afghanistan, and one by a mother whose son has been imprisoned for the rest of his life. In the midst of a season celebrating the birth of the Beloved Son, these two parents struggled with the loss of their children. The father of the fallen soldier described the loss of his son and how he found the precious peace of Christ in the midst of that grief. At the heart of his witness was his assurance that his son's death was part of God's will and that there was absolutely nothing contradictory between his son being a Ranger and being a Christian. To doubt this would be for him to deny Christ.

Images of a good kid with a grin and a hard grip on a rifle surface again as I click on the link for Graham's sermon. Here is the old soldier of Christ introducing his comrades in arms: George Beverly Shea and Cliff Barrows. The two weathered veterans of countless crusades join hands and offer a gesture of thanks to God and the cheering audience. Graham's text is still John 3:16, and his assurance is unshaken. *The Bible still says* . . . (even if he has to keep his eyes on his notes). Graham calls a new generation to get out of their seats and come forward. He lists war and terrorism first on his long list of the sins of the world, but our failure to keep the Ten Commandments is what damns us.

Perhaps he intends for us to decipher the code, "Thou shall not kill," and take the necessary action of applying it directly to a nation as well as a single life. If that is what he means, he never says so. There is no mention of nations; we are personally addressed as he speaks to our need to be forgiven, our hunger to be right, our hope that heaven is assured. He urges us to call on the name of the Lord and promises us that we will be saved. He then quietly waits for the ones, the hundreds, the thousands to come.

I watch them begin to come. They fill the computer screen, and then the image of a man in uniform, a young Ranger lost in Afghanistan, merges with that of a Vietnam soldier marching by himself across a field. I can't tell which feeling is stronger—the anger, regret, respect, or grief as the old Crusader invites: "I'm going to ask you to come. It's a long way, but Jesus went a long way for you. You come."

NOTES

1. Billy Graham, *Just as I Am: The Autobiography of Billy Graham* (San Francisco: HarperSanFrancisco, 1997), xv.
2. Ibid., 163.
3. Deborah Hart Strober and Gerald S. Strober, *Billy Graham: An Oral and Narrative Biography* (San Francisco: Jossey-Bass, 2006), 158.
4. O. C. Edwards Jr., "Evangelism in an Electronic Age," in *A History of Preaching* (Nashville: Abingdon, 2004), 779.
5. Stanley High, *Billy Graham: The Personal Story of the Man, His Message, and His Mission* (New York: McGraw-Hill, 1956), 20.
6. Phillips Brooks, *Lectures on Preaching* (New York: E. P. Dutton & Co., 1907), quoted in Richard Lischer, *Theories of Preaching: Selected Readings in the Homiletical Tradition* (Durham: Labyrinth Press, 1987), 9.
7. Quotations from Graham's sermons are from the frequently repeated telecasts of Graham's classic crusades on Trinity Broadcasting Network (TBN).
8. John Broadus, *A Treatise on the Preparation and Delivery of Sermons* (New York: A. C. Armstrong & Sons, 1889), 28.
9. Charles Finney, "How to Preach the Gospel," *Lectures on Revivals of Religion* (New York: Fleming H. Revell, 1868), 16–17.
10. Ibid.
11. Edwards, "Evangelism in an Electronic Age," 778.
12. H. H. Farmer, *The Servant of the Word* (Philadelphia: Fortress Press, 1964), 122.
13. John B. Cobb Jr., "Law and Faith," in this volume.
14. Strober and Strober, *Billy Graham*, 7.
15. Quoted in ibid., 1.
16. Ibid., 84.
17. Ibid., 87.
18. George W. Bush and Karen Hughes, *A Charge to Keep* (New York: William Morrow, 1999), as quoted in Strober and Strober, *Billy Graham*, 100. The title of Bush's book is from a Charles Wesley hymn with the same title—a matter of some irony, as he consistently declined to meet with United Methodist bishops throughout his first term of office and has granted only a brief hearing in his second term.

3

Law and Faith

JOHN B. COBB JR.

Billy Graham was able throughout his long career to speak as a conservative Christian while giving minimal offense to liberal Christians. He recognized that there is diversity among authentic believers, and he encouraged an ecumenical spirit. He did not join those TV evangelists who rouse their hearers with tirades against liberals and homosexuals. He did not insist on an extreme fundamentalist view of the Bible. He has been a man of integrity, and at times he has acted effectively with great moral courage. For example, while segregation was still dominant in public meetings and churches in the South, he insisted that his campaigns there be integrated. Later he worked for nuclear disarmament.

Accordingly, those of us who appropriate the Bible through eyes informed by critical historical study, often called "liberals," have been hesitant to criticize him. There are so many other conservative preachers who offend us much more and with whom we have much less in common. They seem dangerous, whereas Graham's teaching appears benign. We may be inclined to object to its oversimplifications and to disagree with some of its emphases. But we suppose that overall its impact has been positive. In a world filled with persons who are almost wholly ignorant of the Bible and of Christian ethics and who have little idea about salvation, we appreciate Graham's ability to reach people who need to hear the gospel even if in an only introductory way. For us, who rarely reach these people at all, to criticize one who does so on a large scale seems unfair.

On the other hand, I, for one, hope that people will not stay where Graham leaves them. Indeed, the danger is that they go from Graham to other conservative teachers whose message is less benign. There are already pointers in Graham's teaching that lead in that direction. His simple formulations tend to reinforce ways of understanding the Christian life that are not compatible with the teaching of Paul or even of Jesus, as I understand them.

My focus in this chapter is on Graham's emphasis on law. This is a topic of great importance to all the founders of Protestantism. Indeed, if they had not been troubled by the way law functioned in the church of their time, there would have been no Reformation. They did not take erroneous or misleading formulations lightly, and I fear there is quite a lot in Graham's teaching that they would find unsatisfactory. They tried to be faithful to Paul, and it is by my reading of Paul that I will criticize Graham.

Basically Graham teaches that the Bible is a book of rules or directions for right living.[1] Since he obviously does not expect Christians to abide by all the Jewish laws, he singles out the Ten Commandments as that part of the law book that is universal, timeless, and absolute. He holds that, although we are called to complete obedience to these commandments, they function for us first to show us that we are in fact disobedient. They therefore point us to our need of the forgiveness made available to us by Jesus' atoning death. The new birth that results makes it possible for us to obey God's laws, or at least come much closer to doing so.

If by legalism we mean that we are told what to do and are saved or damned according to whether or not we obey, Graham's teaching is not legalism. Salvation is an unmerited gift of God in Graham's view, and obedience is made possible only by God's grace. However, legalism has another meaning in the Christian context. The more common form of Christian legalism is the understanding that what constitutes one's life as Christian is its conformation to God's laws. No doubt Graham modifies this a little with his emphasis on Christian love, but this legalistic view of Christianity is still the basic picture that many have heard from his preaching. The believer is to obey the laws or follow the rules, and Graham clarifies what these rules are.

Paul would not be pleased. His rejection of the law-bound life was radical. In Galatians he writes passionately against believers returning to the legalistic life. The life into which faith introduces them is life in the Spirit. In Romans he explains in detail that whereas before the coming of Jesus God's righteousness was revealed through the law as wrath, through Jesus it was revealed as love. The one who participates through faith in Jesus' faithfulness, suffering, and death is free from the law.

Some Christians have supposed that Paul thought we are free only from certain Jewish laws, especially circumcision. In particular they assume that

Christians are not free from the Ten Commandments. Billy Graham apparently follows this tradition.

But he gets no support from Paul in exempting the Ten Commandments from the law. Christians need to study Romans 7 again and again. Paul agrees with Graham that the law is holy, just, and good. Nevertheless it is bound up with sin. Graham thinks it functions to make us aware of our sinfulness.[2] Paul says that it actually makes us sinful and thereby brings "death." It is this whole complex of law, sin, and death that he associates with life in the flesh and contrasts with life in the Spirit. When Paul speaks of the positive role of law, it is "the law of the Spirit of life in Christ Jesus" that has set us "free from the law of sin and of death" (Rom. 8:2).

Of course, Paul was accused of antinomianism, that is, of teaching that all things are permitted and thus of opening the door to immorality of all sorts. No one would misunderstand Graham in that way, because he makes clear that in his view the Christian is bound to obey all sorts of laws. But this shows the contrast in the two theologies. Paul is, in one sense, an antinomian. He does declare that laws have no claim upon us. In Romans 14 he makes the point that nothing, in itself, is "unclean," and that means forbidden. But for Paul the issue in the Christian life is not to avoid what is forbidden; the issue is to do what love for the neighbor—and that means for all people—calls us to do.

For Paul, then, the Christian life is not lived by obedience to a series of rules, however wise and good those rules may be. Christians do not need them and are not to be trapped in that kind of life. In Romans 13 he makes explicit that the law—and he specifically refers to some of the Ten Commandments— is summed up in the one "word": "Love your neighbor as yourself." He does not call this a "law" here. If we do speak of the "law of love" fulfilling all laws, we must be clear that this "law" functions in an entirely different way from other laws. We do not love our neighbors in obedience to a divine commandment. We can't. We love our neighbors because we experience ourselves as loved by God and are thereby freed of the need to make ourselves righteous.

Should there be any lingering doubt that, for Paul, the law from which we are freed as Christians includes the Ten Commandments, such doubt should be put to rest by noting the commandment he chooses for his explanation of the interconnection of the law and sin and death: the commandment against coveting found specifically in the Ten Commandments.

One might defend Graham by saying that Paul is too complicated to use as a basis for evangelism, that we must begin with simpler formulations. People already understand the meaning of obedience to law, and most recognize, at least dimly, that they do not always obey all the moral laws. By heightening that awareness, people can be brought to repent and to accept new life through Jesus' atoning death. Then they can again be encouraged to obey the law, and they can be supported by Christian fellowship in doing so. To teach them prematurely about being free from the law could lead to unacceptable behavior.

If one could be sure that Graham intended his legalism as a first step into the richness of life in Christ, the argument would be simply about strategy. But I, for one, cannot be at all sure about that. And I have little confidence that most of those he has drawn into Christian fellowship will be encouraged to move beyond the legalism of this introduction.

If the defense of Graham's legalism in the face of Paul's emphatic rejection of such legalism should be that evangelistic preaching cannot enter into such complexities, I must disagree. I am a product of a great revival movement that was based on a much more Pauline theology—that of John Wesley. I must acknowledge that we Methodists have, time and again, fallen back into legalism, but that was not Wesley's message. I believe that Wesley's success as an evangelist shows that evangelists do not have to preach a legalistic message.

Wesley has a somewhat similar understanding of the law with respect to its making us realize our sinfulness, but he develops it with one major difference. Wesley emphasizes the Sermon on the Mount instead of the Ten Commandments. That all people, even the most virtuous, find themselves sinners in light of the Sermon on the Mount is more evident than is the case with the Ten Commandments. In the context in which they were formulated, the focus was strongly on behavior, and at the level of behavior, obedience to these commandments is not altogether rare. Some of us, even those who are not Christian, avoid stealing and murdering and even bearing false witness. In order to make the commandments seem more demanding, Graham tweaks them in a subjective direction.

The advantage of holding up the Ten Commandments as the summary of the law is that it is understandable that, after regeneration, obedience to them becomes a relatively practical goal. If the Christian life consists in following the biblical way, and that way is understood in terms of rules or laws of behavior, the Ten Commandments work much better than the Sermon on the Mount. And this is the basic pattern proposed by Graham.

For Wesley, however, the Sermon on the Mount provides an understanding of what truly loving our neighbors as ourselves entails. In no way does it function as a set of rules distinct from love. The whole issue of the Christian life focuses on love of God and neighbor. This is an extremely exalted goal.

When one knows God's forgiving love, one experiences justification and begins the process of sanctification. Persons who are justified act as love requires. That is, although love is the governing motive in their lives, it still struggles with other motives. The process of sanctification is one of the growth of love.

I do not propose that we read all this back into Paul. I do propose that it follows Paul in seeing love as central and rejecting legalism. Of course, if one acts as love requires, one will avoid many things that legalists forbid and do many things that legalists require. But the difference is great.

For one who follows Paul, the Bible is not a rule book, as Graham describes it. One does not look for eternally fixed and unchanging principles of morality. Of course, if one wishes, one can discern common patterns in the way love expresses itself always or almost always. But the focus is on the specifics of the concrete situation. That is always changing. It is highly desirable to be well informed, and the information relevant to how best to express love changes. Patterns of behavior that expressed love in earlier days may not do so now. To use the Bible as a rule book can have very damaging consequences.

Jesus saw that clearly. He broke some of the laws of his day. He asserted that the Sabbath exists for the sake of people (Mark 2:23–28). When rules understood to specify how the Sabbath is to be kept end up harming people instead of helping them, they should be set aside. For Jesus, too, love of neighbor is the decisive basis of right action.

Paul's objection to law and his call for the life of love went deeper. He saw that the whole orientation toward law was personally damaging. He expressed this view strongly by saying that it led to death. Love, on the other hand, is healing and maturing, both of the one who loves and of the one toward whom it is directed.

Many people understand Christianity as life lived by a code of rules they were taught as children. Often the moral rules were generally good ones, and to have such a guide stands many in good stead. For Graham to call people back to such a code and sometimes thoughtfully to improve upon it was a service of benefit to many.[3]

But there are many others who have outgrown these childhood codes. They have learned that what was encoded was the wisdom, and sometimes the prejudice, of a particular generation—not the ultimate truth about right and wrong. They have found that subscribing to such a code tends to make them judgmental in relation to those who live by other codes, and they want to see reality from a broader perspective that generates greater understanding and compassion.

Some of these people mature in this way in the church through a deeper understanding of the gospel. But many suppose that to outgrow the original code is to outgrow Christianity. For the sake of the freedom Paul affirms, they cut themselves loose from the community whose rightful task is to nurture that freedom. They turn away from Paul, and often from Jesus too, wrongly supposing that these are supporters of the legalism they now reject.

What happens to these church alumni is quite varied. Many live fruitful lives and serve important causes. Others succumb to new forms of law or lose their moral bearings along with the rules they rightly outgrew. Many adjust to a society in which the pursuit of wealth and sex are primary driving forces.

Even those who are the best models find it difficult to pass on to their children the meanings that have guided them.

Billy Graham is not responsible for the large number of church alumni in our society. But his message has tended to reinforce the reasons that they left the church. Living a Christian life, in his message, seems closely connected to adopting the kind of code many have rightly outgrown.

Just what the laws are that enter into this code is a secondary question. Actually, for one who takes the Bible as the authoritative rule book without much historical reflection, any systematic answer would be very difficult. This is less so for Jews, since orthodox Jews take all the laws, as they have come down to them through an elaborate process of interpretation, as binding. But Graham never advocates that Christians adopt the dietary laws. He may base this on Paul's writings against the law, but he does not explain how that is to be done. Paul never distinguishes the laws that are still valid from those that are superseded. Christian legalists face this task with very little help from the Bible.

Graham wants us to observe a day of rest and worship, but he does not follow the Bible further on this. Observing the Sabbath does not involve obeying biblical laws on the Sabbath. Most important, whereas the only explicit commandment in the Bible about a day of rest specifies Saturday, Graham is comfortable with the early church's shift to Sunday.

In general, the laws Graham emphasizes are the laws that have been emphasized in conservative Protestant circles in the past century. In other words, they reflect recent experience and concern rather than a serious study of the Bible. For example, he shares with most conservative Christians an emphasis on sexuality and what are now called "family values." Since much of the Bible takes polygamy for granted and does not criticize it, for support of what we now mean by family values we are forced to go to the New Testament. There, in both Jesus and Paul, the ideal is celibacy. Since the proponents of family values do not advocate celibacy, wisely, they turn to a few passages they attribute to Paul, mostly from the deuteropauline literature.

Paul's own comments on family values are very limited. He said that although celibacy is better than marriage, it was better to marry than to "burn." If one were to conform to this social custom, one should follow its rules. In both Jewish and Roman society, the only marriage that existed was patriarchal marriage. Accordingly, Paul took male dominance in marriage for granted. His distinctive teaching was to emphasize mutuality within that structure. Paul was not a social reformer. His work was to create a new type of community within the established Roman society. Within his communities women could play leadership roles, but he did not try to impose this pattern on the larger society. His views of patriarchy were like his views of slavery. These were social relationships of no importance within his communities, but they could not be countered in the general society.

In the United States, for a long time Paul's acceptance of slavery in the wider society was taken as justifying the continuation of a much worse form of slavery in American society. Finally, Christians saw that this was a profound misunderstanding of the meaning of the Bible for their time. Similarly, Paul's acceptance of patriarchal marriage is still widely used by conservatives to justify the maintenance of patriarchy forever. This emphasis on just what Paul belittled is not a faithful use of his writings. It is governed by beliefs and attitudes derived from other sources. To Graham's credit, he recognizes and emphasizes Paul's distinctive concern for mutuality within marriage, although he does not allow this to overcome his affirmation of patriarchy.

Once again, one might ask, is this not the necessary role of the evangelist? Must not the evangelist emphasize those moral issues that he sees as most pressing rather than those most important to the biblical writers? I will counter again by pointing to Wesley. Sexual and gender issues were on the minds of English people in the eighteenth century. But it is remarkable how little Wesley attended to them. In this, he followed the Bible, rather than reversing the balance as is the case with so much conservatism today.

I emphasize again that Graham's legalism is moderated by his recognition of the primacy of love. It may be that his recent focus on love has really changed the nature of the Christian life in his view. However, considering his ministry as a whole, the impact has been to strengthen legalism.

Consider the issue of homosexual acts, so important in the church today. Graham has not been among those who play on the widespread homophobia in our society to arouse support for their own campaigns or wider political programs. But Graham certainly understands homosexual acts as against the moral law of God. This has been the primary category within which he has understood them. This illustrates what I mean by legalism.

There are alternatives. One can ask, given a strongly homosexual orientation, how should a Christian live? Suppose we understand the Christian life in terms of love rather than obedience to an unchanging moral code. We might still decide that lifelong celibacy is the best choice. But we might not. We might recommend marriage even if the sexual side of marriage would be unsatisfactory for both partners. But we might not. We certainly would not favor unrestricted promiscuity—for many reasons. We might decide that a faithful relationship with a beloved companion is a better choice. It would not then occur to us to call this choice a sin.

One might respond that at this point I am turning away from Paul. No doubt I am expressing some disagreement with one of Paul's judgments. But I am loyal here to his basic theology. In the famous passage in the first chapter of Romans, so beloved of those who desire to condemn homosexuals, Paul is writing about the corruption of society that follows from idolatry. When society is ordered to something less than God, when it substitutes some creature for the Creator as its object of devotion, it becomes profoundly disordered. This disorder is described in the climax to this passage in verses 28 to 32 in terms of a list of vices and crimes in which sexuality plays no direct role. It then leads to the conclusion, unfortunately now separated from the rest of the passage by a chapter break, that "therefore you have no excuse, whoever you are, when you judge others."

Yet just this passage, in which Paul argues that we should not judge one another, is often taken as the chief basis for condemning homosexuals for acting on their sexual nature. This use of the passage shows the legalistic habits of mind of those who use it for this purpose. It does not point to Paul's intention or meaning.

There is no doubt that Paul regards homosexual practices as important signs of the corruption of society (Rom. 1:26–27). He discusses these in the context of degrading passions to which God has given people up because of their idolatry. Surely Paul is correct that an idolatrous society is one in which degrading passions govern a great deal of practice. He is also correct that this expresses itself in much sexual behavior, including that of homosexuals. This would certainly have been true of male prostitution at the temples—the most public and visible expression of homosexuality at the time.[4]

No doubt Paul shared the Jewish prejudice of the time against any form of homosexual act and therefore regarded all homosexuality as a sign of social corruption. At this point my views are different from his. But this is a difference in factual judgments rather than in theology. The theological position I share with Paul is that all action, including all sexual activity, should be ordered to the love and service of the one God known to us in Jesus Christ and expressed through love and service of all our neighbors. What this means in each individual case is not decided by any book of rules.

If one turns this whole description of the corruption of society into a set of rules, it makes no sense at all. Paul saw it as a description of the society in which we are all enmeshed. Accordingly, no one is in position to condemn anyone else. Legalists turn this passage into a list of sins for which each individual sinner is responsible. Today they usually highlight homosexual acts as the chief of sins. Accordingly, they do not draw Paul's conclusion that we should not judge one another.

That Graham's moderate legalism has shaped his views of public events as well as his private life is also apparent. He recognized that segregation is wrong, and he opposed it effectively. He was not a racist. But when blacks rioted in northern cities, Graham's basic legalism governed his response. He interpreted what happened primarily in terms of the violation of moral requirements. He was critical of those who examined the sociological and economic situation that lay behind the rioting.[5] That does not mean that he failed to love the individuals who rioted. He took seriously the adage to hate the sin and love the sinner. But the primary expression of this double relation was to call the sinner to repentance. Loving individual blacks and behaving justly toward them did not lead to the effort to understand how their situation contributed to their immoral and illegal actions. He did not support the efforts of those who felt called by love to change this situation.

How does biblical teaching stand on this issue? It is hard to say. On the one hand, the individualism that is presupposed by the contemporary forms of legalism is absent from the Bible. God is seen there, for the most part, as dealing with Israel in a collective way. There is a movement toward emphasizing individual responsibility beginning with Jeremiah and Ezekiel, but in Judaism to the present day this movement does not replace the strong sense of the collective identity of Jews. Paul continued to think primarily in collective terms, although individuals were held accountable for their behavior as participants in these collectives, as Jews or Gentiles, for example, or as participants in the new communities of believers.

On the other hand, the possibility of restructuring society or the economy in such a way that the condition of blacks would be improved has only indirect support in the Bible. The prophets viewed their societies in terms of what happened to the poor and the oppressed, and they sharply criticized the economic and legal injustices they observed. These were sins that the societies as a whole committed, of course, *through* individuals. But it never occurred to the biblical authors that a different structuring of society was possible or desirable. That idea developed, almost for the first time, in the eighteenth century. It has led to enormous social experimentation, with very mixed results. In the United States it has led only to modest tinkering.

In my view, any attempt to bring biblical teaching *directly* to bear on basic social and economic issues of our time requires misreading the Bible. I myself stand in the trajectory initiated by the prophets, and I believe that, now that human beings understand that they are able to make major social changes in democratic ways, we should attempt to improve the basic structures of society, albeit cautiously and moderately. But I advocate this not because it is directly biblical but because that seems to me to be what love of fellow human beings, and especially love of the poor and oppressed, calls us to do. The legalistic response is to judge members of oppressed groups as sinners when they respond violently and illegally to those who control them. I do not doubt that personal sinfulness is a factor in that kind of response. But I find it difficult to understand how Christians can see condemnation of this sin and a call to repent of it as the fullest possible expression of love. For this reason I assume that those who respond in this way focus more on other laws than on the "law of love."

Another example of the consequences of legalism can be found in Graham's relations with President Nixon. We know that he felt deeply betrayed when he learned that Nixon had engaged in immoral and illegal acts connected with Watergate. He was also appalled when he heard tapes of Nixon's conversations with his advisors that were filled with profanity and vulgarity. I also respond negatively to all of that. But these personal sins seem to me to be of far less importance than the escalation of war in Southeast Asia. Graham saw sin more in those who vigorously protested the war, disrupted the normal functioning of society, and occasionally resorted to violence than in those who caused the misery and destruction in Vietnam.

Legalism with regard to Christian life is almost inevitably associated with an emphasis on God as lawgiver and judge. I have said that Graham's legalism is moderated by his belief in God's love. But too often it is the legalism that triumphs. God's love is affirmed in Graham's preaching, but it is frequently subordinated to God's justice. It seems that he fears that too much emphasis on God's love will reduce the pressure to observe God's laws. That he does not want to do.

Once again the contrast with Paul is marked. Paul consistently affirms God's righteousness or justice. Before Jesus that righteousness appeared generally as wrath, that is, the proper response to the corruption and degradation of the world. But in Jesus' faithfulness to God, even to death on the cross, God's righteousness is revealed as love. This love does not simply qualify God's justice so that God becomes a bit more merciful. This love *is* God's righteousness and justice. Those who do not participate in Jesus' faithfulness do not yet experience the effects of God's love. But according to Paul's fullest account of what we hope for, in Romans 8, this will be revealed in the end through the resurrection of all and the transformation of the whole world.

Must evangelistic preaching emphasize God's judgment so as to persuade believers to live righteous lives? No. Wesley's approach, for example, was quite different. He, like Graham, was against those who simply proclaimed God's loving acceptance of all, but he did not talk about God as judge. Instead, he held before people an image of the Christian life that made them both desire to be Christian and also recognize the gap between their actual lives and what they were called to be. He drew people into the life of love. He did not drive them by fear into obedience to laws.

In conclusion, I will comment on Graham's relation to Scripture. I have noted that he looks to the Bible as the authoritative source of law, and I have commented that this is very different from Paul's understanding. Graham's legalistic view of the role of Scripture is accompanied in his thought, as in many other instances, by an objectification of the Bible as itself an object of faith. For some fundamentalists the Bible is actually the primary object of faith, but this does not ever seem to have been the case with Graham.

Nevertheless, it has been a very important object of faith. When Graham writes about his struggle to believe, the belief in question is not belief in God or faith in Jesus Christ but acceptance of the idea that everything in the Bible is the authoritative word of God. He struggled with this because there is so much in the Bible that offended his own moral sensibilities and that did not seem to be true. He later considered that to have been a great victory of faith. But still later he became open to a more flexible understanding of the Bible.

There are three troubling elements in the teaching that the Bible's inerrancy should be an object of our faith. First, the Bible and church history do not support such a view of Scripture. Second, there is much in the Bible that one should not believe in any straightforward way. Third, this teaching expresses and encourages an unhealthy understanding of faith.

The first two of these are familiar issues. Jesus is not depicted as taking received Scripture as final and absolute. Incidents in Jesus' life are recounted somewhat diversely in the several Gospels, and all accounts cannot be exactly accurate. Paul's use of Scripture (review Rom. 9–11) is extremely free and creative. "The scriptures" referred to in 2 Timothy 3:16 are quite different from our Bible, and the fact that they are said to be useful is hardly equivalent to declaring them to be inerrant. The process of determining the canon in the early church was not one of discerning God's inerrant authorship but estimates of the probability that the authors of New Testament books were apostles or close to apostles. Such estimates today would exclude a number of the books in our canon. The Catholic canon includes items not in the Protestant one. Luther's exclusion of some of the recognized canon of his day was based on the lack of Hebrew versions. The view that just those books now in our Protestant canon were uniquely inspired by God and that none others were is not supported by any of this.

Secondly, the main concern of Graham himself is that some of the depictions of God, dating from early stages of Hebrew history, are offensive. He may have had difficulty believing that the command to commit genocide attributed to God actually came from the one Jesus prayed to as *Abba*. Actually, there is much more in the Bible that we should recognize as falling short of valid standards today. Much of the Bible was written before monotheism was established and reflects henotheism instead. Much of it takes for granted a polygamous patriarchal culture. Even the Ten Commandments are clearly directed only to male heads of households.

Thirdly, the faith Graham struggled to attain was one that ran, even in his mind at the time, not just beyond reason but against it. This is emphatically not the faith through which Christians are saved. That faith is trust in the God revealed in Jesus. It includes believing that God loves us even when we sin and are wholly unworthy of that love. It emphatically does not include affirming mutually contradictory propositions or assertions that contradict well-established facts. It does not include believing about the Bible what the biblical authors do not claim about their own writings.

Sadly, many have rejected Christianity because they suppose that to be a Christian involves believing what they have no reason to believe is true and considerable reason to believe is false. They are right to reject faith understood in that way. But that is no reason to reject the revelation of God in Jesus Christ or the fellowship of those who seek to participate in Jesus' faithfulness to God.

In no way do I suggest that Graham is responsible for this widespread misunderstanding of Christian faith. It originated with the demand that Christians accept as final doctrine the decisions of church councils. The primary reason for this demand was to put an end to divisive debate. But since the councils put forward their decisions as creeds, faith came to be associated with unquestioning acceptance of some very obscure formulations. Like the compromises expressed in many committee reports, these creeds are often not truly coherent or even intelligible. The resulting faith, far from being directed to God, was directed to church authorities. From my point of view, this faith is idolatrous. One may agree that a conciliar formulation was the best that was possible at that time and under those circumstances, and one may support it as a wise resolution of a particular problem. But one should never direct what Paul calls faith to such a document or to the institution that adopts it.

The Protestant Reformers refused to direct their faith to the ecclesiastical institutions and hierarchies of their day. They insisted that Christians should return to the faith about which Paul wrote. This, of course, involved placing the authority of Scripture above that of current church teaching. They used rhetoric about the Scriptures that led some of their followers, in a succeeding generation, to formulate extreme doctrines of scriptural inspiration.

For some time the issue of just what it means to say that Scripture is inspired was on the periphery of theology. The central focus was understanding the text and developing its implications for the present time. Questions about how the New Testament is related to the Old were important, but in general the inspiration of the Old Testament could be affirmed while also understanding that much of its teaching was superseded by the New Testament. The humanness of the text was largely taken for granted.

The doctrines of inspiration that supported the idea of the inerrancy of Scripture became much more important to some Protestants when scientific accounts of the origin of species and the evolution of human beings challenged the Genesis account. They also took on new energy when historical-critical scholarship was widely applied to the Bible. In the early twentieth century fundamentalism became a self-conscious movement within the churches. Graham was educated in this context.

For this reason he, as a man of integrity, struggled with the notion of requiring that Christians accept the view of Scripture presented to him. I do not intend my comments about this being a misdirection of faith as personal criticism. In his context, Graham has always remained a moderate in his acceptance of fundamentalist doctrine, and he has actually moved away from it in more recent years.[6]

I introduce this topic only because of Graham's vast influence on others. That influence has leaned in the direction of calling for faith in the Bible. I am convinced that the Bible is not the proper object of faith. Such faith is a form of idolatry, that is, of making a god out of a creature. For those who have such faith, it is an obstacle to a full Christian experience and life. It is a form of bondage instead of Christian freedom. For those who suppose that this faith is required of every Christian, it is an obstacle to identifying themselves as Christians at all. Accordingly, Graham's support of this kind of faith, however moderate he has been in promoting it, is not a minor matter.

I conclude with a theme that has run through my chapter. Billy Graham is a man who deserves the respect of his fellow Christians. He has served his Lord honorably and with great success. He has served as a voice of moderation in a community that has become increasingly shrill, a voice of affirmation in a context where negation has become dominant. He has been cooperative on an ecumenical basis where others have sown discord. He has shown moral courage and integrity in a context where that has often been absent. He has accomplished much where others of us have accomplished very little. I take no pleasure in criticizing him.

Nevertheless, just because of his enormous and generally benign influence, it is important to examine his teaching with some care. That it is simplistic may simply go with the territory of popular preaching. I have not been interested in that charge. The question is whether it points in the right direction, and regretfully I have to judge that it does not always do so.

One of the great weaknesses of Christianity in many times and places is that it reverts to the legalism from which Jesus and Paul originally liberated believers. I fear that the preaching and teaching of Billy Graham has tended much more to reinforce that legalism than to challenge it. A second great weakness of Christianity in many times and places is that it reverts to the idolatry that the prophets, Jesus, and Paul struggled against. Among committed Christians the most common idols have been the church and the Bible. I fear that Graham has tended to support the latter form of idolatry much more than to free Christians from it.

I hope no reader will suppose that Graham's teaching has been an egregious case of these failures. He is to be commended for his moderation. But moderation in theological error does not do away with the error. Graham shares the errors with myriads of preachers and laypeople. The result is a serious threat to the ability of Americans to hear the gospel.

NOTES

1. Graham refers to the Bible as "God's rule book" in several published writings and sermons. See, for instance, Billy Graham, "The Game of Life," *Decision*, May 1982, 2. The cover of this issue includes a photograph of a young man holding a black book titled "Holy Rule Book."
2. Graham frequently claims that God gave us the Ten Commandments "in order to show us that we are sinful and weak" (Billy Graham, "Why the Ten Commandments?" *Decision*, April 1989, 3).
3. For Graham, strict adherence to God's code of rules offered moral and spiritual certainty to people living in an "uncertain world" (Billy Graham, "Certainty in an Uncertain World," *Decision*, September 1992, 1–3).
4. See John Cobb, *Matters of Life and Death* (Louisville, KY: Westminster John Knox Press, 1991), 94–120; and *Progressive Christians Speak: A Different Voice on Faith and Politics*, ed. John Cobb (Louisville, KY: Westminster John Knox Press, 2003), 76–88.
5. In a 1967 sermon on riots, Graham stated: "We have been told over and over again by some of our leaders in Washington that poverty is the cause of crime. This is just not true. . . . The problem of rioting and crime is far deeper than just poverty. No amount of money is going to change the present situation. We need new, tough laws against the subversive elements that are seeking the overthrow of the American government" (Billy Graham, *Rioting or Righteousness* [Minneapolis: The Billy Graham Evangelistic Association, 1967], 3–4.)
6. Graham moved away from his fundamentalist colleagues when he adopted an ecumenical approach to his crusade planning. His willingness to work with Catholics received especially harsh criticism from fundamentalist quarters.

Social Issues

4

"Keep Yourself Pure"

Social Justice and Sexual Ethics

KAREN LEBACQZ

Billy Graham's sexual ethic portrays the values on which I was raised: lifelong marriage as the ideal, no sex before marriage, no homosexuality, no adultery, and—above all else—sexual purity as a framing concept. Because I was raised on this ethic, it has deep resonance for me. However, much of my adult life and professional work have been devoted to countering some of the assumptions and conclusions that are so powerfully exhibited by Graham. Thus, I say yes and no to Graham: he is both right and wrong.

The key is to determine where the right and wrong occur. Is he right about divorce? Adultery? Premarital sex? Homosexuality? Temptation? Nudity? While each of these issues might be a chapter in itself, I have chosen a different route. Instead of addressing particular topics, I will assess Graham's underlying vision, captured in the admonition to "keep yourself pure." I will argue that Graham is not wrong to think purity is important, but that he is wrong in his understanding of what purity is and of its place and implications for sexual ethics.

A FEW CAVEATS

I must first offer some caveats. It is never fair to read an author out of context. Graham's ministry continues through the organization that carries his name, but many of his own writings predate some important biblical scholarship and ethical treatises on sexuality. To the extent possible, in my critique I have used

49

materials that might have been available to Graham during his most active years. At the end, however, I will offer a critique that is more contemporary, even while noting that failure to deal with these issues is not altogether a fault that we can rightly lay at Graham's door.

Form shapes function. Graham never sought to write a magnum opus on sexual ethics. While sex is a very common theme in his work, much of that work is done in "question and answer" format. (Even his book chapters on marriage, divorce, premarital sex, and other sexual issues are sometimes crafted as answers to queries submitted by concerned Christians.) This format has its limitations. Like Paul's letters, Graham's advice is often practical, heart-felt, and concrete, but it is also often truncated and lacks extended ethical analysis. A solid ethical critique therefore requires extension from Graham's own work.

The best such extension would demonstrate familiarity with the whole corpus of Graham's writing. This I cannot do. My reflections are based on a collection of writings by and about Graham, all focused on sexual issues.[1] The collection includes a number of Graham's "My Answer" columns; some news clippings; a few book chapters and assorted excerpts, including a selection from Graham's autobiography; and some secondary work on Graham's sexual experiences and sexual ethics. The materials cover a range of issues and decades, but they may not give a full picture of Graham's mature theology and sexual ethics. My analysis is therefore preliminary and subject to revision.

With these caveats in hand, I will summarize Graham's counsel on several key issues, display the underlying ethical and theological framing for that counsel, and then offer a response and critique.

GRAHAM ON SEXUAL ETHICS

Graham's basic vision is both clear and simple. Sex is a gift from God, intended for human fulfillment.[2] It is meant to be an expression of love and is not, in and of itself, dirty or shameful. As with all of God's gifts, however, sex brings the responsibility of proper use.[3] Sex is also powerful. It is one of the ways that Satan works to tempt us, and its power must be harnessed appropriately.[4]

The appropriate harnessing is marriage. Sex outside of marriage—whether before (premarital) or during (adultery) or after (the widowed in later life)—is wrong. The only context that makes sex acceptable is the commitment made in marriage.[5] Homosexuality is therefore wrong, as marriage is only between a man and a woman.[6]

Marriage is ordained of God, not to be entered lightly, and includes a solemn vow to be faithful sexually.[7] Graham is very clear that genuine love is not the same as sexual attraction or romantic love.[8] While the ideal is lifelong marriage, Graham does make some room for divorce where there is abuse or no hope for reconciliation.[9] Nonetheless, before a troubled marriage can be terminated, it should be "taken back to God."[10]

Divorce may be countenanced in some circumstances, but adultery never is. Graham claims that the Bible makes absolutely no allowances for sexual relations outside marriage (1 Cor. 6:18–7:2) and that the act of infidelity is "so destructive" that Christ made it the sole acceptable reason for divorce (Matt. 5:32).[11] To those who have "fallen in love" with someone other than their spouse, Graham's response is clear: breaking the marriage vow to marry another would be wrong (Matt. 19:6: "What God has joined together, let no one separate").[12] On this subject, then, the commandment is absolute, the judgment sure (Heb. 13:4).[13]

Another sure judgment falls on homosexuality, a sin of self-gratification.[14] Paul said that none who are guilty of homosexual perversion will possess the kingdom of God (1 Cor. 6:9). Put simply, "homosexual behavior is wrong in God's eyes."[15]

Because much of his ministry has focused on young people, Graham often has addressed "premarital" sex,[16] and here, too, his judgments have been consistent and strong. Partly because of his own experiences, Graham has recognized just how powerful sexual temptation can be.[17] Nonetheless, he has counseled that God will give youths the strength to follow their convictions if they but turn their lives over to Jesus.

Petting is wrong because it paves the way for sensuality and further sin and will no doubt cause problems in later marriage: "Happy is the person who marries a mate who has not been pawed over."[18] Indeed, Graham has often stressed the bad consequences that he believed would follow any sexual license before marriage: sexually transmitted disease, harm to one's constitution and mental life, lack of trust and eventual breakdown of any later marriage.[19] Ultimately, Graham lays at the foot of the sexual revolution the charge that it will bring about the collapse of our civilization. The greatest threat to democracy, he once declared, is moral decadence.[20]

"In my opinion, sex is probably America's greatest sin," wrote Graham.[21] He also once suggested that most social ills could be cured by covering up the female bosom.[22] We are living in a sex-saturated culture, Graham believes, and that will be our undoing.[23] He contends that America is experiencing not sexual *revolution* but sexual *pollution*.[24] This brings us to his underlying vision.

THE UNDERLYING ETHICAL
AND THEOLOGICAL VISION

Pollution and purity provide the underlying ethical frame for Graham's approach to sex. "Keep yourself pure," taken from 1 Timothy 5:22 and invoked frequently, sums up Graham's vision, passion, and purpose.[25] Graham biographer Marshall Frady even likens the evangelist to Billy Budd, a man possessing "a staggering passion for the pure."[26]

Purity means no hint of sexual immorality (Eph. 5:3); we are not to be enslaved by our lusts.[27] Purity also extends to choosing a sexual partner who shares our faith (2 Cor. 6:14).[28] We should seek a pure heart, and this we receive when we confess our sins and accept Christ. Once we have done so, we must then live a pure life—which will bring us happiness.[29]

A pure life means purity in physical, mental, and moral dimensions.[30] Physical purity includes literal cleanliness but also chastity. Mental purity entails no lust in our hearts or eyes. A lustful look is impure. Dressing immodestly is impure. Reading unclean books is impure. Purity of conduct includes honesty, integrity, and truthfulness.

Graham also claims that impurity *marks* people.[31] The impure develop the shifty glance, the lewd stare, the guilty conscience. Impurity ultimately overcomes people, becoming their master, and they become miserable. Graham's specific proscriptions in the sexual arena are geared toward his underlying concern for purity.

This passion for purity is coupled with an acute understanding that none of us are beyond temptation. We all sin, and therefore we all need forgiveness. Hence, Graham's every admonition and declaration on sexual morality is coupled with the assurance of God's love and desire to forgive. If purity is the underlying ethical theme, it is *forgiveness* that provides the underlying theological theme. God so loves us that God gave up God's precious child for the sake of our sins. If we will but repent and turn our hearts to God, everything will be forgiven.[32]

A RESPONSE AND CRITIQUE

At first glance, Graham's vision and accompanying sexual ethic seem relatively innocuous, possibly compelling. Certainly the approach is not new. Christians have long argued that God's intention for sexual expression is within a lifelong committed marriage. Christians have also long claimed that homosexuality is wrong. Graham's teachings accord with Protestant (and some recent Roman Catholic) tradition in suggesting that sex is not simply for procreation but also for union—for the deepening and fulfillment and enjoyment of the marital relationship. To this extent, he stands solidly within a long tradition.

Where Graham perhaps differs most from some of his contemporaries is in the area of single ("premarital") sex. Numerous boards, commissions, and individual Christian thinkers made room during the 1960s and subsequent decades for some forms of sexual intimacy before marriage and for loving homosexual unions.[33] By contrast, Graham seems to have an "all or nothing" approach: there are no gradations of commitment or of intimacy—it is either all or nothing. Any premarital sex, even for an engaged couple, appears as promiscuity. One is either pure or polluted.

This polarity is a first hint at something troubling in Graham's vision. Reading the material available to me, I first thought that Graham dwelt on sex because his audience so often put sexual questions before him. Increasingly, however, I developed a suspicion confirmed by William Martin's assessment that Graham "devoted what was clearly a disproportionate, if not inordinate, amount of attention to sex-related topics."[34] With poverty, hunger, the aftermath of war, crime, unjust wages, racial tensions, and other social ills abounding, why does sex gain such prominence in Graham's work? He charges that America is obsessed with sex, but the reader cannot help but wonder whether it is not Graham himself who is—or at least was in his early years—obsessed with sex. Despite his acknowledgment that sex is a good gift of God, overwhelmingly Graham stresses its dangers and potential for polluting.[35]

Graham's appeals to the dangerous consequences of sexual license are generally absent any supporting data.[36] They reflect convictions that are not well demonstrated or documented. They are reminiscent of appeals in every generation that civilization is threatened by contemporary movements and changes.[37]

In fairness, Graham has practiced what he has preached. He claims that he never touched a woman wrongly, that his first sexual intercourse took place on his wedding night, and that he has never committed adultery.[38] I believe him. Graham understood the power of sexual temptation in his own life, and he took steps to protect against temptation, going so far as never to be alone with a woman other than his wife and making sure his male colleagues had hotel rooms near his.[39] He made every effort to live out the sexual ethic of purity that he preached for more than half a century. If purity means "celibacy before marriage and fidelity within it," then Graham embodies that purity.[40]

But is this what purity means? Is purity about celibacy outside marriage and fidelity within it? Is purity the important issue for human sexuality? Here is where I have the most difficulty with Graham. And if he is wrong, the implications are profound.

Let me start with purity. Like Graham, I am not a biblical scholar. The much-quoted passage on purity from 1 Timothy 5:22, however, sits in a context that

Graham does not address. The context includes such practical advice as drinking wine as well as water, paying adequate wages to workers, being cautious about accepting rumors of wrongdoing, and acting against partiality. The admonition to purity follows these concerns. The "purity" intended in 1 Timothy, then, seems to have less to do with sex and more to do with avoiding sins committed by others, such as partiality or favoritism or a hasty "laying on of hands" (5:21–22). Yet in Graham's work, "purity" becomes almost synonymous with sexual concerns. This makes it crucial to know whether Graham has interpreted biblical views on sexuality correctly.

The Presbyterian Church (U.S.A.) notes that use of Scripture is always subject to three interpretive difficulties.[41] First, the Bible never comes without prior interpretation. The King James text, for instance, already involves interpretive decisions about translation of Greek terms. Second, there is considerable diversity within Scripture: the Bible often presents powerful theological views in tension with one another. Third, the social and historical distance between the first century and our own setting makes it difficult to know what Paul or his contemporaries really intended.

Graham's use of Scripture exemplifies all three of these interpretive difficulties. He uses the King James text as though it comes without prior interpretation. He takes particular passages out of context and ignores other passages. And he does not address the significant differences between New Testament times and our own time—for instance, the likelihood that "homosexuality" as we know it was not what Paul addressed.[42] Graham's interpretation of the biblical meaning of purity is therefore suspect.

For a better understanding of the biblical meaning of "purity" and its implications, I turn to New Testament scholar William Countryman, who notes that the Bible was always concerned about "dirt" or purity and that most sexual ethics were assimilated under purity rules. However, whereas the code of purity in the United States has become individualized, in the original Holiness Code of Leviticus, purity had to do with separating *nations*, not individuals. Sexual matters were ways of separating the ancient Israelites from other nations—by requiring circumcision of males, for instance. The issue was not individual behavior but social cohesion.[43]

What about Jesus? How did he and his followers deal with the purity tradition they inherited from ancient Israel? Did they come closer to Graham's understanding? Countryman suggests that the inclusion of uncircumcised males (Gentiles) into the early Christian community already meant that "purity" of physical bodies was being replaced by concern for purity of the heart. In Mark's Gospel, the category of physical purity is set aside altogether in favor of purity of intention: only intent to harm renders a sexual act impure.[44] In Matthew's Gospel, Jesus sets purity concerns over against other ethical demands, such as the demand for justice. "The only possible conclusion," suggests Countryman, "is that physical purity is no longer a determinative element in our relationship with God."[45]

Because Paul is so often quoted by Graham on sexual issues, it is important to note that Countryman finds no evidence that Paul ever singled out sexual impurity as a supreme example of sinfulness. Indeed, his list of major sins in Romans 1:28–32 contains no mention of sexuality at all. While Paul differs from the Gospels in retaining the application of "purity" to the physical dimension (Rom. 1:24–27), Countryman argues that *idolatry* is the root sin for Paul and that certain homosexual acts were used as examples of the unclean practices that tend to accompany idolatry.[46] Graham comes closest to this interpretation when he concedes that homosexuality, while a sin in his view, is no worse than any other sin condemned by Paul, such as greed or adultery.[47]

Graham's emphasis on sexual purity and its significance for our relationship with God is therefore significantly challenged by Countryman's analysis. Intentions, not acts, matter most. Homosexuality alone could not prevent a person from entering the reign of God. While many of Graham's pronouncements predate Countryman's scholarship, other significant texts challenging a negative assessment of homosexuality were certainly available to Graham.[48]

However, it is the framing of sexual ethics almost entirely in terms of purity that is the most problematic for me. I stand among authors who argue that any adequate sexual ethic must address issues of sexual injustice.[49] Because he deliberately has avoided discussing politics at certain points, however, Graham often has eschewed important questions of power and its impact on people's lives. He has kept sexuality entirely within the arena of "private" ethics and has failed to see that sexuality is permeated by political realities.

For instance, Graham's view of the family is too irenic: while he urges husbands to protect and provide for their wives, he completely ignores the rate of spousal rape and domestic violence. During the time Graham was writing, rape laws did not cover spousal rape; it was simply assumed that husbands have rights to their wives' bodies.[50] As early as 1981, studies were showing that young people considered it acceptable for a teenager to force intercourse on his partner if they had been dating for a while.[51] As Marie Fortune has noted, sexual violence was "the unmentionable sin."[52] Graham ignores not only the sociological data, however, but also those biblical passages that appear to condone rape of women.[53]

Clearly, his view of sexual encounters between men and women is blind to the social and political context in which men have power over women and use that power to rape and engage in sexual violence. Indeed, one could go so far as to argue that in his insistence that the man is the "head" of the household, Graham has contributed to the social ethos that maintains male power over women.[54] When he counsels women not to divorce philandering husbands but to work on being the "best wife" possible, he contributes to the injustices that women face daily.[55]

Ironically, it is in the very arena of divorce that a more socially conscious reading of Scripture yields a very different view from Graham's. In the Jewish community that Jesus confronted, the husband was the "head" of the household and the wife was but property. Therefore, the husband could divorce his wife, but the wife could not divorce her husband. In other words, divorce was one of the arenas in which male power was most explicitly built into law. When Jesus rejected divorce, then, he took away men's arbitrary power over women and gave women a power that they had not possessed before: no longer could they simply be cast aside as unwanted property.[56] Jesus' rejection of divorce can be seen not simply as support for an ideal of lifelong marriage, then, but as one illustration of his radical empowerment of women.

Although Graham was actively speaking and writing during the time of the second wave of feminism, his views of sexual ethics never incorporated an active concern for the imbalance of power that feminists addressed. But a fully adequate approach to sexual ethics cannot be separated from issues of power. This takes me to the need for *justice* as a frame for sexual ethics.

To give an adequate account of the centrality of justice in sexual ethics is beyond the scope of this short chapter. However, at least a few words should be said. To do so, I begin with a brief word about sin.

Graham claims that the chief sin is idolatry, the worship of false gods.[57] When it comes to naming the next sins in line, he adopts the evangelical practice of equating sin with specific behaviors, mostly drawn from what is usually considered the "private" arena.[58] Graham lists three primary temptations: lust of the flesh, lust of the eye (sometimes equated with curiosity), and "pride of life," or striving for power over others.[59] These constitute a classic listing.[60]

Reinhold Niebuhr, Graham's contemporary, also discusses sin under the rubrics of pride (ego) and of sensuality.[61] However, claims Niebuhr, only "the more Hellenistic and rationalistic forms of Christianity" ever identified sin as primarily sensuality or identified sensuality with sexual license.[62] In Niebuhr's view, the sin of sensuality is not primarily about sexual license but consists in the attempt to lose ourselves in mutable goods. This is a response to the anxiety brought about by human freedom, but it is a wrong response. The fundamental sin, identified by Augustine and others, is the basic sin of pride and self-deification; lusts (especially "unnatural" ones) are the *consequence* of sin, not the locus of sin. The primal sin is rebellion against God.[63] The flesh is not sinful, but good. The issue, then, is not fleshly purity, but spiritual purity—keeping one's focus on God. Here Niebuhr echoes the views later expounded by Countryman.

To some extent, Graham also echoes this understanding. He sees homosexuality, for instance, as a consequence of a disordered love. But Graham lacks

Niebuhr's clear perspective that the moral and social dimension of sin is not primarily lust but injustice. Injustice—the assertion of self and the will to power that disturbs the harmony of creation[64]—occurs in every arena of life, including sexuality. Justice, therefore, must be applied to the sexual arena.

Two contemporary authors have done so with considerable power. One is Marvin Ellison. According to Ellison, human sexuality has been distorted by various forms of social oppression, and no discourse about sexuality will be adequate unless it attends to the political dimensions of injustice and imbalance of power.[65] Religious communities that react with fear and fixation and that reduce morality to "private" matters are complicit with the larger culture. Sexuality has been depoliticized, and this has led to a failure to understand how "the quality of personal life is dependent on the wider social order."[66]

Most striking in Ellison's work is his method. Where Graham follows tradition in beginning with biblical pronouncements (often out of context and sometimes wrongly interpreted but nonetheless considered authoritative), Ellison proposes that an adequate sexual ethic must begin with recognition of the concrete suffering of people.[67] Ellison would probably place Graham among the sexual traditionalists who believe that the problem with sexuality is an abandonment of traditional values; they "long for a romanticized past of cultural homogeneity" and seek to restore a presumed context for appropriate sexual expression.[68] He notes that most "sexual ethics" in Christian tradition has really been an ethics of *marriage* rather than an ethics of *sexuality*.[69] The main problem, Ellison believes, is that voices from the margins—from the unmarried, from gay and lesbian and disabled and older people who do not fit the paradigm—are missing.[70]

Compulsory heterosexuality is then one of the contemporary forms of sexual injustice. In contrast to Graham, Ellison would not advise gay men and lesbian women to give themselves up to God, praying for God's forgiveness. Rather, he would counsel that it is the heterosexual majority who need to seek God's forgiveness for the injustices perpetrated on those on the margins.

Mark Jordan would go even further. The problem, claims Jordan, is not simply that voices from the margins are missing, but that voices from the margins have been deliberately excluded by discursive maneuvers or rhetorical devices. The way sexual questions are framed limits the possibilities for answers to those questions. For instance, when homosexuality is viewed as "incurable pathology," even scientific findings will be distorted to support the idea that gay and lesbian people are "objectively disordered."[71] Parents are told that they will inevitably be sad if their child is gay; such pronouncements do not simply *describe* parental response—they *prescribe* that response.

The net result is that we have no idea what "true" homosexuality is, for even people's experiences are delimited by the structures and constraints of society.

We cannot simply "discover" our true sexual selves, as the results of oppression distort our experiences to the point where experience itself becomes untrustworthy as a guide. The injustice is not simply stifling voices of those on the margins, but it amounts to a kind of societal surgery on all our vocal cords. No voices can speak clearly, because of the injustices and oppression that surround all sexual discussions.

Jordan's piercing critique of sexual ethics in the Roman Catholic Church— and by implication in society at large—uses contemporary methods that were not prominent in the days of Graham's prime. Nonetheless, the underlying concern for justice as the major form of social sin is something that must not be omitted in any contemporary discussion of sexual ethics.

CONCLUSION

We can therefore conclude the following: Graham is right primarily in his underlying theological framing. God's love is so great that God wants to forgive us our sins. Graham is also right that all of us are sinful and stand in need of that forgiveness. He is wrong, though, in his understanding of what constitutes the sins for which we need forgiveness. Graham reduces sin to specific behaviors such as homosexuality or premarital sex. He ignores the social context and political dimensions of oppression and injustice. While some of our understanding of those dimensions is more recent than much of Graham's ministry, the feminist and gay rights movements should have been a signal to look at sin in more structural and social terms, rather than in the individualistic and "privatized" terms that Graham consistently adopted.

Graham is wrong about purity. Purity does not mean celibacy in singleness and fidelity in marriage. Purity is not about the private use of our bodies. It is primarily about the orientation of our spirits to God. If God seeks justice, then we are impure when we fail to do justice. Justice applies to the sexual arena as to every other arena. We need a new beginning place for sexual ethics, and we will find that place best in the underlying theological vision of God's love, not in the specific pronouncements about sexual rights and wrongs that have been so central to Graham's ministry.

NOTES

1. I am indebted to Mike Long of Elizabethtown College for pulling together all of this material and getting it to me. Without his assistance, I could not have agreed to undertake the task of writing this chapter.

2. Billy Graham, *Answers to Life's Problems: Guidance, Inspiration and Hope for the Challenges of Today* (Nashville: W Publishing Group, 1988), 28.

3. David Frost, *Billy Graham in Conversation* (Oxford: Lion Publishing, 1998), 109.

4. Larry King, "Interview with Billy Graham," CNN transcript, http://transcripts .cnn.com/TRANSCRIPTS/0506/16/lkl.01.html; William Martin, *A Prophet with Honor: The Billy Graham Story* (New York: William Morrow, 1991), 158.

5. Graham, *Answers to Life's Problems*, 28; Billy Graham, *The Journey: How to Live by Faith in an Uncertain World* (Nashville: W Publishing Group, 2006), 250.

6. Graham's writings predate the legality of homosexual unions, but there is reason to believe that he would not approve such unions.

7. Billy Graham, "My Answer," http://www.bgea.org/MyAnswer_Article.asp? ArticleID=2225. Subsequent citations to Graham's "My Answer" column will give just the article ID number.

8. Graham, *Answers to Life's Problems*, 32–33.

9. Ibid., 27.

10. Ibid., 36; Graham, *Journey*, 260.

11. Graham, "My Answer," no. 46; Graham, *Answers to Life's Problems*, 24.

12. Graham, "My Answer," no. 2225.

13. Graham, *Answers to Life's Problems*, 44. However, judgment will be coupled with the possibility of forgiveness, as we shall see.

14. Billy Graham, "Sex," in *Blow, Wind of God: Selected Writings of Billy Graham*, ed. Donald E. Demaray (Old Tappan, NJ: Fleming H. Revell, 1975), 17.

15. Graham, *Answers to Life's Problems*, 228.

16. I find this term problematic. It assumes that everyone will marry! I think it better to talk about "single" sexuality.

17. Marshall Frady relates a story in which Graham and his friend were accosted by prostitutes. When one took off her coat, revealing that she had nothing on underneath, Graham simply turned tail and ran (*Billy Graham: A Parable of American Righteousness* [Boston: Little, Brown, 1979], 168–70). In his own autobiography, Graham talks about crying to God for strength to resist sexual temptation as a teenager.

18. Billy Graham, *My Answer* (New York: Pocket Books, 1967), 50.

19. On disease, see Graham, *Answers to Life's Problems*, 125; harm to one's constitution, *My Answer*, 65; lack of trust, "My Answer," no. 2063, and *Answers to Life's Problems*, 26.

20. Billy Graham, "The Sickness of Sodom," *Time*, July 11, 1969, http://jcgi .pathfinder.com/time/magazine/printout/0,8816,901007,00.html.

21. Billy Graham, *Find Freedom* (Grand Rapids: Zondervan, 1971), 47.

22. Martin, *Prophet with Honor*, 257; "Graham Sees Sex Mania: Advocates Stronger Laws against Pornography," *New York Times*, May 23, 1958, 27.

23. Graham, "Sex," in *Blow, Wind of God*, 18.

24. Billy Graham, *The Jesus Generation* (Grand Rapids: Zondervan, 1971), 75.

25. Graham, *Answers to Life's Problems*, 24; "My Answer," nos. 2061 and 2063.

26. Frady, *Billy Graham*, 596.

27. Graham, "My Answer," nos. 2061 and 1990.

28. Graham, "My Answer," no. 1957; *Answers to Life's Problems*, 25.

29. See Billy Graham, *The Secret of Happiness: Jesus' Teaching on Happiness as Expressed in the Beatitudes* (New York: Pocket Books, 1964), chap. 7.

30. Ibid., 97–104.

31. See Graham, *Find Freedom*, chap. 4.

32. The only sin that lies beyond God's forgiveness is the refusal to accept that forgiveness (Graham, "My Answer," no. 2546).

33. In an agonizing first departure from absolute prohibition, for example, the Society of Friends developed a thoughtful paper suggesting that engaged couples could enjoy a certain amount of sexual intimacy before marriage (see *Towards a Quaker View of Sex*, ed. Alastair Heron [London: Friends Home Service Committee, 1964], excerpted in *Social Ethics: Issues in Ethics and Society*, ed. Gibson Winter [New York: Harper & Row, 1968], 24–43). The eminent Christian ethicist Paul Ramsey critiqued the Friends by suggesting that such couples were already "married" in the eyes of God. Later groups extended sexual intimacy toward principles such as that adopted by the United Church of Christ in which the level of intimacy should mirror the level of commitment. On this point, see Karen Lebacqz, "Appropriate Vulnerability: A Sexual Ethic for Singles," *Christian Century*, May 6, 1987, 435–38.

34. Martin, *Prophet with Honor*, 158.

35. I could not help but think of Augustine's *Confessions* as I read Graham. Both seem sometimes overwhelmed by the power of physical feelings, attraction, and lust.

36. In one place (*Jesus Generation*, 72–73), Graham does offer supporting data. In arguing that peer pressure is an almost irresistible force for young people, he appeals to sociological studies on the topic. Ironically, however, on the previous page he dismisses sociological studies regarding premarital sex in other cultures. Thus, his use of data appears to be selective: he adopts it when it serves his purposes and dismisses it when it does not.

37. One thinks, for example, of Francis Fukuyama's recent claims that we have entered a "posthuman" world because of the impact of biotechnology (Fukuyama, *Our Posthuman Future: Consequences of the Biotechnology Revolution* [New York: Farrar, Straus & Giroux, 2002]). Further, the appeal to pragmatic considerations might make it seem that Graham's sexual ethics is grounded in utilitarian concerns. This, however, would not be accurate. His counsel is often peppered with biblical references, as we saw above in the discussion of adultery.

38. Frost, *Billy Graham in Conversation*, 106.

39. Ibid., 105.

40. Ibid., 109.

41. See also Stephen Sapp, *Sexuality, the Bible, and Science* (Philadelphia: Fortress Press, 1977).

42. William L. Countryman, *Dirt, Greed, and Sex: Sexual Ethics in the New Testament and Their Implications for Today* (Minneapolis: Fortress Press, 1988), 118; and Mark D. Jordan, *The Silence of Sodom: Homosexuality in Modern Catholicism* (Chicago: University of Chicago Press, 2000), 60.

43. Interestingly, however, adultery was *not* a purity concern. Adultery fell into property rather than purity rules. Because women were considered property, the offense in adultery was not lack of purity but rather the stealing of another man's property.

44. Countryman, *Dirt, Greed, and Sex*, 86.

45. Ibid., 94.

46. Countryman's argument is too intricate to be repeated in detail here. See *Dirt, Greed, and Sex*, 109–23.

47. Martin, *Prophet with Honor*, 585.

48. See Sapp, *Sexuality, the Bible, and Science*; Ralph W. Weltge, ed., *The Same Sex: An Appraisal of Homosexuality* (Boston: Pilgrim Press, 1969); and Dwight W. Oberholtzer, ed., *Is Gay Good? Ethics, Theology, and Homosexuality* (Philadelphia: Westminster Press, 1971). Graham is known to have retracted statements when he was wrong. On one occasion he suggested that AIDS might be a punishment for the sin of homosexuality; he retracted that statement, which he clearly regretted, and attempted to make clear that homosexuality is no more sinful than other transgressions, such as lying (United Press International, October 9, 1993). Failure to retract his general judgment against homosexuality, therefore, suggests that he never has taken seriously the scholarship that challenges his views.

49. See Karen Lebacqz, "Love Your Enemy: Sex, Power, and Christian Ethics," *Annual of the Society of Christian Ethics* (1990): 3–23; Marvin M. Ellison, *Erotic Justice: A Liberating Ethic of Sexuality* (Louisville, KY: Westminster John Knox Press, 1996); and Marvin M. Ellison, John C. Carey, and Sylvia Thorson-Smith, *Keeping Body and Soul Together: Sexuality, Spirituality, and Justice* (Louisville, KY: Presbyterian Church (U.S.A.), 1991).

50. See Camille E. LeGrand, "Rape and Rape Laws: Sexism in Society and Law," *California Law Review* 61, no. 13 (1973): 919–41.

51. Laurel Fingler, "Teenagers in Survey Condone Forced Sex," *Ms.*, February 1981, 23.

52. See Marie Marshall Fortune, *Sexual Violence: The Unmentionable Sin* (New York: Pilgrim Press, 1983).

53. See Phyllis Trible, *Texts of Terror: Literary-Feminist Readings of Biblical Narratives* (Philadelphia: Fortress Press, 1984).

54. Martin, *Prophet with Honor*, 159.

55. Graham, *Answers to Life's Problems*, 34–35.

56. Countryman, *Dirt, Greed, and Sex*, 149–50.

57. Richard Scheinen, "Evangelism: Graham Finds New Techniques in Trio of California Cities," *Christianity Today*, December 8, 1997, 68, http://ctlibrary .com/print.html?id=1006.

58. Martin, *Prophet with Honor*, 158.

59. Frost, *Billy Graham in Conversation*, 104.

60. Compare Augustine of Hippo, *The Confessions of St. Augustine*, trans. E. B. Pusey (New York: E. P. Dutton & Co., 1951), book 10.

61. Reinhold Niebuhr, *The Nature and Destiny of Man: A Christian Interpretation*, vol. 1, *Human Nature* (New York: Charles Scribner's Sons, 1941), 186ff.

62. Ibid., 229.

63. Ibid., 230.

64. Ibid., 179.

65. Ellison, *Erotic Justice*, 1.

66. Ibid., 9.

67. Ibid., 11.

68. Ibid., 20.

69. Ibid., 26.

70. Ibid., 23.

71. Jordan, *Silence of Sodom*, 29.

5

You Shall Have No Poor among You

DOUGLAS STURM

For well over half a century, Billy Graham has been a name to reckon with in religious circles. His unique crusades, designed with the single purpose of converting individuals to faith in Jesus Christ as their personal savior, have attracted massive crowds of people in virtually every land across the globe. In recognition of his highly visible and widely publicized efforts as a Christian evangelist, he has, over these years, been consistently listed as "One of the Ten Most Admired Men in the World" by the Gallup association.

THE PROBLEM OF POVERTY

It is therefore no small matter that when he was asked at a press conference during his 2005 New York City crusade to name the most critical societal problems of our time, he responded, "Well, the greatest problem that we have is poverty." He continued, "And I believe that the Gospel of Christ is the answer. Not part of the answer, but the whole answer. We don't have any possibility of solving our problems today, except through Jesus."[1] In what follows I intend to take a close look at that claim—what Graham seems to mean by it and whether it is the most satisfactory way to view the problem of poverty and its elimination.

That poverty is indeed a dominant problem in our times is often indicated through the citation of a range of remarkable statistics. Of the total population of the world—now over six billion—half of them are living in dire poverty (less than two dollars a day), including one billion children. In 2003, nearly 11 million children annually (30,000 a day) died of poverty prior to their fifth birthday. Over one billion people are without access to clean water, and three billion lack proper sanitation facilities. Nearly one billion people are illiterate, unable to read or even to sign their names.

The contrast between rich and poor is striking. Whereas the richest 2 percent of the world's population own over 50 percent of the world's wealth, the poorest half of the human community control but 1 percent of its assets.[2] The wealth of the world's three richest individuals surpasses the gross domestic product of the 48 poorest countries of the world.

In the United States, given current official measurements of wealth in the nation, 37 million citizens live in poverty—12.7 percent of the total population. That number has increased annually since 2001. The proportion, it is often noted, differs according to racial and ethnic identity. The poverty rate among blacks is approximately 25 percent, among Hispanics 22 percent, and among non-Hispanic whites, less than 8.5 percent. Among children under 18 years of age, nearly 18 percent are living under conditions of poverty (nearly one of every five). According to one calculation, among industrialized nations, the widest gap in wealth between the richest and the poorest fifth of the population is located in the United States.

Given these shocking statistics, it is no wonder that the United Nations, at the start of the twenty-first century, declared as the first of its Millennium Development Goals to "eradicate extreme hunger and poverty" and initiated an impressive program, working country by country, to move steadily toward the attainment of that end.

It is no wonder that a number of groups within the Christian community—including, for instance, the World Council of Churches and the National Council of Churches of Christ in the USA—have joined in the UN program. That action proceeds from an impulse integral to Christian faith in its beginnings. Since the time of the primitive Christian community, the concern to care for persons in poverty has occupied a central role in the church's ministry: "All who believed . . . had all things in common; they would sell their possessions . . . and distribute the proceeds to all, as any had need" (Acts 2:44–45). Monastic orders have long had a reputation for offering hospitality and charitable services to the poor. With the emergence of modern denominationalism, virtually all denominational groups, whatever their theological differences, have provided assistance to the needy—for example, the United Methodist Committee on Relief (UMCOR). In recent times, religious associations cutting across denominational lines have been created to strengthen their several endeavors in the struggle against poverty—for instance, Bread for the World, Habitat for Humanity, and World Vision.

Hence, when Billy Graham, nearing the end of his famed career as perhaps the preeminent Christian revivalist of the past half century, declares that poverty is the greatest of social problems we currently confront throughout the world, his voice seems, at first blush, to join in a common chorus of Christians bending their energies and resources to respond to the plight of desperately needy peoples.

TWO MODELS

I suggest that there is good reason, however, to distinguish different ways within the Christian community of comprehending the meaning of poverty, and therefore different ways of approaching poverty as among the most critical of social problems in our time. The seemingly common chorus among Christians, that is, may not all be singing in the same key. Indeed, its voices may not all be singing the same song.

In order to identify—and to assess—Billy Graham's specific contribution to the cause of alleviating poverty, I would contrast two models of Christian understanding, representing distinctively different (though not wholly incompatible) constructs of the human condition from the perspective of the Christian gospel that result in different ways of approaching poverty: the conversion model and the prophetic model.

Billy Graham is representative of the conversion model. In contrast, I propose that the prophetic model provides a more adequate characterization of the impact of poverty on human life and of the responsibility of Christians in its elimination—although I do so without intending to deny the contribution those representing the former model have made to mitigating the suffering of poverty-stricken peoples throughout the world. The models hold in common the conviction central to the Christian gospel that the world as it exists is in profound need of transformation, but they diverge from each other in their determination of what sort of transformation is needed and how that transformation bears on conditions of poverty.

The conversion model, as the customary usage of that term conveys, focuses on the transformation of the singular soul. It concentrates primarily on the relationship between God and the individual self. The prophetic model, on the other hand, focuses dominantly on the quality of life prevailing across the whole community of creatures, acknowledging that often the institutions of our common life are seriously flawed, cause undue suffering, and are in need of radical social reconstruction. It concentrates on the God-world relationship, incorporating notions of social sin and social salvation.

The conversion model presents a way for the individual self to gain release from the clutches of sin and thereby to find salvation. The prophetic model instead considers ways to transform the community, making it more conducive to the flourishing of each of its members, recognizing that the struggle to create a just and sustainable world is an ever continuing vocation of us all who respond to the call of God.

During modern times, the former model is characteristic of the tradition of evangelistic revivalism, a tradition that became prominent in the eighteenth and nineteenth centuries on the European continent and in America, continuing throughout the twentieth and into the twenty-first century. The latter model was articulated keenly in the development of the Social Gospel beginning at the end of the nineteenth century, a tradition born in response to the ill effects of industrial capitalism and reappearing subsequently in a series of developments such as various forms of political theology and liberation theology beginning in the mid-twentieth century. The Social Gospel and its successors are, in spirit and effect, participants in the modern progressive movement, an aggregation of associations all committed in one way or another to the creation of a new public order more conducive than industrial capitalism to the welfare of all peoples (as well as other creatures).

Both the conversion and the prophetic models declare allegiance to the twofold Great Commandment traditionally affirmed as a central proposition of the Christian gospel: to love God unconditionally and to love our neighbors as ourselves. Both believe that that commandment is applicable to our everyday life. Yet they tend to diverge on the question of what it means to love our neighbors. The conversion model tends to stress acts of charity, whereas the prophetic model is more prone to stress acts of justice. So, in response to poverty, the former promotes voluntary donations of goods and services to the needy. The latter promotes a reconstruction of political and economic relationships to approximate as nearly as possible a kind of community through which all participants are treated as copartners in the ongoing adventure of life.

I present these two models as typifications in an effort to illuminate a broad difference among persons of faith in the modern Christian community in the way they interpret poverty and propose to respond to its devastating impact on human lives. I do not mean to intimate that these two models are exhaustive of all possible approaches to poverty as a social problem. Nor do I present them as wholly exclusive of each other. Nonetheless, I believe the contrast between these two models might enable us to comprehend Graham's way of treating poverty and how it might be considered inadequate.

BILLY GRAHAM AND THE CONVERSION MODEL

Billy Graham has been keenly aware of the turbulence of the times throughout his ministry. His initial carefully crafted evangelistic crusade—the kind of revivalist event that constituted the centerpiece of his long ministry—was held in 1947, at the beginning of the Cold War. As he conducted his crusades from land to land, including those behind the Iron Curtain, and expanded his ministry through his Billy Graham Evangelistic Association (BGEA), he did not shy away from addressing significant travails from which peoples were suffering across the world—manifest in persisting tensions between the free world and the communist world, struggles of organized labor to improve working conditions, the ravages of racism, or the pains of poverty. Invariably, however, his message was at all times governed dominantly by a single theme, namely, that every one of these travails is grounded ultimately in the sinfulness of individual souls.

Graham, quite properly, did not consider himself a systematic theologian. Yet he insisted his presentation of the gospel was rooted in a biblically based philosophy of human nature and destiny. World events over the course of time, however they differ, are reflective of fundamental principles declared throughout the biblical text, namely, that in the beginning God created the universe and all that is therein; that humankind, commencing with our first parents, exists in a state of rebellion against the divine law; and that, nonetheless, out of his continuing love for humankind, God sent his Son to redeem us through his sacrifice on the cross.

Throughout his career, Graham insisted that these three fundamental propositions—creation by God, rebellion by humankind, redemption through Jesus Christ—constitute the underlying truths of all human history whatever its seeming variations from culture to culture. Only if we comprehend how that dynamic works out can we understand the massive social problems we confront and what, in the final analysis, is required to resolve them. Graham's crusades were geared exactly to clarify what is entailed in this dynamic and, most importantly, to urge each individual soul to embrace its third stage through conversion from the state of sin to the state of salvation. Conversion, in Graham's construction of the revivalist tradition, consists of three components: repentance (renunciation of one's sinfulness), faith (confidence in the efficacy of Christ's sacrifice), and regeneration (infusion of divine life into one's soul).

That dramatic change of heart—the dominant intention of Graham's crusades—is the crux of the gospel and marks the necessary means for the resolution of whatever problems plague human life. The upshot is that, in Graham's own language, his is an "individualistic gospel." Since sin is personal and all problems are rooted in sin, so those problems may be resolved only through personal conversion. Social groups of all kinds—nations, corporations, clubs—consist of individuals, and it is only through the transformation of the human heart that the pains and sufferings that accompany their impact on our lives may be redressed. Political and economic systems are unjust only because the hearts of those in control of them are twisted by sin. Efforts to change such systems through legislation or social engineering invariably fall short or may even worsen conditions. Only conversion—through a radical change of heart by each individual—holds the key to the creation of a new world, a world in which peace and harmony might prevail.

ASSISTING THE POOR

Conversion, so understood, must therefore be the key to resolving the problem of poverty. We should note at this point that Graham never, so far as I can discover, explores the existential meaning of poverty. He seems to assume that poverty in its strictest sense consists dominantly, if not solely, in the lack of sufficient resources to sustain physical life. He seems also to assume that the problem of poverty is secondary to a far more important matter. That is, within the framework of Graham's biblical philosophy, the preeminent problem we confront is whether and how we might gain purchase on eternal life. That is the problem of problems whose resolution is assured exclusively through the conversion experience itself, and that is attainable solely within the context of the Christian faith.

With that assurance, the regenerated must find a way of coping in a history riddled with sinfulness. In doing so, they must at the start acknowledge that all the problems of our temporal life—including poverty—are diminished in their importance, given their guarantee of eternal life. As such, those problems become less urgent and less painful than before.

As I comprehend the logic of Graham's perspective, the regenerate, if living in poverty, may appropriately seek some way to improve their condition by mitigating their lack of resources—but they must do so without in any way causing harm to others, disrupting the social order, or acting contrary to God's imperatives. That is the backdrop of what some commentators have labeled Graham's political conservatism, reinforced, we might note, by his family background on a dairy farm during Depression years and by his close associations with persons in power throughout his professional life.

As an instance of his conservatism, he is fond of citing Paul's declaration, "I have learned to be content with whatever I have" (Phil. 4:11). Hence, when confronted with a discrepancy between what we desire and what we have, we should simply cut back on our desires. In sum, contentment is Graham's dominant advice to the poor once they have accepted Christ as their savior.

This is not to say that Graham has been oblivious to the sufferings of the poor. Through the years he and his son Franklin have initiated programs connected with the BGEA to assist peoples existing in poverty, particularly those in economically underdeveloped lands, and they have urged Christians to engage in similar charitable programs. However, charitable assistance to the needy as a means of responding to persistent poverty, though not unimportant, has always been considered by Graham a matter secondary to the primary mission of the Christian community: to save individual souls from sin. First conversion, then charity, particularly provided to the "deserving" poor.

During the mid-1960s—at the time of the urban race riots in America, the turning of the civil rights struggle toward issues of economic deprivation, and the subsequent introduction of legislation during the Johnson administration promoting a "war on poverty"—Graham seemed to waver for a while from his counsel of contentment and charity. At first during this period, Graham dismissed a report that declared the race riots disrupting urban areas (in Watts, Detroit, and elsewhere) were in large part caused by poverty, insisting instead that they were more likely provoked by subversive political forces whose anarchic intentions might require suppression through tough governmental action to preserve law and order. He was even critical at this time of nonviolent methods of civil disobedience led by Martin Luther King Jr. and others to advance the cause of civil rights. This criticism grew out of his concern for social control—a concern arising, I suspect, from his conviction that, given the pervasiveness of sin, an enforced social order is better than the kind of chaos that tends to follow efforts at radical social change, however peaceable and however seemingly justified. He also initially opposed Lyndon B. Johnson's proposal for a "war on poverty" on several grounds: its reliance on governmental coercion, its naive supposition that poverty could be eliminated in this world, and its seemingly exclusive emphasis on conditions of physical life to the neglect of spiritual need.

During the late 1960s, however, Graham seemed for a brief time to have a change of mind. His direct experience of a newly instituted governmental program on equal economic opportunity in the United States, accompanied by his rediscovery of the hundreds of biblical texts mandating care for the poor, steered him to endorse legislative efforts to overcome the incidence of poverty in the nation through the creation of new governmental agencies and programs (Head Start, legal services, food stamps, etc.). He even collaborated in a direct lobbying campaign in Washington in support of this "war on poverty." He endorsed the programs of the Office on Economic Opportunity. He expressed the need for a special federal tax to eliminate urban ghettos and slums. He gave his approval of a proposal for a Poor People's Campaign in the nation's capital.

That rush of activity, which seemed to signal a new approach to the problem of poverty—moving beyond personal charity toward reconstructive public policy—was, however, short-lived. Before the end of the decade, Graham reverted to his counsel of contentment and his ministry's dominant emphasis on conversion.

Yet, once again, in 2005, Graham was persuaded to join other evangelicals supporting a broadly sponsored campaign, "To Make Poverty History," launched in collaboration with the United Nations' Millennium Development Goal to rid the entire world of extreme poverty in the foreseeable future. With others, he signed a request addressed to President George W. Bush to designate 1 percent of the federal budget annually to this ambitious program. It is doubtful, however, that Graham's action in this case marks a thoroughgoing radical change in his basic orientation to the problem.

Even in these brief episodes of a seeming change of mind on his approach to the problem of poverty, I would guess he retained his longstanding conviction that the issue of poverty is distinctively secondary to his preeminent mission of conversion. His seeming changes of mind were episodic, not systemic, and most likely were influenced by respected colleagues.

INSTRUCTING THE RICH

Graham insists repeatedly that God's saving grace is available impartially to poor and rich alike. In his biblical philosophy, there is nothing inherently sinful in the possession of wealth. The wealthy even while wealthy may be saved. He does not consider the stark declaration of the Sermon on the Plain—"Woe to you who are rich" (Luke 6:24)—as condemnatory of the wealthy class. In fact, he avers that Jesus (in contradistinction to the communist doctrine of class struggle) refuses to pit class against class. Moreover in his rendition, Jesus' admonition to the rich young ruler to sell all his goods and give the proceeds to the poor is case-specific. It is not to be taken as a universal principle.

However, Graham does not avoid addressing persons of the wealthy class with a range of vital moral concerns intended specifically for them, concerns whose logic, pursued to its full implications—a pursuit he does not himself undertake explicitly—might be construed as critical of capitalist culture.

In instructing the rich, Graham focuses on three basic moral concerns: the acquisition of wealth, its status, and its use.

Acquisition. While the possession of wealth is not intrinsically sinful, wealth must not be acquired dishonestly, declares Graham. What precisely he means by "dishonestly" he does not say. Presumably he would contend, at least as a minimal measure, that the wealthy must adhere to given legal constraints in their pursuit of the accumulation of their riches. But he does not, for instance, address with any greater particularity matters of resource exploitation, marketing exaggeration, treatment of workers, competitive strategies—at which points, along with others, thoroughgoing honesty might mandate far-reaching change in the prevailing practices of business within a capitalist system, particularly in its current historical stage. However, in keeping with his usual reluctance to rely on governmental action save to maintain rigorous social order, he fails to address whether it might not be appropriate to institutionalize such changes through legislation.

Status. Repeatedly, in his concern about the status of wealth among the rich, Graham invokes the New Testament epigram from 1 Timothy: "The love of money is the root of all evil" (6:10 KJV). In a discussion of the Seven Deadly Sins, he declares that avarice, manifest in the scramble to accumulate money whatever it takes, is America's deepest flaw, its dominant sin. Love of money, so pervasive throughout American culture, is sinful because it detracts from the love of God: "You cannot serve God and wealth" (Matt. 6:24).

Intriguingly, in a sermon developing his concept of a "Kingdom Society" (which he sets over against Lyndon B. Johnson's slogan of a "Great Society"), he pronounces that the profit motive, as an obvious instance of the love of money, is antithetical to the love of God and neighbor.[3] On this point, he seems to cast serious doubt on the legitimacy of a keystone principle of the capitalist credo. Within that credo, the pursuit of optimal return on investment is the driving force of the system whose prime objective is the continuing growth of the wealth of nations. Yet Graham seems to shy away from developing that implication explicitly—perhaps because throughout his career he has often stated his support of free enterprise (especially in contrast to communism).

Use. Regarding the use of wealth, Graham explicitly and frequently condemns the propensity for materialism that pervades American culture (and, in his reading, that pervades the philosophy and practice of communism, given its principled atheism) as a modern case of the deadly sin of gluttony. Wealth expended merely for the pleasures and comforts of the body is the height of self-centeredness, an archdenial of the love of God.

In contrast, Graham proposes that wealth be used to advance God's purposes. In particular, he contends that the principle of stewardship should govern the expenditure of wealth, promoting the sharing of one's wealth with the needy and the suffering. Sometimes he proposes the principle of stewardship pragmatically as a way to deflect the poor from the lure of communism, manifesting thereby his political sympathies favoring the free world during the time of the Cold War. Yet beyond that pragmatic consideration, the ultimate ground for the principle of stewardship in Graham's theology is not pragmatic; it is moral, rooted in the biblical mandate to love our neighbors.

In a remarkable address to the 1975 annual convention of the American Bankers Association, Graham, acknowledging the economic crisis of the time, announced that the crisis would be resolved only through a spiritual revival empowering persons, one by one, to surmount the materialism with its allied love of money that had so thoroughly ensnared the culture. He advocated a "new Puritanism" induced by conversion to Christ and characterized, presumably, by personal virtues he often praised: honesty, frugality, stewardship, hard work, industriousness, acceptance of one's place in life, and contentment.[4] These are, of course, qualities of the "Protestant work ethic" (although he does not use this language), which has long been held by some economic historians to have been essential to the rise of modern capitalism.

As an aside, however, while Graham's call for a new Puritanism seems at initial glance to be supportive of capitalism on its productive side, it is, in its intended effect, antithetical to capitalism on its traditional distributive side which, as practiced over the decades, has spawned an extensive consumerist culture on which the success of that system is dependent. Graham, in this respect, is fond of citing John Wesley's maxim "Earn all you can, save all you can, give all you can" without recognizing how that maxim jars with the workings of the prevailing economic system in the United States.

At all three points of Graham's moral instruction to the rich, it seems strange that he is not more forthright about the deep moral deficiencies of modern capitalism as a system in need of significant reconstruction. He might, of course, deflect that observation by insisting that such a change is only possible through the conversion of individuals one by one.

There is a further curiosity in Graham's writings about his understanding of God's will regarding the status of the poor and the rich and their interrelationship. Early in his ministry, in a 1952 sermon on organized labor, he observed that whatever degree of wealth one possesses is a gift of God's bounty—which would seem to imply that whether one is poor or rich is ordained by God and presumably therefore to be embraced as such.[5] However, various comments he has made throughout his ministry about the poor and the rich seem to suggest that, given the dynamics of regeneration, the relationship between rich and poor should be complementary, leading to an improvement in the conditions of the poor, even, ideally, to the elimination of poverty.

By definition the poor are in need, but, if regenerate, they must be content with their lot in life. Yet the rich are, if regenerate, mandated to share their surplus resources voluntarily and generously with those in need as a matter of charitable stewardship. Hence, were all the rich to take action of this sort, then, under ideal conditions, it would seem the poor might surmount their poverty, although Graham does not take his speculation to that point.

In any case, the more that wealthy converts adopt the principle of stewardship, the more the differential between rich and poor will begin to approximate conditions Graham attributes to the "Kingdom Society"—where, he affirms, "brotherhood" will prevail, there will be no poverty, and, as well, the profit motive will be absent. To be sure, so far in the world's history, charitable giving, however much enjoined by congregations of faith, has failed to overcome the miseries of abject poverty in the world.

What are we to conclude from all these observations of Graham? Are we to assume that, in Graham's biblical philosophy, God ordains that failure since God determines our economic status in this world, whatever it is? Or is it God's will that humankind take action to surmount the sufferings of the poor so far as possible? In this connection, we should take note of those few scattered passages in Graham's writings where he praises concerted actions of organized groups—religious reformers and labor unions—to improve the state of laboring peoples: their wages, hours, working conditions, and treatment on the job.

In sum, Graham seems conflicted over whether the poor must accept their poverty as God's will though remain hopeful of assistance, or whether poverty, at least when it is the result of social forces beyond the control of the poor themselves, runs contrary to what God intends and constitutes a moral problem to be resolved by forceful political action. Graham seems reluctant to adopt the latter alternative without hedging. On the other hand, those favoring the prophetic model of Christian understanding promote it wholeheartedly as a moral mandate.

THE PROPHETIC ALTERNATIVE

From the perspective of the prophetic model, poverty, given its full existential significance, is more than a secondary concern. It is indicative of a fundamental fracture in the human community. We must, of course, make an exception in cases of voluntary poverty adopted as a special way of life by individuals or groups to signify a cause—religious or political—to which they are committed.

Setting those cases aside, when the presence of poverty within a group—clan, nation, region—manifests an appreciable gap between the wealthy and the poor, it betrays a system of relationships privileging some persons over others, resulting in the distress and destitution of the latter. Systems of this sort are sustained by their participants, especially their more powerful class and greatest beneficiaries. Nonetheless, as they have been created and are maintained by human action, they are therefore susceptible to transformation—even if, in many instances, that transformation may be painstaking in accomplishment and may encounter forcible resistance. In this manner, poverty, like slavery and patriarchal institutions, is a social sin—an unjust social form that, while held as favorable by some, causes others to suffer.

To the ancient Hebrew prophets, such a gap between rich and poor within the nation was among the key marks of a broken covenant. Consider, as an example, Isaiah's pronouncement of the Lord's judgment against "the elders and princes of his people: It is you who have devoured the vineyard; the spoil of the poor is in your houses. What do you mean by . . . grinding the face of the poor?" (Isa. 3:14–15). Consider as well the declaration of Amos that the Lord will punish those "who trample the head of the poor into the dust of the earth" (Amos 2:7).

In judgments of this kind against the privileged, the prophets claim to be giving voice to the Lord's judgment that in any deep division in a nation between an elite class and an oppressed class, that nation has deviated from the covenant that brought it into being—a covenant intended to result in the well-being of the whole community. It has broken the promises of that covenant. It has violated the quality of peoplehood envisioned and proclaimed at its genesis.

A prophet's vocation is to call a people back to the principles of its beginning—that is, principles of justice and solidarity, mutual respect and togetherness—principles of a genuinely vibrant community. Jesus, in Luke's rendition of the gospel, identified himself with this understanding of the prophet's vocation during the initial days of his active ministry, drawing on words inherited from Isaiah: "The Spirit of the Lord is upon me, because he has anointed me to bring good news to the poor[,] . . . to proclaim release to the captives . . . [,] to let the oppressed go free" (Luke 4:18).

From a prophetic perspective, poverty entails a rending of the moral fabric of a people. Customarily poverty is measured by a narrowly defined economic metric. However, its full meaning in the lived experience of the poor is far more devastating than merely the lack of resources to secure the necessities of daily life, though it includes that as one of its more obvious features. Poverty constitutes a form of dehumanization. Its components in the daily life of the poor are threefold: a deprivation of economic sustenance, a denial of political agency, and a diminishment of those mutually enriching interactions that, when extended throughout all participants in the community whatever their status, enliven them all.

First, the economic metrics usually employed to define poverty point to, but fail to represent sufficiently, the crushing impact of a lack of resources to meet the basic requisites of life. The poorest of people in the world—currently attempting to meet the bare necessities of themselves and their families on less than two dollars a day—teeter on the edge of survival, often slipping over that edge. Even the working poor living within otherwise affluent societies encounter a constant strain to care for their needs for housing, health care, proper nutrition, and minimal education. The slightest crisis—caused by natural catastrophe, changes in government policy, corporate restructuring, or economic recession—may cast them into a life-threatening whirlpool.

Second, poverty is almost certainly accompanied by an inability to access those locations where major social decisions are made—the legislative forum, corporate boardroom, business roundtable, city hall, or housing authority. These are locations where fundamental policies are determined that have a direct impact on the lives of the poor. Yet even where principles of democratic governance are touted, a power elite tends to rule. And that power elite tends to be occupied by a wealthy class or those who have its support. The poor, save in those instances where they are organized specifically to articulate their cause, have little opportunity to participate meaningfully in making basic decisions about matters that shape their day-to-day lives, all too often to their detriment.

Third, the deep cleft between rich and poor has rightly been designated by some commentators to be a form of apartheid that creates a wall of separation between populations who live and work in different locations throughout the nation. The gated neighborhoods and private clubs designed by the rich, often policed with private security forces, are symbolic of that separation. In contrast, the poor are clustered in enclaves of their own, deficient in the kinds of amenities that make up a comfortable life and lacking in the kinds of cultural opportunities that might enrich their lives. To be sure, many of the poor find invigorating companionship with one another and, on occasion, initiate associations to press their grievances and conditions on decision makers lest they be totally ignored. But given this kind of apartheid to which they are subjected, the poor are relegated to a diminished status in the community—marginalized, ostracized, fated to live in a kind of internal exile, devoid of opportunities that might broaden and deepen their experience and give expression to their distinctive genius.

It should be clear at this point that charitable offerings to the poor, however generous and however welcome, do not come anywhere close to solving the full problem of poverty. What is needed is a reconstruction of the fundamental forms of our living together out of concern for the health and welfare of all. That is the focus of the prophetic perspective as I am representing it.

From that perspective, a nation has as its underlying purpose the common good—that which contributes to the vitality of all participants within a context of mutual support and interaction. In our day and age, the common good must embrace, as a means of doing justice, the full range of rights indicated by the modern human rights movement—political and civil, economic and social.

In the Universal Declaration of Human Rights—adopted by the United Nations in 1948 in direct response to the defeat of fascist powers in World War II as "a common standard of achievement for all peoples and all nations"—Article 1 states, "All human beings are born free and equal in dignity and rights. They . . . should act towards one another in a spirit of brotherhood" (and, we should add, "sisterhood"). That is a way of construing a central covenantal principle for the contemporary world embracing the entire human community. Expanding this opening affirmation in a litany of particulars as it proceeds, the Declaration insists in Article 25 that all individuals and their families have "the right to a standard of living adequate for [their] health and well-being"—which implies clearly that nations have a moral responsibility to eradicate poverty.

Therefore, governments, understood as agents of the community, hold as their preeminent responsibility the securing of these rights. That affirmation contrasts with Billy Graham's assertion that the dominant purpose of government is the maintenance of law and order. Instead, from the prophetic perspective, the function of government is collaborative and directive, channeling the associative energies of the people toward the enhancement of lives of the whole community. Not orderliness and quietude but social justice is the business of governing.

Charitable gifts by individuals and groups may and do serve to alleviate the immediate sufferings of the poor. They are to be applauded and encouraged. However, they alone cannot substitute for public policies directed toward the redesign of social and economic practices that perpetuate the miseries of millions of persons living in poverty across the world. That is the reason why those of the prophetic persuasion, out of a strong commitment to do justice—derived from their response to God's calling (Mic. 6:8)—concentrate their energies on social reconstruction while not ignoring, in the short range, the immediate needs of suffering peoples.

The difference between the approaches of the conversion and the prophetic models to the problem of poverty in the world today is acute. To be sure, both are, in a sense, ways of reading the Christian gospel. Both manifest concern over the sufferings of oppressed peoples. Both are efforts to take the Great Commandment seriously. However, they diverge radically in their comprehension of the faith and what it means in our day-to-day life.

The conversion model presents to each individual a means of escaping from the clutches of a life of sin through repentance and regeneration conjoined with a promise of eternal life. The comfort of that promise enables those who are saved to accept their historical circumstances whatever they might be even as it instructs the regenerate who are able to mitigate the personal suffering of the needy. But the ultimate hope of the regenerate rests in a world beyond history, a "Kingdom Society" offered by God transcending the here and now.

The prophetic model, in contrast, calls us to pursue a special vocation in the thick of history, working out in the here and now what it means to embody the reign of God in that context. It calls us to follow in the path of peace and justice, doing whatever we can to create ways, personal and social, of enhancing the whole community of life and thereby responding to the intentionality of God within an ever evolving world. Those whose faith assumes this form find their joy in the constant presence of God who, as a creative and redemptive force, would have us collaborate in the advancement of the common good. Their ultimate hope resides not in their accomplishments but in the acknowledgment that God cherishes the engagement of all those who follow in this path, however much they may succeed or fail.

Billy Graham, of course, must be commended for the energy and integrity with which he has pursued the conversion model throughout his professional life. Undoubtedly through his crusades he has brought a renewed zest for life to many in lands across the globe. And through the charitable works of his associations and of those converted under his leadership he has contributed much to persons living in poverty. Moreover, on occasion, as we have seen, he has seemed to discern the need in the contemporary world for extensive political reform to alleviate their suffering and has also, in his own way, been critical of the limitations and flaws of modern-day capitalism even though these aspects of his ministry are peripheral to his primary concern.

However, in the final analysis, I find the prophetic perspective to be a far more convincing comprehension of the Christian gospel and a far more sensitive discernment of the problem of poverty in the world and the moral responsibility we bear for its eradication.

NOTES

1. These quotations are from Billy Graham's June 21, 2005, press conference in New York City and can be read and heard at http://www.beliefnet.com/story/169/story_16954_1.html.
2. Office of Communications, *United Nations University Annual Report 2006* (Tokyo: United Nations University, 2007), 17, http://www.unu.edu/publications/annual reports/files/UNU_ar2006-extended.pdf.
3. See Billy Graham, *The Kingdom Society* (Minneapolis: Billy Graham Evangelistic Association, 1965); and Graham, "The Kingdom Society," *Decision*, September 1965, 1, 14–15.
4. Billy Graham, *The Economics of the Apocalypse* (Minneapolis: Billy Graham Evangelistic Association, 1975), 9.
5. Billy Graham, *Organized Labor and the Church* (Minneapolis: Billy Graham Evangelistic Association, 1952), 6.

6

A Matter of Pride

A Feminist Response

ELLEN OTT MARSHALL

In 1969 and 1970, Billy Graham published two pieces responding directly to the women's liberation movement. The first, "A Vocation of Honor," appeared in the May 1969 issue of *Decision*, a magazine started by Sherwood Wirt in 1960 at Graham's invitation. By 1965, this publication reached five million homes.[1] The second piece, "Jesus and the Liberated Woman," appeared in the *Ladies' Home Journal* in 1970. Both pieces advance the same argument. "The Word of God teaches that the primary duty of a woman is to be a homemaker."[2] "Wife, mother, homemaker—this is the appointed destiny of real womanhood."[3]

Graham supports this argument in three ways. First, he secures the homemaker argument to the anchor of divine order and obedient response, two of his core theological convictions. Second, he explains this order through literal interpretation of the Bible, particularly Genesis 1:27–31; 2:18; 3:16; and Ephesians 5:22–33. Third, he stresses the morally essential role of "consecrated Christian mothers" in the home and the influence they have on society by fostering a godly home. In sum, wife, mother, and homemaker are divinely ordered, biblically mandated, and morally essential roles for women. After examining each of the three planks of this argument, I will look at the wiggle room surrounding it before offering a more critical response.

DIVINELY ORDAINED

Graham begins "Jesus and the Liberated Woman" by considering women who feel unfulfilled as homemakers and dismissing their complaints as forms of boredom or envy, both of which are spiritual problems that arise when we fail "to comply with spiritual laws laid down in the Old and New Testaments." Like all social problems, the plight of women arises from prideful disobedience: "We moderns have substituted pleasure for discipline, success for duty" (40).

When a social movement challenges these laws and promises liberation from them, it undermines morality. Indeed, Graham writes, "I believe the women's liberation movement is an echo of our overall philosophy of permissiveness" (44). Although such statements did little to engage feminists in dialogue, they did appeal to a more conservative base that shared Graham's understanding of the Christian life as faithful obedience to timeless divine laws and roles. As Graham puts it:

> I am not against freedom for women. But I believe that the Bible teaches that women have a role, that it is a noble role, a God-given role, and they will be happiest, most creative—and freest—when they assume and accept that role. The same goes for men. Their chief roles are father and breadwinner, according to the Bible, and it has ever been so in history. (114)

Regardless of gender, we all have a "Biblically prescribed vocation" (114). And divine judgment, not human liberation, awaits those of us who seek to extricate ourselves from our vocational roles.

BIBLICAL MANDATE

God's plan for the lives of men and women is no mystery. It is made plain in Scripture. According to biographer William Martin, Graham "shied away from the shibboleth term inerrancy, by which conservatives mean the Bible contains no scientific or historical error." However, he adamantly believed the Bible to be the actual and inspired word of God, and he approached it literally.[4] In Martin's words, Graham "never wandered far from his conviction that when he used the phrase, '*The Bible says* . . . ,' it was tantamount to saying, 'The Bible means . . .'"[5] On the subject of women's work, Graham drew most heavily from the Genesis passages to explain biological roles and to argue for complementarity, and from the Ephesians passage to describe the loving Christian household.

In Genesis, God creates man and woman, each with a distinct biological function: "The biological assignment was basic and simple: Eve was to be the child-bearer, and Adam was to be the breadwinner." Graham also asserts that men and women are not in competition with each other but are complementary to one another: "both equal, yet each with his own station and role." Biological differences ensure that men and women have what the other needs. Drawing on Genesis 2:18, Graham comments, "Man, biologically and emotionally strong, needed the seasoning of tenderness that woman alone could provide, and she in turn required man's strength and leadership qualities to complete her, to give her fulfillment." Moving on to Genesis 3:16, Graham explains Eve's assignment more fully: "Eve's biological role was to bear children—'in sorrow thou shalt bring forth children' (Genesis 3:16). Her romantic role was to love her husband—'Thy desire shall be to thy husband' (v. 16). Her vocational role was to be second in command—'and he shall rule over thee' (v. 16)" (42).

Graham then links Genesis 3:16 directly to Ephesians to describe this complementary relationship in more detail: "The Lord God decreed that man should be the titular head of the family" and that the husband should love the wife (Eph. 5:24–25). Graham continues, "And, in defense of women's liberation, I also suggest that a man's love for his wife should include recognition of her as an individual, with her own personality and her own needs, including the need for appreciation, understanding and real respect" (42). For this reason, Graham's advice columns repeatedly insist that the decision about when to become pregnant finally rests with the woman.[6]

I do think he sincerely believed that there was equality in the home where husband and wife fulfilled their respective functions with love for each other, both submitting to God. But he initially distinguished between equality in treatment of and respect for each other and equality in the governance of the household. As Martin explains:

> Given his own marriage to a strong and capable woman, Graham had to admit that "in one sense, the husband and wife are co-equal in the home; but when it comes to the governmental arrangement of the family, the Bible, from Genesis to Revelation, teaches that man is to be the head of the home. . . . He is the king of the household, and you, his wife, are the queen." A proper queen, he said, would prepare the king's favorite dishes, have the meals on time, make their home as attractive and comfortable as possible, and feel "it is her duty, responsibility, and privilege to remain at home with the children."[7]

Martin claims that this sense of hierarchical governance lessened in the mid-1970s when Graham suggested that he had misinterpreted the Bible in calling for women to be subject to their husbands. Rather, Graham wrote, "'the Biblical position on women's rights is that the husband and wife are equal.'"[8] He continued to see the husband as the governing head of the family, but now he described husband and wife less as king and queen and more as "vice-presidents in a corporation" in that "they have equal status but manage different divisions." Husbands and wives thus submit to each other.[9]

Graham consistently affirms the political rights and equality of women. In several places he suggests that Christianity has been good for women's political freedom because Jesus' message of the worth of every individual is extended unequivocally to women. From Graham's perspective, Jesus already did the work of women's liberation. The evangelist also went on record early on as supporting "equal pay for equal work."[10] However, Graham's insistence on political freedom and economic equality did not mean that he endorsed a woman's freedom to pursue a vocation outside of the home. According to Martin, Graham "decried a feminist tendency to devalue the role of wife and mother as 'a Satanic deception of modern times.'"[11]

MORALLY ESSENTIAL

Graham believes that homemaking is not only the woman's "Biblically prescribed vocation" (114) but also the only vocation that could be truly fulfilling to her. As the faithful response to a loving God, homemaking is the one place where a woman can really make a difference in the world. Repeatedly, Graham praises the influence of "consecrated Christian mothers" on their children and, consequently, on society. Indeed, he writes that women's greatest power is "the power of shaping the world through the influence of a Godly home" (114). This is, following the title of his 1969 essay, a "vocation of honor."

There may be women who need to work outside of the home for financial reasons, Graham acknowledges. And there may even be women

> possessed of unusual talents or drives, who can so arrange their lives, even with husbands and children, to work outside the home and still maintain their family responsibilities. For these women who work, there must be respect, and dignity, and equal rewards. But in the larger perspective, I feel they should not lose sight of the fact that a career alone can never bring total fulfillment. (42)

With rhetorical flourish, Graham suggests that homemaking "can be embroidered on and supplemented, but the fabric underneath must be preserved" (42).

I will take up this language of embroidery in a more critical way shortly, but first I should acknowledge these comments as providing some wiggle room for working mothers. As we have just seen, Graham does acknowledge circumstances in which women must work outside the home. They may need the income, they may be widowed or divorced, or they may be possessed of "unusual talents or drives." Although I have not read everything Graham ever wrote on the subject, I have yet to see or hear him question a woman's ability or intellect for work beyond the domestic sphere. He does reference feminine qualities as making women more suitable to homemaking, but I have not seen him argue that a woman is incapable of professions outside the home.

Indeed, part of his biblical literalism includes a litany of great women in the Bible "whom God used to advance His kingdom": Miriam, Ruth, Esther, Mary, Mary Magdalene, Dorcas, and others not given names in the texts. Of course, he praises some of these women for their roles as mothers, but he also lauds actions they took outside of their own domestic realms.

I do not want to misrepresent him here. He follows this litany with the statement already quoted: "The Word of God teaches that the primary duty of a woman is to be a homemaker."[12] But I mention the litany because it illustrates an important argument running through Graham's writings on women. Early on he recognized the important role that women play in the work of Christian ministry, primarily but not exclusively in the home. This recognition made him open to women's ordination, one of many positions that distinguishes Graham from more conservative evangelicals. As early as 1977, as recorded by William Martin, he said:

> "I don't object to [women's ordination] like some do because so many of the leaders of the early church were women. They prophesied. They taught. You go on mission fields today and many of our missionaries are women who are preachers and teachers." As for women as pastors, "I think it's coming probably, and I think it will be accepted more and more. I know a lot of women who are far superior to men when it comes to ministering to others." Men might resist giving them full rights in the church, but such women "are ordained of God whether they had men to lay hands on them and give them a piece of paper or not. I think God called them."[13]

Incidentally, this language parallels Anne Graham Lotz's own response to the question of seeking ordination in a much more recent interview with CNN's Larry King. Lotz states that the argument against women preachers is one of the "things out there that have been passed down from generation to generation that aren't true." What one must do, she says, is look to Scripture and listen to what God is saying to you. Like her father, Lotz hears a compelling call from God: "We just feel we're under compulsion. We have a message that we want to give out, and we believe God's called us to do it, and we're trying to be obedient to God." When asked about ordination, she replies that ordination itself (whether for men or women) has no scriptural basis. "I just don't feel that's what God has for me," she states. "You know, in the Bible, ordination, I don't see that in the Scripture. In the Bible it's whether you're filled with the Holy Spirit, whether you're anointed by God, whether you're called by God, whether you're obedient to him. I want to be those things, but I don't see any purpose for me in being ordained."[14]

Most striking to me after reading these passages is Martin's claim that Graham never considered handing his ministry to Anne, in spite of her obvious gifts as a preacher. Graham and his inner circle believed that the choice of successor was really God's and therefore a mystery. They would await God's instruction on the question of successor and, more generally, what the future of BGEA should be. And all signs apparently indicated that God wanted a man. Graham and his team never mentioned either the name of Anne Graham Lotz or the possibility that the next leader might be a woman. Quite the contrary, they simply assumed that God's mystery could not extend that far. The common consensus was that God would "lay his hand on the right man at the right time."[15]

CRITICAL RESPONSE

From a feminist perspective, there are many ways to disagree with Billy Graham. That is, feminism is so terrifically varied at this point that one might critically respond to him in any number of ways. For example, it is possible to accept his premise that women are more nurturing and reject his conclusion that we are therefore better suited for homemaking. One could argue, for example, that women's caring nature means that we are best suited to be in positions of public authority where we can more effectively care for the well-being of the polis.

Many other feminists, however, would reject the premise that women are naturally more nurturing, arguing instead that society has socialized women to behave this way. Marxist and socialist feminists, for example, argue that such caretaking traits are a function of economics more than anything else. That is, capitalist societies need women to function in a supportive, domestic role, and so we have developed qualities necessary for taking care of children and household. From this point of view, "feminine qualities" result from our prescribed social role rather than testify to our biological fittingness for it.

More recently, feminists resist any sweeping claims about women as a group, regardless of what they are. They argue that it is simply inaccurate and indeed another form of oppression to speak of women as a monolithic group. We are too heterogeneous, and any sweeping claim about the essential woman marginalizes those who by experience, social location, or worldview do not fit that description.[16] From this perspective, Graham's descriptions of "womanhood" become problematic because they are essentialist.

While I believe all of the preceding criticisms are warranted, my greatest concern with Graham's writings on women emerges from liberal feminism, which focuses primarily on matters of equality and freedom for women and men. I ground my critical comments here not only because these concerns are the most pressing for me personally, but also because I think that they would be most persuasive to those sympathetic to Graham's views on women and women's role in society.

I do truly believe that Graham values equality and freedom for all people and that he believes that Christianity ensures these things. And yet his argument for gender-prescribed vocations is deeply inconsistent with these core commitments. To put it simply, one cannot simultaneously affirm equality and freedom and prescribe vocation according to gender.

Regardless of gender, all people must have equal freedom to pursue their own sense of vocation, whether that is primarily in the home or not. Vocational discernment is not a matter of fulfilling a biblically prescribed duty but of prayerful consideration of one's gifts, attentiveness to one's calling, and accountability to one's deepest commitments to self, to family, and to community. Vocational discernment is not a matter of adhering to rules. It is about crafting a life that is authentic and meaningful.

In the remaining pages, then, I dissent from Graham's biblically prescribed vocations. Before I do so, I want to be very clear about the difference this makes. It is the difference between asking the following question authentically or not: What do you want to be when you grow up? Either this is a genuine question, followed by the sincere affirmation "You can be anything you want to be," or it is not. Either we take all children's dreams seriously and affirm their pursuits, or we do not. If we begin this exchange with a prescription, we say to all children that their bodies determine their vocation, and we toy with the dreams of our daughters.

With that overarching response, I offer a more particular critique of the three planks supporting Graham's argument. I begin with a response to his appeal to divine order, then raise questions about his use of Genesis and Ephesians, and conclude with a counterproposal about the moral function filled by mothers who also work outside the home.

DIVINE ORDER

Billy Graham's response to feminism in 1970 is a standard response to movements of liberation, offered by those who benefit from the status quo. Graham's early position on women's liberation as a prideful and disobedient response to a divinely ordered structure places him in bad company. And, although the analogies are harsh, they illuminate the problems with his argument. When Graham preaches of a divine order that relegates women to a subservient position, he echoes anti-abolitionist ministers offering biblical justification for slavery. When he softens this position a bit to affirm some kind of equality while maintaining separate vocational tracks assigned by gender, he echoes the apartheid theology of the Dutch Reformed Church in South Africa. And when he scolds women for desiring a vocation outside the home and tells them to accept their homemaking role with joy and thanksgiving, he joins the ranks of every minister who has admonished the poor to accept their poverty and await riches in heaven rather than work to lessen their suffering in the here and now.

The easy rebuttal is to say that the loving Christian home that Graham wrote about is far from slavery, townships, and deep poverty. Maybe so, but that rebuttal misses the point of the analogy, which is not to equate Graham's relegated homemakers to slaves, township dwellers, and the poor, but to challenge the form of his argument. Examples like this show that appeals to a divine order maintain repression and advance the interests of the most powerful members of society. Therefore, such arguments should always be treated with suspicion. In addition, the starkness of the apartheid example illustrates the impossibility of separate but equal. One simply cannot affirm human equality and simultaneously limit people's pursuits according to physiology, be it according to race or gender. Either we are all equal, with the same range of freedom, or we are not.

I offer the third analogy because it demonstrates the paternalism of a pastoral response that promises happiness to those who accept their lot in life. The pastoral response—the assurance that one will only experience fulfillment when one submits—is particularly insidious because it sounds so caring. If I am making decisions for and recommending a course of action to someone who is unable to determine and pursue her or his own well-being, we call this caring. But if I do the same thing to people who are able to determine and pursue their own well-being, then it becomes paternalism. When one ascribes a role to men and women without recognizing their own autonomy, one exemplifies paternalism. And when this person then scolds those who make their own way as being prideful and disobedient, the paternalism becomes repression.

One of the most important responses to Graham's admonition against pride is to say, with Susan Nelson Dunfee, that Christianity has encouraged "woman to confess the wrong sin."[17] Those who attempt to exert themselves against the confines of their society, whether those confines are buttressed by convention or tyranny, are not guilty of pride. It is not prideful to declare one's somebodiness and strive to realize one's full potential. Rather, the sin for those less powerful is that of "hiding," of not establishing a self, of not claiming one's full humanity with all of its rights and responsibilities.

There is a false dichotomy in Graham's writing that asserts that one either dutifully submits to the biblically prescribed vocation or one is prideful and disobedient. However, between these two options is a full range of behaviors. Determining one's vocation is not a matter of fulfilling a duty, but a process of prayerful discernment and ongoing conversation with loved ones.

BIBLICAL PRESCRIPTION

We must, however, deal with the biblical prescription itself, the texts that Graham cites as describing God's intended role for women (Gen. 1:27–31; 2:18; and 3:16; and Eph. 5:22–33). What is most striking here is the tremendous power that this argument holds when its biblical warrant is so thin and Graham's own argumentation so tenuous. It is a very good example of how little work one has to do to make the case for convention. It is also a good illustration of something Martin points out—namely, Graham's conviction that what people really need is not careful argumentation and thoughtful exegesis but something preached with conviction. Martin quotes him as follows: "'People want to be told authoritatively that this is so,' he said, 'not be given pro and con arguments. . . . The world longs for finality and authority. It is weary of theological floundering and uncertainty. Belief exhilarates people; doubt depresses them.'"[18]

Using this authoritative tone, Graham has told people some rather remarkable things. For example, there is Graham's comment on Genesis 2:18, quoted earlier: "Man, biologically and emotionally strong, needed the seasoning of tenderness that woman alone could provide, and she in turn required man's strength and leadership qualities to complete her, to give her fulfillment" (42). At this point in the story, of course, we know nothing of Adam and Eve's temperaments. When we do get to know them in the garden narrative, Adam is hardly the leader and Eve is anything but tender. Genesis 2:18 does not assign gender traits to the partners; rather, it acknowledges human need for relationship. Yet Graham reads into it a strong distinction between masculine and feminine traits, a distinction that the most literal read of Adam and Eve cannot possibly sustain.

A second remarkably powerful yet tenuous statement from Graham equates anatomy with a moral imperative. Because women have wombs, we must use them. Indeed, we are incomplete and even disobedient if we do not. In his language, it is women's "biological assignment." Women are literally made to be mothers. But even that does not quite capture Graham's position, which is not only that women have a biological imperative to be mothers but that we are under divine mandate to be stay-at-home mothers. He goes so far as to argue that Jesus may have liberated humanity from sin, but he "did not free [women] from the home" (43–44). Again, I am not sure where the scriptural support for this statement comes from. It reminds me of a student who told me once that homosexuality is the one unforgivable sin because Jesus never talked about it. I suggested that Jesus did not talk about it because it was not a concern for him, and the student said he had never thought of it that way.

Clearly, the position that nature determines destiny (let alone profession) flies in the face of the fundamental concept of human freedom. Yet here, once again, Graham makes an argument that places him in bad company. Like those who supported slavery, segregation, and apartheid, Graham says, "Jesus freed you *in spirit*" (42). There is a natural order, ordained by God. Jesus freed you in spirit but did not liberate you from this divinely appointed order. He did, however, make this order more loving, as the Ephesians passage shows: "Wives, be subject to your husbands. . . . Husbands, love your wives" (Eph. 5:22, 25).

Graham comments on Ephesians, as I noted earlier, by saying that man's love for his wife includes "recognition of her as an individual, with her own personality and her own needs, including the need for appreciation, understanding and real respect" (42). However, this love—like Graham's understanding of Jesus' freedom—is narrowly circumscribed. For example, Jesus frees the woman in spirit to order her commitments as she chooses, but this freedom "urges her to keep those commitments. Wife, mother, homemaker—this is the appointed destiny of real womanhood" (42). Somehow, Graham describes here a love and a freedom that do not threaten structure. The structure is a heterosexual couple with children, all of whom maintain their stations and functions. This structure holds firm, but in doing so, it calls into question the real meaning of love and freedom.

Not long after becoming a grandfather, my father went golfing with a younger man who participated in the Promise Keepers movement. Dad remarked, "You can never anticipate how your children are going to change your life." His golfing partner strongly objected, insisting instead that his children do not change his life, but rather fit into the life he and his wife established for them. Like Billy Graham, this man believes that a Christian home is one in which each member fulfills his or her function in a loving way. There may be freedom in spirit, but there is order in the home.

I have experienced, and I hope that I express, such a different kind of love. It is a love that shapes commitment but does not enforce a structure. It is a love that sustains relationships but does not order them. It is a love that opens up the future rather than mapping its route. It is a love that enables true freedom rather than delineating choices. And it is a love that is open to being changed by the relationships one holds most dear.

MORAL ROLE OF MOTHERS

When we embody this kind of love, mothers play a morally essential role. However, one does not need to use or even have a womb to play this role. People can embody this kind of love through all kinds of relationships. So, while I agree with Graham that mothers play a morally essential role, my agreement is narrow. Consequently, my disagreement ranges broadly.

Recall Graham's point that homemaker, wife, and mother are not only biblically prescribed but also the only truly fulfilling jobs for women. Work outside the home may be "embroidered" onto this fabric, but it must never replace it. Moreover, Graham asserts that homemaking is the site of women's greatest power, "the power of shaping the world through the influence of a Godly home" (42, 114). I do think that Graham truly believes what he says here, and his description of this vocation of honor has helped many stay-at-home mothers believe in the importance of their work. Moreover, I appreciate the positive impact that his words have had on husbands who acknowledge not only the amount but also the value of work in the home.

However, his words also remind me of the time my older brother convinced me that paddling the canoe for him while he fished was really more fun than fishing myself. I "bit" once but never failed to take my own rod after that. So let me respond to Graham as I should have responded to my brother: If paddling is so much fun, why don't you do more of it? If the work of the home is so deeply fulfilling, why not take part in it?

The answer returns us to the biological assignment and to Graham's sharp distinction between masculine and feminine traits that suit us to separate spheres of work. And it clarifies the inequality in Graham's equality. Praising the helper still relegates her to a supporting role. Lauding the power of a consecrated Christian woman in the home still limits that power in scope and keeps her influence on society indirect. Her locus of power does not extend beyond the front yard. She can make a difference in the world only through her children and, honestly, only through her male children.

When Graham talks about the influence that women have on their children in the home or in their spiritual lives, he refers inclusively to "children." But when he talks about the influence that mothers have on public figures—on people who "make an impact on the world"—he talks exclusively about sons. "Men who have made an impact on the world have had good, faithful, and attentive mothers" (114). This is logical, since women are not prescribed public vocations and lack the traits necessary to make an impact on the world directly.

Graham's position begs the question: What difference does a mother's work make in the life of her daughter? If a good, faithful, and attentive mother can rear a son to make an impact in the world, what does she do for the daughter?

In Graham's system, she teaches her daughter how to support men. But I come from a long line of women who also worked outside of the home, and I have been taught other things. So I dissent from Graham on this last point not only as a feminist Christian but also as a daughter, granddaughter, and great-granddaughter of women who also worked outside the home, and as a mother who tries every day to balance my own family's needs with my sense of vocation.

My mother received a PhD in biology and taught at the university level for thirty-five years. What difference does a mother's work make in the life of her daughter? When she told me I could be anything I wanted to be, I had no reason to doubt her. She modeled for me the unleashed potential of women, and I am fiercely proud of her accomplishments as a mother and as a professor. She was and is a good, faithful, and attentive mother who also had a life of her own. By living her own life, she encouraged me to craft my own too.

I do not work outside the home out of economic necessity or because I have "unusual talents and drives." Rather, I maintain my professional life because it is deeply meaningful to me. I also have potential beyond my biological capacity to bear children, and I believe that my traits (whether one labels them "masculine" or "feminine") serve me as well in the classroom as they do in the home. I spent years preparing for this profession, and I believe that I make a contribution to the world when I do it well. Moreover, being a teacher is part of who I am. It is not embroidery on the fabric of my life, but one of its central threads.

Like many mothers who also work outside the home, I find myself bending over backward to convey to stay-at-home mothers how thoroughly I respect their decision. I usually say things like, "It's great that you can stay home with her/him" and then comment on how hard being a full-time mother must be. But I also think that it is important to say that working mothers are also good mothers. That is, having a profession outside the home does not detract from mothering. I am not talking here about all of the mothering one does before and after her other job, but rather about the message that a mother's outside vocation sends to her children. It is the message that I received from my mother, and the message that I hope to give to my daughter. It is this:

> *You are an amazing person with potential that we cannot imagine. Your future is wide open. Take your dreams seriously and pursue them with all your being. Attend closely to the needs of those you love, but do not lose yourself in them. I am your mother and your daddy's wife, and I am my own person too. You are our daughter, and you are your own person too. We cannot anticipate how you will change our lives. We cannot anticipate what you will do and who you will become, but we love you and support your endeavor to discern your own vocation and craft a life that is meaningful for you.*

There is nothing disobedient or prideful here. There is nothing in this that makes me less of a woman or less of a Christian.

I have noted the places where I appreciate Graham's contributions, but I must close by saying that he was utterly wrong about the "destiny of real womanhood." There is no divine prescription for vocations determined by gender any more than there is a divine prescription for station based on race. The task and responsibility of all children of God is to discern a vocation that is meaningful to them, faithful to commitments they hold dear, and in balance with the needs and hopes of those people with whom they bind their lives. There is nothing in this thoughtful pursuit that is disobedient or prideful. Indeed, it is in the midst of this process of discernment that one is brought into a more meaningful relationship with God and family.

NOTES

1. William C. Martin, *A Prophet with Honor: The Billy Graham Story* (New York: William Morrow, 1991), 250.
2. Billy Graham, "Vocation of Honor," *Decision* 10, no. 5 (May 1969): 14.
3. Billy Graham, "Jesus and the Liberated Woman," *Ladies' Home Journal*, December 1970, 42. On March 18, 1970, two hundred feminists showed up unannounced at the *Journal*'s offices to protest the magazine's editorial content. One of the results of this action was the *Journal*'s decision to publish "'The New Feminism': A Special Section Prepared for the *Ladies' Home Journal* by the Women's Liberation Movement" (August 1970). Graham's article served as a rebuttal to this section and to the wider feminist movement. Subsequent citations to Graham's article appear in parentheses in the text.
4. Martin, *Prophet with Honor*, 156, 575.
5. Ibid., 575.
6. Ibid., 159–60.
7. Ibid., 159.
8. Ibid., 586.
9. Ibid.
10. David Frost, *Billy Graham Talks with David Frost* (Philadelphia: A. J. Holman, 1971), 40.
11. Martin, *Prophet with Honor*, 586.
12. Graham, "Vocation of Honor," 14.
13. Martin, *Prophet with Honor*, 587.
14. From a transcript of *Larry King Live*, "Anne Graham Lotz Offers Insights on the Health of Her Father, the Reverend Billy Graham," May 18, 2000, http://transcripts.cnn.com/TRANSCRIPTS/0005/18/lkl.00.html.
15. Martin, *Prophet with Honor*, 608.
16. See, for example, Elizabeth Spelman, *Inessential Woman: Problems of Exclusion in Feminist Thought* (Boston: Beacon Press, 1988).
17. Susan Nelson Dunfee, "The Sin of Hiding: A Feminist Critique of Reinhold Niebuhr's Account of Sin," *Soundings* 65 (fall 1982): 317.
18. Martin, *Prophet with Honor*, 164.

7

Truth and Power

Reflections on the Graham Enigma

J. Philip Wogaman

After a quarter century of appearances in many other cities, Billy Graham announced that his first Washington, DC, crusade would occur April 27 to May 4, 1986. I had been no great fan of his through the years. But as a professor of Christian ethics at Washington's Wesley Theological Seminary, I felt the need to show up at least one night to see for myself and to be able to critique the evangelist responsibly. The evening I chose turned out to be a kind of military emphasis service, with thousands of soldiers and veterans bused in from nearby military installations. I found an elevated seat with an excellent, close-in view from behind the platform.

There were various preliminaries, including an address by a wheelchair-bound veteran who had, as I recall, lost both legs in Vietnam. In the course of offering his Christian testimony, the veteran lashed out at the Soviet Union and called for intensified war preparations. In particular, we should be prepared to use nuclear weapons against this wicked enemy. The largely military audience responded with an enthusiastic ovation.

Billy Graham was not scheduled to speak at that point, but he went to the microphone to respond to this wounded veteran. Commending the man for his Christian witness and his sacrifice, Graham then spoke of the prospect of nuclear war with the Soviet Union. He had been to Russia several times, he said, and he had met there with thousands of fellow Christians. He could not imagine the horror of our dropping nuclear bombs on these brothers and sisters in Christ. His rejoinder was received by the audience with polite hand clapping. Clearly I had just witnessed an incontestably prophetic moment, and I would have to adjust my attitude toward Billy Graham accordingly.

I have since learned that even before that night, Graham had advocated nuclear disarmament, and that his access to the Soviet Union was partly based upon that. Pragmatically, his continued access to an Eastern European audience—which had come to mean so much to him—depended upon his keeping faith with that emphasis upon peace. Possibly he could not have afforded to allow heavy Cold War rhetoric on his own stage to go unchallenged. Whether or not that is so, he had to know that his gentle remonstrance was directly opposed to the attitudes of most of the audience that night. So he was keeping faith with the truth of the gospel, as he understood it, and that got my attention.

PROMINENT CONSERVATIVE SPONSORS

That experience also helped me see the great complexity of this man. He had burst onto the national scene in 1949 with his highly successful Los Angeles crusade (boosted by newspaper chain owner William Randolph Hearst's legendary "puff Graham" telegram to his string of editors) and by his obvious oratorical talents. Already a star evangelist for Youth for Christ, the young Graham quickly became a national figure, hyped in national media (beginning with the Hearst newspapers). His simple message, contrasting the wages of sin and the corruptions of modern life with salvation and new life through accepting Christ, doubtless accounted for much of his appeal. The simplicity of his words was enhanced all the more by his personal charisma and by every appearance of integrity; from the beginning he and his associates adopted and kept faith with clear guidelines to protect themselves from the kinds of temptations that have corrupted so many charismatic evangelists.

But the sponsorship providing Graham with access to mass audiences had a distinctly conservative ideological slant. That was certainly true of Hearst. Early on, Graham also enjoyed the patronage of Texas billionaire H. L. Hunt, whose money sponsored numerous right-wing causes in this country. (Hunt even tried to persuade Graham to run for president, offering an initial guarantee of $6 million in campaign funds.) Oil tycoon J. Howard Pew was another early supporter. During the 1950s Graham was instrumental in the founding of *Christianity Today* as a conservative alternative to the *Christian Century*, and Pew provided the initial funding that made it possible for the new magazine to be sent free of charge to every Protestant minister in the country for whom an address could be located. Pew had already made similar provisions for the extremely conservative *Christian Economics* journal.[1] Graham also received early support from Henry Luce, founder and publisher of *Time* and *Life*, both of which frequently featured the evangelist and his ministry.

The support of such wealthy conservatives in the early years of Graham's ministry most likely had at least two roots. First, Graham shared with them an almost Manichean anticommunism. The struggle against communism was, he declared, "a battle to the death—either Communism must die, or Christianity must die because it is actually a battle between Christ and Anti-Christ. . . . I think it gets its power from the devil."[2] Graham was also late and lukewarm in any criticism of Sen. Joseph McCarthy and what came to be called McCarthyism, having endorsed McCarthy's call for changes in the Fifth Amendment. Such anticommunism could only have delighted his conservative sponsors.

Apart from that, there was Graham's basic message, which emphasized personal conversion and the belief that the only way to change society was through changed individuals. Implicit in that theme was the rejection of efforts to change society through governmental intervention, as called for by the Social Gospel movement and enacted by New Deal legislation. Thus, the Billy Graham of the 1950s and early 1960s was not sympathetic to civil rights legislation and the actions of the civil rights movement. He was particularly unresponsive to acts of civil disobedience carried out by the movement. Insofar as he expressed views on public issues, he was generally conservative. But his pietistic individualism had the effect of diminishing Christian support for collective action in behalf of social justice even when he did not make that explicit.

GRAHAM'S RELATIONSHIPS
WITH MAJOR POLITICAL FIGURES

Notwithstanding that, Graham cultivated relationships with political leaders of every persuasion, including all of the U.S. presidents from Harry Truman on.[3] His relationships with Lyndon Johnson and Richard Nixon were probably his closest, although he seems to have been on fairly intimate terms with Ronald Reagan, George H. W. Bush, and George W. Bush as well. Given the great differences in political viewpoint of the presidents over these decades, one wonders how he could have squared his own convictions with theirs. Perhaps he would simply say that he was concerned only with relating to them pastorally. But then why devote so much time to these powerful leaders? In his 1997 autobiography, he wrote:

> most of my ministry has not been spent with famous people, whether in the entertainment field or the financial or political arenas. Over the years, I have met so many of the rich and famous in many countries

that it's impossible to mention—or even remember—them all. But presidents and royalty aren't typical of the people I've had contact with. . . . 98 percent of my time has been spent with people who were never in the public eye [and] I never go to see important people—or anyone else—without having the deep realization that I am—first and foremost—an ambassador of the King of kings and Lord of lords. From the moment I enter the room, I am thinking about how I can get the conversation around to the Gospel.[4]

One can be forgiven for not taking those words entirely at face value. In fact, most striking about the taped conversations of Nixon and Graham is the absence of the gospel. The subject of their conversations is typically political strategy, trends, and personalities. Aside from this, Graham's own recounting of many relationships with presidents and other world leaders indicates that his relationships were not as exclusively spiritual as might appear.

Was he simply being used by these leaders? Conservative columnist Cal Thomas seems to think so. In a Beliefnet interview with Deborah Caldwell, Thomas sought to explain why Graham had said very negative things about American Jews, as had just been made public in a 1972 Nixon White House tape. The recording caught Graham saying that Jews had a "stranglehold" on the American media that had "to be broken or the country's going down the drain."[5] After noting that Graham "deeply regrets" the remark, Thomas went on to speak of the evangelist's relationship with presidents:

> It demonstrates again that no matter who you are, but especially if you are a clergy person, conservative or liberal, any president can seduce one into supporting his policies or even himself, by this offer of access to his presence. . . . Let's just take Nixon for example. I used to go to these Sunday so-called church services which were held in the White House by Nixon, and he or his people would screen the clergy. He had a Catholic Cardinal there once, and Graham was there on several occasions. . . . And you didn't get in there unless you were a Nixon supporter of course. . . .
>
> The same thing happened with Bill Clinton. His collection of supposed spiritual advisors following the Monica Lewinsky affair was all used as religious cover. All political people want to have the covering, the protection of religious authority on their side.[6]

That got my attention, since I was one of those Clinton advisors![7]

It was obvious to me at the time that Clinton was indeed seeking to "use" the spiritual advisors in communicating with the public. Having acknowledged, with remorse, the immorality of his behavior, he needed to communicate to the American people that he was doing something about it. Otherwise people might easily have concluded that his contrition was not sincere. When challenged about my role by a *Newsweek* writer on an MSNBC national "town meeting" program, I remarked that I was certainly willing to be used by the president to convey his remorse—which I was doing at his specific request. This was, I thought, different from the broader question of political leaders using religion to cloak actions arising from very different motives.

Religion can be a very effective political tool. Machiavelli advised his prince that of all things, he must "appear" to be religious in seeking the support of religious people. Political power is largely constituted by the support of people whose values can be appealed to in one way or another by their leaders. Economic values are important here, as are values of patriotism or ethnic loyalties. But religion can be especially important, as Machiavelli observed. Contemporary struggles in the Middle East, the Balkans, Ireland, and the United States make that very clear.

Given Graham's enormous influence over millions of people, it is certainly no wonder that successive presidents have found relationships with him to be politically convenient. But what about Cal Thomas's questioning whether religious leaders themselves are too easily seduced by access to a president? Based on my own experience, I have to say that there is some truth to this criticism. There is, to be sure, a certain aura about the presidency that can affect you. What does that mean? I suppose it may be something like this: The president represents the entire nation. That one person is the focal point of the whole community. To be in a close relationship with a president is to participate in that. To a lesser degree, the same kind of reflected glory is characteristic of proximity to other celebrities—in sports, entertainment, literature, media, religion, or any other aspect of life commanding wide attention.[8]

I had to deal with some of these feelings in myself. In time, it helped to see the president as a human being like all the rest of us. One of the gifts of religious conversation is a mutual understanding that in the long run we shall all be forgotten, at least on earth. That is even true of a president of the United States.[9] What does endure is the good or the harm we have done.

I suspect that Billy Graham was indeed able to remind his various presidential friends that the eternal perspective is the only thing that matters. What ultimately counts is God's eternal purposes. For Christians, those purposes for humanity are most fully disclosed in the deep love of Jesus Christ, the sublime expression of God's grace to broken humanity. In conveying this kind of spiritual message, Graham might have been able to get beyond the vanities associated with being related to prominent and powerful people—and the spiritual consequences of constant adulation by very large numbers of people. Perhaps that has also been for him more of a struggle than his most enthusiastic followers understand. In any event, most of us would find that to be a recurring spiritual problem, and I doubt whether many people are in a strong moral position to criticize Billy Graham on that point.

HAS GRAHAM'S MINISTRY BEEN PROPHETIC?

The more relevant question is whether, within the pastoral context, Billy Graham was able to bring deep theological insight to bear upon the problems of the day. Is it enough for a pastor to encourage spiritual centeredness and the moral integrity that entails? Spiritually centered motivations are clearly important. But there is more to moral decision-making than being well-motivated. One recalls the adage that the road to hell is paved with good intentions. Haven't we all made really poor decisions, not because our motives were impure but because our information and perspective were faulty? We must cultivate and celebrate good intentions. But we must also acknowledge a distinction between goodwill and wise judgment.

Then how are we to understand the relationship between truth and power? Perhaps we can speak of "truth" as the clear perception of reality. In its simplest form, a Christian will perceive ultimate truth as God's creation and grace and the array of theological formulations derived from that. The central problems of life come down to how we are to understand and act within that perspective, both within the most intimate aspects of personal existence and the broadest social context. Even at its best, our knowledge is bound to be imperfect, as noted by the apostle Paul in his memorable line: "For now we see in a mirror dimly. . . . Now I know in part; then I shall understand fully, even as I have been fully understood" (1 Cor. 13:12 RSV). So none of us can pretend to have the whole truth.

But in relationship to the presidency, the worst form of untruth would be to view its exercise of unparalleled power as irrelevant to what ultimately matters. A few years ago Graham was quoted as saying that he was not an Old Testament prophet but a New Testament evangelist. That comment, which he probably would not offer today, raises the question whether the ministry of a prophet is fundamentally different from that of an evangelist or a pastor. Is it possible for an evangelist to call people to repentance and new life while getting specific about the evils in need of correction?

It is, of course, a part of the stock in trade of evangelists—definitely including Graham—to characterize the sins and corruptions of the old life from which people need to turn in accepting Jesus Christ and the new life. The old nineteenth-century revivals included a moment of "conviction," when the people, having been sufficiently challenged by the preacher, were led to see the realities of the old life for what they were. To be convicted of sin was to come to see, inescapably, that one really is a sinner in need of redemption. That would appear to be the very essence of evangelism, as practiced for more than half a century by Billy Graham.

That would also appear to be "prophetic" in the broadest sense, deeply characteristic of the prophets of ancient Israel and of subsequent generations of Jews and Christians. The word "prophet," derived from the Greek *prophetes*, means one who speaks in behalf of another, and in the Hebrew-Christian tradition, it means one who speaks in behalf of God—who conveys to people what God wants to be said. Authentic evangelists have certainly aspired, in that sense, to be prophets.

Can one also be a pastor and prophet, in particular as a pastor to persons (such as presidents) who exercise great power? Such Old Testament prophets as Amos and Nathan do not come across as particularly pastoral, if "pastoral" refers to one who sympathetically seeks to minister to a person's spiritual life. Graham's own pastoral relationship with presidents is well characterized in the expanded version of the quotation citied earlier:

> I never go to see important people—or anyone else—without having the deep realization that I am—first and foremost—an ambassador of the King of kings and Lord of lords. From the moment I enter the room, I am thinking about how I can get the conversation around to the Gospel. We may discuss a dozen peripheral things first, but I am always thinking of ways I can share Christ and His message of hope with them. I make every effort to be sensitive to their position and their viewpoint, but I rarely leave without attempting to explain the meaning of the Gospel unless God clearly indicates to me that it is not the right time for this person.[10]

Aside from acknowledging Graham's high degree of confidence in knowing the mind of God, one can note that he has exactly stated the meaning of "prophetic": to be an ambassador, or spokesperson, for the King of kings. But what about the relationship between the gospel and the issues with which important people have been grappling? Would that include some of the "peripheral things" to which he refers? Not having been present at any of those sessions, I cannot know. His further remark that "no one has ever rebuffed me or refused to listen to me" could either mean that he had spoken a pertinent prophetic word that was taken seriously, or that he was being treated with kid gloves because of his great popular influence, or that he was inhibited from saying things important people might not want to hear, out of fear of diminishing further access to those people. Probably the truth includes some mixture of these possibilities, as it likely would with most of us, if we were in his position.[11]

Still, with few exceptions, one searches Graham's life and works in vain for serious study of the great issues of the day in the light of the gospel. For example, most Christians would agree that communism posed a serious challenge to the Christian faith. Its avowed atheism was but a part of the picture, possibly not even the most important part, since there were Marxists who continued to believe in God and much of the atheism was a response to idolatrous forms of worship. It seems to me that Reinhold Niebuhr was exactly on target in identifying Marxism's denial of original sin as the larger problem. If human evil is altogether a matter of wrong institutional relationships, then the Marxists were right in saying that revolutionary action to change those relationships would immediately restore the full goodness of humanity. In fact, as Joseph Stalin illustrates, even the revolutionary Communist Party, once in power, could do evil things. A classless society could not dispel human sinfulness. Hence, all leadership must be held accountable. (As the democratic socialist Michael Harrington once remarked, if the state owns the economy, we must ask who owns the state.) On these points, Marxism as an ideology or religion could be rejected. But Marxism contains insights that an absolute rejection, such as Graham voiced in his early career, would miss. His 1980s experience in Russia must have taught him a few things about that.

Much has been made about Graham's refusing to hold segregated campaign services, even in the South during the 1950s and 1960s. That is, of course, to be commended, particularly since so much of his support base has been southern. He coupled this, however, with criticism of the civil rights movement. He is quoted as telling a 1962 press conference that "Jim Crow must go, but I am convinced that some extreme Negro leaders are going too far and too fast." And while Martin Luther King Jr. was in jail in 1963 (during which time he composed his famous "Letter from Birmingham Jail"), Graham advised him to "put on the brakes a little bit." Then, during the summer of 1963, in response to King's "I have a dream" speech, Graham said that "only when Christ comes again will the little white children of Alabama walk hand in hand with little black children."[12] These quotations and others in a comprehensive and basically friendly biography illustrate Graham's reluctance to address social justice questions from a theological perspective.

Contrast that with the explicit—and, I believe, profound—theological grounding of the civil rights movement. King and others spoke directly to the spiritual brokenness of a racist society. The cause of desegregation was not only for the oppressed African Americans; it was also necessary for the spiritual liberation of the white majority. When we are racially alienated from others, we cannot even affirm our own sacred worth as human beings. Human worth is reduced to the accidental characteristics of skin color; deeper spiritual realities are lost. The civil rights movement was able to express its love of the oppressor, even as it acted resolutely and effectively to end the oppression.

At great movement locales, such as Selma, Alabama, in 1965, the combination of deep spirituality with effective social action left an indelible impression upon participants. As one of those participants, I found it a whole lot more compelling than a walk down the aisle to the music of "Just as I Am." If the altar call had included deep conviction about the gaping national sin of racism, it would have been so much more real. And if the reluctance to include such a message was fear that it would turn off potential converts, then that in itself raises questions about how deep the conversion experience was. I do not wish to overstate this, since the integrated setting was itself an important message. But neither should the failure to address racism more directly be excused. If clear social justice issues had been a part of Graham's evangelistic message, it might have made a difference.

Arkansas governor Orval Faubus had himself attended a Graham crusade service at Madison Square Garden only months before his infamous resistance to the racial desegregation of Little Rock's Central High School. Faubus was, in any event, playing the demagogue with the racial prejudices he perceived in Arkansas voters. At the time, that was an altogether accurate perception, and it is more than questionable whether even the most compelling appeal by Graham at Madison Square Garden would have made the slightest difference. But confronting power with the truth is not just a matter of confronting powerful political leaders. Political power is ultimately derived from the dominant will of the whole community. To a surprising degree that is even true in a totalitarian state, where even the dictator has to receive a modicum of support and more than a modicum of acquiescence by the people. It is all the more true that in a democracy leadership must command wide support. Thus, in measuring power, one looks to the multitudes who sustain the few in visible positions of authority.

It is here that one must ask the searching questions about Billy Graham's ability to speak truth to power. He has commanded huge audiences in this country and abroad. I do not question for a moment the estimate that he has spoken directly, in person, to more people than anybody else in human history—and that can be multiplied many times over by television, the emergence of which coincided with the beginnings of his evangelistic ministry. Could he not have said more? Could he not have created more sympathy for the marginalized and stigmatized people of his times and thus effected more lasting change? This is not to discount the times when he did address issues, including the night in Washington I described at the beginning of this chapter. From time to time he spoke of the impoverished and hungry people of this nation and the rest of the world, though rarely did he voice the hope that the nation could act in concert through public policy to address their needs.[13] And I am not aware of any president's having become more motivated to deal with social justice issues as a result of Graham's friendship and pastoral relationships.

GRAHAM'S INVOLVEMENT IN PARTISAN POLITICS

There is a further question. Did Billy Graham seek to affect the outcome in presidential elections? Occasionally he was criticized for seeking to do exactly that, especially in relation to his friend Richard Nixon. Toward the end of his autobiography, Graham remarks that "if I had it to do over again, I would also avoid any semblance of involvement in partisan politics. . . . There have been times when I undoubtedly stepped over the line between politics and my calling as an evangelist. Becoming involved in strictly political issues or partisan politics inevitably dilutes the evangelist's impact and compromises his message. It is a lesson I wish I had learned earlier."[14]

He appears, in fact, to have been deeply involved in partisan maneuvering. One significant illustration of that was his providing Richard Nixon a place of prominence at a Pittsburgh crusade service shortly before the 1968 election. While also reading a telegram from Nixon's opponent Hubert Humphrey, Graham used the occasion to extol Nixon effusively.[15] Earlier, when asked by Nixon for advice in the choosing of a vice presidential running mate, Graham enthusiastically supported Senator Mark Hatfield.

Four years later, as President Nixon sought reelection, Graham was clearly in his camp. I find a paragraph from Nixon's presidential memoir to be especially revealing. The context is Nixon's effort to gain the tacit support of Lyndon Johnson, who evidently disliked the 1972 Democratic nominee, Senator George McGovern. Johnson had already indicated to Nixon that his support for fellow Democrat McGovern would be entirely *pro forma* and that he would not interfere with any other Democrats opposing the Democratic nominee. Nixon's memoir continues:

> A few weeks later Johnson sent me some campaign advice through Billy Graham: "Ignore McGovern, and get out with the people. But stay above the campaign, like I did with Goldwater. Go to ball games and factories. And don't worry. The McGovern people are going to defeat themselves." Billy said that when he had raised the question of the Watergate bugging business, Johnson had just laughed and said, "Hell, that's not going to hurt him a bit."[16]

Is it proper for a religious leader to endorse or otherwise support a presidential candidate, as Billy Graham has been criticized for doing? If not, I am not in a very good moral position to cast the first stone. During the 1968 campaign, while Graham was supporting Richard Nixon, I was actively lining up signers for a statement supporting his opponent, Hubert Humphrey.[17] I have felt it improper for church bodies, as such, to endorse candidates except in truly extreme circumstances, but it is another matter when religious leaders voice their personal view. The only question then is whether that view is sufficiently discerning.

Graham can, at least in the case of his support for Richard Nixon, be criticized for not seeing through Nixon's basic character. Later, after the Watergate scandal, Graham expressed some disillusionment with his friend's behavior. Might he not have perceived the roots of that in Nixon's whole political career, including the mean-spirited campaigns of the early Nixon against Gerald Voorhis and Helen Gahagan Douglas? Of course, Nixon's strident anti-communism in those campaigns was closely paralleled by Graham's own views in the late 1940s and 1950s. He failed to perceive the hardness of Nixon's political ambitions. On the other hand, he did see more positive aspects in Nixon's personality that often escape more liberal critics.[18]

CONCLUSION

While much about Billy Graham's long evangelistic career and his personal integrity can be respected, his limitations have greatly diminished the good that a person of his charismatic gifts and with his vast following might have accomplished. The basic problem theologically has been a failure to see the social interconnectedness of all life. He has emphasized the importance of our decision to turn to God, as revealed in Christ; he has neglected the fuller purposes of the God to whom we must turn. The basic problem politically has been naiveté about power. That is astonishing, given the unprecedented exposure he has had to powerful leaders for half a century. He has seemed but dimly aware of the vast influence he could have over the large public or upon the decision makers with whom he interacted pastorally. He seemed scarcely aware at all of the extent to which he was used by political leaders for purposes that were remote from the gospel.

Still, Graham's life and his legacy remain something of an enigma. He has always been more complex than the simple message of his typical evangelistic sermon. His calls for nuclear disarmament illustrate that, even though he does not seem to have thought through the connections between the evangelistic message and its social implications. Whatever his limitations, he has shown a capacity to grow, and I am reluctant to define him by his limitations.[19] I suspect, in the end, that the enigma presented by this man's long evangelistic career may be, as some have suggested, the persistent, unresolved tug within his own nature between a sincere commitment to the gospel—however narrowly he has perceived that—and a simple desire to be liked by masses of people and by persons of great power.

NOTES

1. As a young pastor in Massachusetts during the mid-1950s, I received both of these publications, which were critical of liberal tendencies in denominations associated with the National and World Councils of Churches.

2. Quoted in William Martin, *A Prophet with Honor: The Billy Graham Story* (New York: William Morrow, 1991), 165. The quotation is from a printed Graham sermon entitled "Christianity versus Communism."

3. Truman appears to have been the only one of these who specifically distanced himself from Graham, evidently feeling that Graham was attempting to use a relationship for his own ends and maybe also sensing, correctly, that Graham's political views were not consonant with his own. See Martin, *Prophet with Honor*, 131–32. Martin quotes Truman as saying about Graham that "he claims he's a friend of all the Presidents, but he was never a friend of mine when I was President. I just don't go for people like that" (144). The relationship between the two mellowed in later years.

4. Billy Graham, *Just as I Am: The Autobiography of Billy Graham* (San Francisco: HarperSanFrancisco, 1997), 683–84.

5. Confronted with the tape recording, Graham apologized but said he could not remember the conversation. See Eric J. Greenberg, "Graham Apology Not Enough," *Jewish Life*, http://www.ujc.org/page.html?ArticleID=29272.

6. Cal Thomas, "A Little Glitch," interview by Deborah Caldwell, Beliefnet, http://www.beliefnet.com/story/102/story_10214_1.html.

7. President Clinton and his family were regulars at Foundry United Methodist Church, which I served from 1992 to 2002, and at his request in August 1998, I agreed to be one of his three spiritual advisors (the other two being Tony Campolo and Gordon McDonald).

8. Many members of a church in Virginia were attracted to a neighboring church that was visited by President-elect Clinton a few days before Clinton's first inauguration. The pastor well understood why his people would want to be in the same church with the new president. It was a historic occasion, and he offered no criticism. He remarked to his people, however, that the Holy Spirit was present in their church *every* Sunday.

9. President Clinton used to show a five-billion-year-old moon rock to visitors in the Oval Office with the remark that "we're only a passing scene."

10. Graham, *Just as I Am*, 684.

11. In "An Open Letter to Billy Graham," Will Campbell and James Holloway express sharp criticism of Graham's uncritical "worship of politics; the shoring-up to political gods, leaders, powers, and principalities; the service to the Baals in the chicanery, flimflam, deceit, and murder that defines the present political process." In *The Failure and the Hope: Essays of Southern Churchmen*, ed. Will D. Campbell and James Y. Holloway (Grand Rapids: Wm. B. Eerdmans, 1972), 115.

12. Quoted in Martin, *Prophet with Honor*, 295–96.

13. His public support for President Johnson's "war on poverty" was a striking exception. In his autobiographical comments on Johnson, Graham writes that "he wanted to harness the wealth and knowledge and greatness of this nation to help the poor and the oppressed here and around the world. That hope must be revived by every President and kept alive in the hearts of all citizens" (Graham, *Just as I Am*, 418).

14. Graham, *Just as I Am*, 724.

15. Martin, *Prophet with Honor*, 353.

16. Richard M. Nixon, *The Memoirs of Richard Nixon* (New York: Grosset & Dunlap, 1978), 673–74.

17. The statement was published with the signatures of such religious leaders as Reinhold Niebuhr, John C. Bennett, Abraham Heschel, and Martin Luther King Sr. (whose son had been assassinated half a year earlier).

18. I was late coming to this broader perspective on Richard Nixon myself. One of my parishioners at Foundry United Methodist Church in the 1990s was the late Arthur Flemming, who had been a member of President Eisenhower's cabinet and was a friend of Nixon's. Flemming was a very progressive Republican, liberal enough to be fired from his later post as head of the U.S. Civil Rights Commission by President Reagan. Over a long lunch one day, Flemming spoke of Nixon as being a kind of "Dr. Jekyll and Mr. Hyde." The dark side of his personality, illustrated by the whole Watergate scandal, was an important character flaw. But he was also capable of kindness and even political generosity. The latter was illustrated by Nixon's comment to him that he would not pursue possible electoral fraud in Illinois during the 1960 election since that would destabilize the country. Billy Graham's problem was that he saw only the positive side, at least until the Watergate scandal could not be ignored.

19. For a perceptive discussion of Graham's evolving views, see Thomas Paul Johnston, *Examining Billy Graham's Theology of Evangelism* (Eugene, OR: Wipf & Stock, 2003).

8

Religious Sanctity
and Political Power

Leslie C. Griffin

> It is wonderful what a simple White House invitation will do to dull the critical faculties, thereby confirming the fears of the Founding Fathers.
>
> *Reinhold Niebuhr*

So wrote Reinhold Niebuhr about the worship services conducted in the Nixon White House by "representatives of all the disestablished religions," especially Billy Graham. The famous Protestant theologian worried that Graham's participation in the White House services "established a conforming religion" in clear violation of the First Amendment.

Niebuhr's concern was primarily theological, not legal. Citing the biblical prophets, he feared that religion lost its critical voice when it was allied too closely with the power of the state. Quoting Thomas Jefferson on the "wall of separation between church and state," Niebuhr also asserted that the American constitutional system "encouraged the prophetic radical aspect of religious life, which insisted on criticizing any defective and unjust social order."[1]

Jimmy Carter's argument about the White House services was more straightforward; he was devoted to the separation of church and state because of his Southern Baptist heritage. When he moved into the Georgia governor's mansion in 1971, he cancelled church services there, preferring to worship in Atlanta's Northside Baptist Church. Carter repeated that action in the White House after he was elected president in 1976.[2] Although the Georgian had

spoken openly of his evangelical faith on the campaign trail, he discontinued
his predecessor's worship services as soon as he became president, choosing
instead to attend the First Baptist Church in Washington, DC, or (when the
Carters were in Georgia) the Plains or Maranatha Baptist Churches, where
the president had long taught Sunday school.[3] In contrast to Nixon, who "told
the press he had established these services in order to further the cause of
'religion,'"[4] Carter believed that the government should not support religious
worship at all. Consequently, Billy Graham did not preach in the Carter White
House.

Niebuhr's explicit and Carter's implicit criticism of the White House services echo a long-asked question about the purposes of the First Amendment's
religion clauses: do they protect religion from the state, the state from religion, or both?

Progressive criticism of Billy Graham's public career as confidant of presidents from Dwight D. Eisenhower to George W. Bush typically has arisen
from a concern that religious faith not be corrupted by political power. Progressives like Niebuhr thus have questioned whether White House invitations
dulled Graham's critical faculties and encouraged him to conform prophetic
Christianity to the demands of the state. While that question is important, we
should also ask the converse—whether Graham's career as America's pastor
harmed or compromised the state in any way. If some of Graham's conduct
confirmed the fears of the Founding Fathers that prophetic religion would be
corrupted by the state, it is also probable that Graham's career demonstrates
that too much public religion is bad for the state.

It is important to note here that a progressive interpretation of the First
Amendment focuses on both potential problems—religion's corruption by the
state and the state's corruption by religion. For religious progressives in particular, both problems warrant attention because of their belief that religion
and the state have important yet distinctive roles to play in the formation of a
tolerant community. Hence, my chapter will seek to address both concerns in
the politically significant aspects of Graham's career—his spiritual and political advice to presidents, his endorsement of presidential candidates, and his
involvement in the nation's civil religion.

SPIRITUAL AND POLITICAL ADVICE

The interaction of church and state is seen most clearly in Graham's career of
giving spiritual and political advice to presidents. Research about Billy Graham has demonstrated that Graham was both a spiritual and political advisor
to Richard Nixon and to other presidents.

In many ways, Graham's spiritual legacy seems secure; he was a "counselor in prosperity and a comfort in care and sorrow" for presidents from Dwight D. Eisenhower to George W. Bush, both Republican and Democratic. He offered spiritual advice to Richard Nixon before the 1960 election and after the close loss to John F. Kennedy (which he urged Nixon to view as "a stepping stone to new spiritual experience").[5] He consoled Nixon upon the death of his mother, Hannah; he comforted Lyndon Johnson during the travails of the Vietnam War and became his spiritual counselor; he offered Bill Clinton forgiveness during the Monica Lewinsky scandal; and he planted the mustard seed of faith in George W. Bush's heart during a walk in Kennebunkport, Maine. According to George H. W. Bush, "When my soul was troubled . . . it was Billy I reached out to, for advice, for comfort, for prayer."[6] Graham's legacy of spiritual solace to the powerful is strong.

The record also indicates that Graham loved politics and was an astute political observer and advisor. His correspondence with Vice President Nixon during the 1950s included commentary on farm policy, Cuba and the Congo, the U-2 incident, and Nixon's choice of running mate.[7] Nixon wrote Graham, "I have often told friends that when you went into the ministry, politics lost one of its potentially greatest practitioners!"[8]

Although Graham's role as political counselor certainly annoyed progressives, it might not have been especially controversial, at least from the standpoint of the First Amendment. If Graham had an avocation for politics and loved to talk about it with his political friends, in the same way that athletic amateurs love to discuss professional sports, Graham's political behavior was wholly unremarkable and uninteresting for First Amendment purposes.

The potential for controversy arises not over Graham's spiritual advice or his political hobby, but in his mixing of spiritual and political roles. Clearly, this mingling was evident in Graham's early letters to Richard Nixon, which counseled the vice president to give lectures to religious groups, to use more religious language in his public speeches, and to speak more openly of his own religious faith. Graham also volunteered to make arrangements for Nixon to speak before groups of Presbyterians and Baptists, and to meet individual religious leaders from the Episcopal, Methodist, Presbyterian, and Baptist churches. The evangelist even advised Nixon on what to say in these meetings.[9] As Graham bluntly wrote in 1956, "Very frankly, you are in need of a boost in Protestant religious circles. . . . I think it is time you move among some of these men and let them know you."[10]

Although some observers may find it uncontroversial for Graham' to have introduced a presidential candidate to religious groups, the historical context makes his remarks about the Protestant groups especially troubling. John Kennedy's Catholicism was the religious issue in the 1960 campaign, and many

Protestants feared that a Catholic leader would follow the Vatican and not the American system of government. Graham understood those fears, and although he frequently noted that he did not want to act in an anti-Catholic manner, his comments to Nixon about the 1960 campaign effectively divided the country into Protestant and Catholic voters.

Early on, he suggested that having a Catholic opponent could help Nixon secure the Protestant vote.[11] Then he strategized at length with Nixon about the voting breakdown, assuming that, because Catholics would vote for Kennedy no matter what, Nixon should work to secure the ballots of all the Protestant groups. In a letter to Vice President Nixon, Graham wrote:

> If Senator Kennedy is nominated, he will capture the Catholic vote—almost 100 percent of it! No matter what concessions you make to the Catholic church or how you play up to them—even if you had a Catholic running mate, you would not even crack five or ten percent of the Catholic vote. Therefore you must count on almost a solid Catholic vote for Kennedy throughout the Nation. . . .
> Since the Protestant voters out-number the Catholics three to one, you must concentrate on solidifying the Protestant vote. In my opinion, if you make the mistake of having a Catholic running mate, you will divide the Protestant vote and make no inroads whatsoever in the Catholic vote. Therefore I hope you will discard this idea at all cost. Therefore it becomes imperative for you to have as your running mate someone the Protestant church can rally behind enthusiastically.[12]

Graham also warned that the vice presidential choice was important and that he was "desperately afraid that there is a possibility of your not only losing all the Catholic votes but much of the tolerant Protestant vote." Graham's own suggestion for a running mate was Walter Judd, a former missionary who was a member of the House of Representatives from Wisconsin from 1943 to 1963. Nixon, of course, did not select Judd; nor did he destroy Graham's political letter, as the evangelist had requested.

Although at the beginning of the campaign Graham had focused on the religious issue and tried to get Nixon to use it to his advantage, he and the vice president were unhappy in later months when it appeared that Kennedy was more successful than Nixon in using religion for political benefit. By October, Graham warned Nixon that "some leading person in the Republican Party must show that the religious issue has been deliberately used by the Democrats to (1) solidify the Catholic vote, (2) split the Protestants, (3) make a martyr out of Kennedy, and (4) obscure the more basic issues in the campaign." Voters needed to learn that both Protestants and Catholics were caught "in a deliberate political trap made for them" by the Democrats.[13] Graham also thought there was evidence that Democrats were spreading anti-Catholic literature for their political advantage, in order to "solidify the Catholic vote and split the Protestants."[14]

In spite of all this work for Nixon, Graham met with Kennedy shortly after the election, even while reassuring Nixon of his loyalty. And at a news conference with Kennedy, the evangelist stated that the election "proved there was not as much religious prejudice as many had feared, and probably had reduced forever the importance of the religious issue in American elections."[15]

It was not only Catholics that Graham feared at the height of his public ministry, however. Recently the evangelist was caught in the most difficult moment of his career when tapes from the Nixon White House revealed that he had exchanged anti-Semitic remarks with President Nixon. Although those comments were of a different order from the ones about Kennedy and the Catholics, they reinforce the point that it is dangerous to base political participation on religious loyalties.

Graham's career of giving spiritual and political advice to the powerful rightly meets with criticism from both religious and political perspectives. The major criticism from the religious perspective, of course, is that close access to power corrupted Graham's spiritual judgment. As Richard Pierard wrote in 1980, not too many years after Watergate:

> Further, it appears that Johnson and Nixon turned to Graham for spiritual counsel because he did not really call them to account for political sins. Since he conceived himself to be a "New Testament evangelist not an Old Testament prophet," a "nonpolitical Apostle Paul living in the Roman Empire of Caesar," political leaders had little reason to expect his censure of their activities. In this context, then, could Graham speak the word of truth—especially when that word may be critical or slashing—to the man in the White House when he is on such friendly terms with him? On the basis of the evidence now available, the answer must be no. Hopefully, out of the purifying fires of Watergate has emerged a different Graham, one who no longer feels a need to identify with presidents and others in positions of power and authority.[16]

For political criticism, we would do well to recall the words of U.S. Chief Justice Warren Burger. In the leading Supreme Court case about the Establishment Clause, Burger warned that "political division along religious lines was one of the principal evils against which the First Amendment was intended to protect."[17] Although Billy Graham is not a state actor who can violate the Establishment Clause, his actions in the 1960 campaign, especially those encouraging Nixon to secure the Protestant vote while letting the Catholic vote fall by the wayside, illustrate both the temptation of attracting and keeping voters based on their religious affiliations and the danger of doing so—that political discourse will become divided along religious lines and that government will be based on Protestant, Catholic, or anti-Semitic principles rather than constitutional ones.

Both sides of the First Amendment—corruption of religion by the state and corruption of the state by religion—were implicated in Graham's long career of giving spiritual and political advice to the powerful. Problems occurred both when he let his religious judgment be guided by politics and when he let his political judgment be directed by religion. Graham's advice about religious audiences and voters, and his intermingling of religion and politics, also culminated in the most difficult question of spiritual and political support—whether it was appropriate for him to endorse presidential candidates.

POLITICAL ENDORSEMENTS

From Nixon to George W. Bush, Billy Graham was ambivalent about endorsing candidates while nonetheless managing to do so in one way or another. In May 1960, for instance, he wrote to Nixon about a *New York Times* article: "While I did not call you by name, yet I left the implication. I think this strategy carries greater strength than if I came all out for you at the present time."[18] While doing everything but calling Nixon by name, Graham offered a virtual endorsement when he publicly stated, "This is a time for a man of experience and world stature, and not a novice."[19] Any reasonable person would have concluded exactly what Graham meant—that he strongly preferred the vice president of the United States over the junior senator from Massachusetts.

Graham also weighed a direct endorsement of Nixon over the ensuing months of 1960. In September, however, loud criticism greeted Norman Vincent Peale when his group, the National Conference of Citizens for Religious Freedom (NCCRF), endorsed Nixon over Kennedy. According to the *New York Times*, the NCCRF stated, "A Roman Catholic President would be under 'extreme pressure from the hierarchy of his church' to align the foreign policy of the United States with that of the Vatican."[20]

In response, Reinhold Niebuhr and others argued that NCCRF had "'loosed the floodgates of religious bigotry'" through their actions.[21] Peale eventually volunteered to relinquish his pulpit because of the widely publicized controversy, and although he was able to keep his job, the public turmoil shook Graham, causing him to anguish over backing Nixon explicitly. Beyond his personal aversion to conflict, Graham and his advisors feared that an endorsement might detract from his ministry or lead people to view him as anti-Catholic.

Graham's anguish became all the more apparent after he submitted a lengthy commentary backing Nixon for *Life* magazine. The evangelist was unsure about the wisdom of publicizing his endorsement, and even after he had submitted it, he prayed about whether the article should be published. When *Life* postponed publication due to complaints about equal treatment from the Kennedy campaign, Graham interpreted the action as a miracle of God and refused to grant permission for *Life* to publish the article in any forthcoming issue.[22] Nonetheless, in November 1960 Graham offered an invocation for Nixon at a late campaign rally in South Carolina while at the same time informing "leaders of the South Carolina Democrats for Nixon-Lodge that 'my appearance in Columbia should not be politically interpreted, however.'"[23]

Graham's endorsement practices became even more explicit in years to follow. Toward the end of the 1968 presidential campaign, for instance, he announced that he had voted by absentee ballot for Nixon, thus showing his support well in advance of Election Day. Nixon aide Harry Dent later declared, "That was all I needed. I used it in all our TV commercials right down to the end."[24] And although Graham refused to endorse a candidate in 1976, he returned to endorsements in 2000 when he repeated the absentee ballot announcement, this time on behalf of George W. Bush.[25] It is easy to see why Richard Pierard concludes that "any disclaimers that Graham is 'neutral in politics' may safely be ignored."[26]

The endorsement of politicians by religious individuals and organizations is a controversial issue in U.S. tax law. According to Internal Revenue Service guidelines, tax-exempt, section 501(c)(3) organizations, including churches and religious organizations, must follow certain rules, including one that instructs them not to "participate in, or intervene in, any political campaign on behalf of (or in opposition to) any candidate for public office," in order to retain their tax-exempt status.[27] "By its terms, the statutory prohibition of participation in political campaigns is absolute; the charity can not so much as utter a peep in support of (or in opposition to) a candidate running for office."[28] The prohibition on intervention in political campaigns is the quo for the quid of being tax-exempt. Although churches rarely lose their tax-exempt status, in 2000 Branch Ministries' tax-exempt status was revoked for placing ads in newspapers that "urged Christians not to vote for then-presidential candidate Bill Clinton because of his positions on certain moral issues."[29]

The IRS explains the scope of the political campaign rule in the following illustrations:

> Minister C is the minister of Church L and is well known in the community. Three weeks before the election, he attends a press conference at Candidate V's campaign headquarters and states that Candidate V should be reelected. Minister C does not say he is speaking on behalf of his church. His endorsement is reported on the front page of the local newspaper and he is identified in the article as the minister of

Church L. Since Minister C did not make the endorsement at an official church function, in an official church publication or otherwise use the church's assets, and did not state that he was speaking as a representative of Church L, his actions did not constitute campaign intervention attributable to Church L.

Minister D is the minister of Church M. During regular services of Church M shortly before the election, Minister D preached on a number of issues, including the importance of voting in the upcoming election, and concludes by stating, "It is important that you all do your duty in the election and vote for Candidate W." Since Minister D's remarks indicating support for Candidate W were made during an official church service, they constitute political campaign intervention attributable to Church M.[30]

According to these standards, Billy Graham's virtual endorsements are acceptable under the provisions of the tax code; all he did was to announce the content of his absentee ballots, and he did not do so as an official representative of, or at events sponsored by, any charitable, educational, or religious organization. Graham himself believed that he was acting as an individual citizen, and in his unpublished article for *Life* magazine, he rightly observed that Reinhold Niebuhr and John Bennett of Union Theological Seminary were openly campaigning for Kennedy and that he "was also taking [his] right as a citizen of the United States to express his conviction."[31]

Some commentators believe that the political activity prohibition in U.S. tax law is a good idea, because it keeps church and state from becoming too intertwined, while others argue that it intrudes upon the independence of religious organizations. According to John Fritze, for example, "Critics of the nonprofit tax code say it stifles the free speech of religious leaders and undermines the role churches play as advocates for their communities. Others argue that allowing congregations to become politically active could turn the collection plate into a vehicle for tax-free campaign finance."[32]

Texas Democratic senator Lyndon Johnson sponsored the political activity limitation of section 501(c)(3) in 1954, reportedly because he was unhappy about opposition by tax-exempt groups to his reelection in Texas. Ann Murphy, however, has argued that Johnson and other senators were in fact worried about left-wing and right-wing groups sponsoring critics of the American government while receiving tax exemptions.[33]

Current critics of the tax provision argue that the IRS rule inappropriately muzzles ministers and that their free speech rights should be returned by ending the political activity prohibition for churches. In 2003 Republican representative Walter Jones of North Carolina proposed, in the Houses of Worship Free Speech Restoration Act, that the code be amended to allow endorsement of political candidates from the pulpit. The Jones amendment allows political endorsements during church services "in the content, preparation, or presentation of any homily, sermon, teaching, dialectic, or other presentation made during religious services or gatherings."[34] If it becomes law, this amendment would allow Graham or his son Franklin to endorse candidates at crusade services sponsored by BGEA and televised across the globe. Under the Jones standard, however, ads like the one run by Branch Ministries are still not allowed.[35]

The endorsement questions are difficult. If the predominant concern of the First Amendment is about the corruption of religion by politics, then ministers should not be encouraged to endorse candidates in any setting. This seems to be the position of U.S. representative John Lewis, who has argued that the Jones amendment "threatens not only our quest for meaningful campaign finance reform, but threatens the very integrity and independence of our churches and others [sic] houses of worship."[36]

But a tension arises when we consider the Free Exercise and Free Speech Clauses, which encourage church speech about important social issues. Moreover, individual churches may differ theologically about how much political intervention they deem appropriate and what counts as corruption. Some churches may view their endorsement of candidates as fulfilling and not threatening their integrity, while other churches may be hesitant even when a candidate walks through their doors in election season. This suggests that the corruption of religion question may differ from church to church, from community to community, or even from religion to religion.

Once again, the legal question has a different focus, as expressed most notably in the famous sentences from James Madison's "Memorial and Remonstrance against Religious Assessments":

> Who does not see that the same authority which can establish Christianity, in exclusion of all other Religions, may establish with the same ease any particular sect of Christians, in exclusion of all other Sects? That the same authority which can force a citizen to contribute three pence only of his property for the support of any one establishment, may force him to conform to any other establishment in all cases whatsoever?[37]

If the churches' tax exemptions are a government subsidy that reduces the government's tax benefits, then the government should not subsidize religious organizations' political activities.[38] From the political perspective, one problem with church endorsements is that they come from institutions that have the benefit of being tax-exempt; other taxpayers' religious freedom may be violated by the indirect support of the religious endorsement. A progressive First Amendment is wary of such support.

CIVIL RELIGION

Beyond the religious and political problems posed by Graham's endorsements, we must also question his pastoral leadership of a nation guided by civil religion. Robert Bellah, the author of the classic 1967 article "Civil Religion in America," has argued that "the separation of church and state has not denied the political realm a religious dimension" and that there is "a set of beliefs, symbols, and rituals" that accompany the political sphere.[39] In American political life, examples of civil religion—sometimes called "ceremonial deism"[40]—include inaugural prayers, State of the Union addresses, and presidential proclamations on Thanksgiving, Christmas, and the National Day of Prayer. Other examples abound: Congress opens with a chaplain's prayer, "In God We Trust" appears on coins, "under God" is recited in the Pledge of Allegiance, and "so help me God" concludes the presidential oath of office (but not because these words are present in the text of the Constitution).[41] God's name, then, is invoked time and again even though civil religion is the ritual of politics, not of organized religion.

As America's pastor, Billy Graham has been an active participant in the nation's civil religion. In fact, the National Day of Prayer was partly his idea; he lobbied Congress for its passage in 1952 so that there would be "a day 'in which the normal pursuits of the American people would be forgotten, so that there would be a day of confession of sin, humiliation, repentance and turning to God.'"[42] Of course, Graham also preached at White House services during the Johnson and Nixon years.

Perhaps his most visible participatory role, however, has been in presidential inaugurals—one of the most important practices of civil religion. According to Bellah, "The inauguration of a president is an important ceremonial event in this religion. It reaffirms, among other things, the religious legitimation of the highest political authority."[43] Graham has participated in this practice of legitimation by delivering the inaugural prayers for Presidents Nixon, George H. W. Bush, and Clinton (after becoming ill, Graham was replaced at the inauguration of George W. Bush by his son Franklin), and by preaching at private inaugural church services for Presidents Johnson, Nixon, and Reagan.[44]

On a general level, Graham's participation in our nation's civil religion may not be constitutionally questionable. Consider Steven Epstein's sharp analysis of the constitutional status of ceremonial deism:

> The Supreme Court has utilized the concept of ceremonial deism to immunize a certain class of activities from Establishment Clause scrutiny. This class of activities seems to have or is perceived to have certain defining characteristics . . . :

1) actual, symbolic, or ritualistic;
2) prayer, invocation, benediction, supplication, appeal, reverent reference to, or embrace of, a general or particular deity;
3) created, delivered, sponsored, or encouraged by government officials;
4) during governmental functions or ceremonies, in the form of patriotic expressions, or associated with holiday observances;
5) which, in and of themselves, are unlikely to indoctrinate or proselytize their audience;
6) which are not specifically designed to accommodate the free religious exercise of a particular group of citizens; and
7) which, as of this date, are deeply rooted in the nation's history and traditions.

Practices which fit this definition can be divided into two categories, the first of which I label "core" ceremonial deism. . . .

"Core" ceremonial deism includes practices which have been non-controversial, have resulted in very little litigation, and have *never* been held unconstitutional by any court. . . . including: (1) legislative prayers and prayer rooms; (2) prayers at presidential inaugurations; (3) presidential addresses invoking the name of God; . . . [and] (8) the National Day of Prayer; . . .[45]

By Epstein's (and the Supreme Court's) standard, Billy Graham has appeared to participate—constitutionally—in core ceremonial deism, both in the creation of the National Day of Prayer and in his inaugural prayers and sermons. Meeting this constitutional standard, however, does not rightly free Graham of all criticism.

Bellah later wrote that his essay "was not intended to celebrate the civil religion but to describe it and to see if it had resources for the work of national self-criticism."[46] The critical question that arises here is whether Graham's participation in civil religion has given the nation resources for self-criticism.

The content of his sermons and prayers at inaugurals and private White House worship services shows that America's pastor consecrated, blessed, and legitimated presidents and their policies much more effectively than he subjected them to any sort of criticism. In fact, one would have to search long and hard in these sermons and prayers, all of them available at the Billy Graham Archives at Wheaton College, for any sort of criticism that goes beyond calling the nation to repent of its sins and to turn back to God.

A detailed look at Graham's White House sermons during the Nixon years, for instance, turns up nothing critical about the Vietnam War, even while hundreds of thousands protested just steps away from the front door to the White House. And a detailed analysis of Graham's inaugural prayers suggests that the evangelist simply neglected to pray about major issues plaguing the nation at different times—Watergate among them. Niebuhr was thus on target when he criticized Graham for practicing a conforming religion without prophetic criticism.

Equally troubling, but from a different perspective, is the sectarian quality of some of Graham's participation in civil religion. Consider his inaugural prayers alone. In the 1969 inaugural, his prayer made reference to Jesus ("the Prince of Peace who shed His blood on the Cross") several times. And although his prayers became shorter and more general in 1989 (without any reference to Jesus), in 1993 he invoked the "one that's called Wonderful Counselor, Mighty God, the Everlasting Father and the Prince of Peace," and in 1997 he prayed in "the name of the Father, Son and Holy Spirit."[47]

Graham has not been the only one to pray to or about Jesus at national events; the name of Jesus has been invoked in prayers at most presidential inaugurals.[48] From the standpoint of a purely civil religion, of course, such naming is controversial because Jesus Christ is not a figure of American civil religion but is instead the founder of a specific religious tradition to which many Americans do not belong. Simply stated, praying to Jesus is not a practice shared by U.S. citizens who express their faith through, say, Judaism, Islam, or Hinduism—which means that Christian prayers effectively exclude or alienate these citizens. A similar point holds true of all sectarian prayers at public events. These prayers are troubling because they cannot by definition include all members of the population—because they exclude members of the body politic. In that sense they appear to "send a message to nonadherents that they are outsiders, not full members of the political community, and an accompanying message to adherents that they are insiders, favored members of the political community,"[49] which, according to Justice Sandra Day O'Connor, always violates the Establishment Clause.

Further, it is not clear that nonsectarian prayers, which Graham has also used, are any more helpful or good for the political order. In *Lee v. Weisman*, 505 U.S. 577 (1992), the Supreme Court ruled that a high school could not provide a "nonsectarian" prayer for its graduation ceremony. Theoretically, a nonsectarian prayer should not violate the Establishment Clause, either because it is not really religious or because it is a ritual of civil religion. Justice Kennedy, however, addressed the issue of civil religion in his opinion for the court, writing:

> We are asked to recognize the existence of a practice of nonsectarian prayer, prayer within the embrace of what is known as the Judeo-Christian tradition, prayer which is more acceptable than one which, for example, makes explicit references to the God of Israel, or to Jesus Christ, or to a patron saint. There may be some support, as an empirical observation, to the statement of the Court of Appeals for the Sixth

Circuit, picked up by Judge Campbell's dissent in the Court of Appeals in this case, that there has emerged in this country a civic religion, one which is tolerated when sectarian exercises are not. [Citations omitted] If common ground can be defined which permits once conflicting faiths to express the shared conviction that there is an ethic and a morality which transcend human invention, the sense of community and purpose sought by all decent societies might be advanced. But though the First Amendment does not allow the government to stifle prayers which aspire to these ends, neither does it permit the government to undertake that task for itself.

Nonsectarian prayers are not an effective solution to the problems posed by sectarian prayers; both involve the government in a religious practice that inevitably excludes certain members of the body politic. To push the issue even further, we should ask whether there can really be a nondenominational or nonsectarian political prayer. What would be its content? The answer seems as elusive as the goal of advancing the common good through any type of political prayer.

In the final analysis, the political system is not about religious faith at all but about "constitutional faith"—the "wholehearted attachment to the Constitution as the center of one's (and ultimately the nation's) political life."[50] If it is religiously wrong for Graham to preach constitutional faith, it is politically wrong for him to preach faith in Jesus. As Niebuhr put it:

This constitutional disestablishment of all churches embodied the wisdom of Roger Williams and Thomas Jefferson—the one from his experience with the Massachusetts theocracy and the other from his experience with the less dangerous Anglican establishment in Virginia—which knew that a combination of religious sanctity and political power represents a heady mixture for status quo conservatism.[51]

Progressives, of course, should oppose this lethal combination for both religious and political reasons.

NOTES

1. Reinhold Niebuhr, "The King's Chapel and the King's Court," *Christianity and Crisis*, August 4, 1969, 211.
2. Betty Glad, *Jimmy Carter: In Search of the Great White House* (New York: W. W. Norton, 1980), 333.
3. Jimmy Carter, *Christmas in Plains: Memories* (New York: Simon & Schuster, 2001), 143.
4. Niebuhr, "King's Chapel," 212.
5. Graham to Nixon, November 28, 1960, National Archives and Records Administration, Laguna Niguel, California (NARALN). See also Graham to

Nixon, November 2, 1960 ("cast yourself before the Lord and trust in Him"), NARALN.

6. Quoted in Jon Meacham, "God, the Bushes, and Billy Graham," *Newsweek*, April 11, 2006, http://www.msnbc.msn.com/id/12271894/site/newsweek.

7. See Graham to Nixon, October 17, 1960; May 27, 1960; June 21, 1960; July 22, 1960, NARALN.

8. Nixon to Graham, January 15, 1961, NARALN.

9. See Graham to Nixon, June 4, 1956, and July 14, 1956, NARALN.

10. Graham to Nixon, June 4, 1956, NARALN.

11. Graham to Nixon, December 2, 1957 ("Contrary to popular opinion, when the chips are down I think the religious issue would be very strong and might conceivably work in your behalf"), NARALN; Graham to Nixon, May 27, 1960 (on the 15,000 delegates at the Southern Baptist Convention: "Nearly all seemed to be strong Nixon supporters—if Kennedy is the Democratic nominee! I think there is a distinct possibility that you can capture several Southern states if Kennedy is your opponent"), NARALN.

12. Graham to Nixon, June 21, 1960, NARALN.

13. Graham to Nixon, October 17, 1960, NARALN.

14. Graham to Nixon, November 2, 1960, NARALN.

15. "Dr. Graham Says Election Aids Church Amity," *New York Times*, January 17, 1961.

16. Richard Pierard, "Billy Graham and the U.S. Presidency," *Journal of Church and State* 22, no. 1 (winter 1980): 126.

17. *Lemon v. Kurtzman*, 403 U.S. 602 (1971).

18. Graham to Nixon, May 27, 1960, NARALN.

19. Quoted in Marshall Frady, *Billy Graham: A Parable of American Righteousness* (Boston: Little, Brown, 1979), 442; and Pierard, "Billy Graham and the U.S. Presidency," 119.

20. Peter Braestrup, "Protestant Unit Wary on Kennedy: Statement by Peale Group Sees Vatican 'Pressure' on Democratic Nominee," *New York Times*, September 8, 1960.

21. John Wicklein, "Niebuhr and Bennett Say Raising of Religious Issue Spurs Bigotry," *New York Times*, September 16, 1960, 1.

22. Graham to Nixon, June 12, 1961, NARALN.

23. "Dr. Graham to Aid Nixon Rally," *New York Times*, November 2, 1960, 19.

24. Frady, *Billy Graham*, 450.

25. "Bush Makes a Final Push in Florida," salon.com, November 5, 2000, http://archive.salon.com/politics/feature/2000/11/05/florida.print.html.

26. Pierard, "Billy Graham and the U.S. Presidency," 111. The embedded Graham quotation is from the *London Daily Herald*, February 26, 1954.

27. See Internal Revenue Service, *Tax Guide for Churches and Religious Organizations*, Pub. 1828, 5, http://www.irs.gov/pub/irs–pdf/p1828.pdf.

28. Johnny Rex Buckles, "Not Even a Peep? The Regulation of Political Campaign Activity by Charities through Federal Tax Law," *Cincinnati Law Review* 75 (2007): 1071.

29. *Branch Ministries v. Rossotti*, 211 F.3d 137 (D.C. Cir. 2000).

30. *Tax Guide for Churches and Religious Organizations*, 8.

31. "Billy Graham's Story LIFE Magazine did not use," NARALN.

32. John Fritze, "Political Gifts by Churches Break IRS Rules," *Baltimore Sun*, February 26, 2006, 1A.

33. Ann M. Murphy, "Campaign Signs and the Collection Plate—Never the Twain Shall Meet?" *Pittsburgh Tax Review* 1 (Fall 2003): 35.
34. See H.R. 235, 108th Cong. §2 (2003), http://www.govtrack.us/congress/bill .xpd?bill=h108-235.
35. Murphy, "Campaign Signs and the Collection Plate," 41.
36. Ibid., 78.
37. *The Writings of James Madison*, vol. 2, *1783–1787*, ed. Gaillard Hunt (New York: G. P. Putnam's Sons, 1901), 186.
38. For a description of different rationales for the political campaign activity prohibition and a proposal for rewriting the tax requirements, see Buckles, "Not Even a Peep?"
39. Robert N. Bellah, "Civil Religion in America," *Dædalus* 96 (winter 1967): 3–4.
40. Steven B. Epstein, "Rethinking the Constitutionality of Ceremonial Deism," *Columbia Law Review* 96 (1996): 2083.
41. Ibid., 2095–96.
42. Pierard, "Billy Graham and the U.S. Presidency," 114.
43. Bellah, "Civil Religion in America," 4.
44. The chronology and texts of these addresses can be found in the Billy Graham Center Archives, http://www.wheaton.edu/bgc/archives/inaugural101.html.
45. Epstein, "Rethinking the Constitutionality," 2094–96.
46. See Robert Bellah and Steven M. Tipton, eds., *The Robert Bellah Reader* (Durham, NC: Duke University Press, 2006), 221.
47. See these texts at http://www.wheaton.edu/bgc/archives/inaugural101.html.
48. See Epstein, "Rethinking the Constitutionality," 2107.
49. This sentence expresses the so-called endorsement test by which Justice O'Connor decided whether a government practice violated the Establishment Clause. See *Lynch v. Donnelly*, 465 U.S. 668, 688 (1984).
50. Sanford Levinson, *Constitutional Faith* (Princeton, NJ: Princeton University Press, 1988), 4.
51. Niebuhr, "King's Chapel," 211.

Contemporaries in Conflict?

9

Billy Graham in a Secular Society

The Greater London Crusade of 1954

MARK D. CHAPMAN

On May 22, 1954, an unseasonably cold day with sleet and driving rain, Geoffrey Fisher, archbishop of Canterbury, sat on the same platform as Billy Graham at the Empire Stadium, Wembley, the largest stadium in England and home of the FA Cup Final.[1] When the addresses were over, Fisher, a broad churchman and Freemason,[2] pronounced the final blessing on the crowd of over 110,000 people, "simply, clearly, movingly," according to Ruth Graham.[3] This official sanction given to the 1954 Greater London crusade by such an establishment figure might have come as something of a surprise, especially given the initial lukewarm response by many English church leaders and bodies, including the archbishop himself and the British Council of Churches, to Graham and his crusade.[4]

Many had been suspicious of what they perceived to be the brash and inappropriate techniques of American mass evangelism.[5] Memories of Americans were still colored, no doubt, by the large numbers of GIs who had been stationed in Britain during the war. Furthermore, during the preparations for the crusade, the Graham team had blundered in failing to excise a piece of antisocialist propaganda from one of its publicity calendars, which claimed that "when the war ended a sense of frustration and disillusionment gripped England and what Hitler's bombs could not do, Socialism with its accompanying evils quickly accomplished."[6] While possibly suitable for the American context, this sort of overt political message was hardly likely to endear Graham to the British audience—Britain had, after all, warmly embraced the moderate socialism of the postwar government of Clement Attlee. In the end, the word "socialism" was changed to "secularism."

Writing in the *Daily Herald*, the leading socialist newspaper, Hannen Swaffer consequently called on Graham to "apologize . . . or stay away!"[7] He also directed his attention to the bishop of Barking in the Diocese of Chelmsford, Hugh Gough, asking him "to disown all this ignorant nonsense before the Big Business evangelist whom he sponsors opens his crusade," and to "call Billy Graham to repentance before he has the effrontery to start converting us!"[8] Gough was one of the key English figures behind the crusade, having become acquainted with Graham at Syracuse.[9] He was also one of the leading conservative evangelical spokesmen on the episcopal bench and later became archbishop of the archconservative diocese of Sydney.

Graham and his team probably learned an important political lesson from this initial faux pas. Graham's apologies were masterful (although hard to believe, given his earlier track record),[10] and he continued to express political caution throughout the crusade. This was symbolized by the bipartisan presence of the two U.S. senators accompanying him: Stuart Symington (Democrat from Missouri) and Styles Bridges (Republican from New Hampshire).[11] Graham also avoided most of his earlier apocalyptic Cold War rhetoric, which he had continued to express as late as October 1953 in the preparatory propaganda flysheet, *London Crusade News*.[12] Instead, he focused far more on a vaguer and more general message of the evils of the world, coupled with the typical message of repentance and personal salvation. In a hagiographic biography prepared just before the crusade "to bring the story to life," Charles T. Cook expressed something of the general narrative of moral disillusionment that dominated Graham's preaching:

> The need for Billy Graham's message is beyond question. We live in an age of disillusionment, fear and frustration. There are many indications that very many among the churchless masses, despite their appearance of indifference to things divine, are ready to listen to anyone who will speak with authority and passionate sincerity about the ultimate realities. . . . That is why scores of thousands have flocked to Graham's meetings in America.[13]

The sins of the world were characterized less by overt evil and more by a widespread moral indifference on the part of the masses. Thus, people throughout the country—although they might not have been aware of the fact—were clamoring for the certainty that comes through repentance and conversion to Christ.

The extraordinary success of the London crusade won over virtually every senior church leader in all the major denominations, except the redoubtable socialist Donald Soper, president of the Methodist Conference, who claimed that "there is not a single reputable theologian who agrees with what is promulgated at Harringay."[14] Despite the initial reservations, words of criticism after the crusade are almost impossible to find. A good example of the change of opinion about Graham comes from the secular press. At the beginning of the campaign, Frank Martin had written in the *Sunday Graphic*, "This Billy Graham line just won't do! I went to hear him at Harringay—and felt as if it were 1890, not 1954." By the end of Graham's visit eleven weeks later, however, he had completely changed his mind: "Thank you, Billy. You have done us a power of good. Come again soon."[15] From within the churches, C. A. Martin, bishop of Liverpool, also expressed a change of mood:

> In the first place, some people went to Harringay very prejudiced against American evangelism. They found there nothing to which they could take exception. I have spoken with many people of different traditions of churchmanship, and have yet to hear from anyone who has actually been present one word of serious criticism. At one Anglican church in the London area the vicar announced that 150 newcomers to the church now worshipped there regularly as a result of this Crusade.[16]

Hugh Gough spoke of the crusade as "the outstanding spiritual movement in the lifetime of many of us. . . . London was stirred in a way which few could have believed possible. Indeed, in some measure, the whole country was affected."[17] He saw the crusade as bringing about a "real revival" in English religion.

While Gough obviously was not immune from the triumphalism of the time, there is more than an element of truth in his assessment. Crucially, Geoffrey Fisher had changed his opinion. He felt that Graham did not succumb to American razzmatazz but instead gave a "plain delivery of a plain message concerning some of the fundamental Christian truths about God's Gospel and man's need."[18] Like many other commentators, Fisher pointed to Graham's "great humility and sincerity." He succeeded in teaching the church to go back to basics by speaking, in Bryan Green's words, of "sin and righteousness and of judgment."[19] Indeed, "sincerity"[20] rather than "sensationalism"[21] became one of the key epithets used to describe Graham throughout the 1954 crusade. Commenting on his performance on BBC television, for instance, the *News Chronicle* noted, "The TV camera notoriously picks up the faintest shred of insincerity. It did no such thing with Mr. Graham."[22] Graham, it seemed, toned down his style throughout the crusade and even bought some less flamboyant ties.[23]

From a different perspective, Beverley Nichols felt that it was "petty and puerile" to criticize Graham, who used "all the apparatus of the atom era to spread the Gospel of the eternal era."[24] Similarly, John Betjeman, writing from a somewhat idiosyncratic Anglo-Catholic perspective, "to whom the revivalist approach is unattractive," noted in the *Spectator* that "all churches should be grateful for the work being done for them."[25]

This success, symbolized by the archbishop's final blessing, marked a major change of direction in the fortunes of English conservative evangelicalism (or what Major-General Donald J. Wilson-Haffenden, chairman and leading layman on the planning committee, called portentously, "the history of our nation and our church").[26] The London *Evening News* produced a Billy Graham souvenir edition after the final rally, which noted that the "church acknowledges its debt to him, as the presence of the Archbishop of Canterbury at Wembley this evening testifies."[27] What had for the most part been a relatively marginal movement in the mainline churches was for the first time suddenly in the ascendant.[28] The mood had changed, which allowed evangelicalism to move from the periphery to the center. "Feeling" proved more important than intellect. Prebendary Colin C. Kerr, a leading evangelical Anglican clergyman and vicar of St. Paul's, Portman Square, captured this change well:

> Billy Graham, under God, has created an *atmosphere* which, like the dew, has quietly fallen upon London, and indeed many other parts. There has been created something only just short of a widespread *awareness of God*! . . . Almost overnight people have found that they could talk about religion without embarrassment. But there is more in it than this. God has once more become vital in the consciousness of a great number of people. . . . Almost overnight a *movement* of God had started. It can rightly be said that there has been great publicity and organizing of the highest order; but this cannot, as I see it, account for the fact that something has started to move right through the country. Harringay has not started a machine destined for three months to give effective evangelism, it has released a power which has spread with incredible speed to many parts.[29]

Probably for the first time in the twentieth century, especially in the Church of England, a distinct form of enthusiastic, experiential, and revivalist conservative Christianity gained the official seal of approval. What had usually defined itself negatively against other competing versions mutated into a "normal type" of Christianity. As the BBC assistant head of religion, the Reverend E. H. Robertson, put it, "[Graham] has brought a breath of America's activism into our tired and slightly bored atmosphere. . . . He has permanently influenced the preaching of many thousands of our preachers."[30] For many, Graham's simple and sincere variety of Christianity was widely regarded as the most effective and appropriate form to overcome something of the spiritual malaise in postwar Britain. Consequently, it is not implausible to see the 1954 crusade as the most significant event in the reorientation of English Christianity away from the dominant public theology of the interwar era epitomized by William Temple[31] and toward an enthusiastic version of conservative evangelicalism (or what the *Manchester Guardian* called "a holy simplicity" with "lots of common sense").[32] F. Townley Wood, president of the Baptist World Alliance and minister of Bloomsbury Central Baptist Church, noted:

> Harringay has shown that the direct challenge to the will has proved effective where "intellectual" presentations of Bible teaching have left many unmoved. Finally, of course, appeals to "will" and "mind" must be harmonized; but in an age when we have been greatly concerned with the intellectual presentation of the Faith, the Harringay experience has recalled us to the need for direct and warm-hearted evangelism.[33]

One of the leading Methodists, Leslie Weatherhead of the City Temple, remarked that he could not "understand the hostile critics. . . . What does fundamentalist theology matter compared with gathering in the people we have all missed, and getting them to the point of decision? Theology comes much later."[34] The changes brought about by the crusade led in part to the gradual loss of theology from public discourse and its replacement, at least among a significant proportion of churchgoers, with a more subjective religion of the heart that offered solutions to the problems of the world. Christopher Chavasse, the evangelical bishop of Rochester, suggested that the success of the crusade showed that

> multitudes who are only on the fringe of the churches, and more especially young people . . . are realizing increasingly that in a world of wars and atom bombs God and his way are the only hope. Movements and campaigns like Mr. Graham's have helped to give an impetus to this increasing predisposition among people to try and find an answer in Christianity to life's problems and their own personal dilemmas.[35]

Similarly, the bishop of Norwich, Percy Herbert, wrote in the *Norwich Diocesan Leaflet* that the

> campaign happened at precisely the right moment. There is, and for some time has been, a hunger for religious guidance, for a firm basis on which life can be built in this uncertain world, and congregations have been found increasing wherever sincerity of word and worship are found. . . . It is indeed a challenge to every clergyman and congregation to get back to the fundamental truths of God and man, sin and righteousness, this life and the life to come.[36]

In an insecure world, solutions to personal feelings of insecurity seem more pressing than political solutions to the world's problems. Consequently, religion is primarily a form of escape, as Graham admitted in an interview given soon after the crusade:

> The human mind cannot cope with the problems that we are wrestling with today. And when our intellectual leaders begin to admit that they

don't know the answer, and that fact reaches the masses on the street, then they are going to turn somewhere. They will turn to all sorts of escapisms. Some will turn to alcohol. Others will turn to religion in the want of security and peace—something to hold onto.[37]

For this reason, Billy Graham was "probably the most important factor" in the resurgent vitality of the conservative evangelical tradition.[38] At the same time, his success marked an end to the dominant public theology of the interwar years.

THE 1954 CRUSADE

The 1954 crusade was marked by meticulous planning, careful public relations, and efforts to win over the churches by involving as many as possible from the outset.[39] One commentator noted that the "whole burden of the message is that people should return to their particular churches."[40] Bishop Wand of London similarly observed that the key to the success of the crusade was the mass participation in counseling and the direction of large numbers of inquirers to local churches.[41] The Evangelical Alliance was responsible for the planning, and organized as representative a group as possible with a strong Church of England presence, including many prominent laymen (but no women).

Techniques that had been honed in America were adapted for the English context. These included a number of prayer meetings, as well as a vast publicity campaign budgeted at £30,000 but that in the end cost £50,000.[42] Posters were put up in 1,500 locations, as well as on the sides of 750 buses and trolley buses and 500 sites on the Underground.[43] There were also a number of scheduled screenings of *Oil Town USA*, which told of the story of the conversion of an oil magnate.[44] To prepare the ground, the planning group published the *London Crusade News*, 180,000 copies of which were distributed free of charge. Offices were rented in central London, and huge numbers came forward for training as volunteer counselors in five London churches of different denominations. Classes of 600 were held at St. Paul's, Portman Square, and St. Mary Woolnoth, one of the City of London churches, proved too small for the numbers attending. This provision of counselors helped revive congregations. Maurice Wood, rural dean of Islington and vicar of St. Mary's, one of the leading centers of evangelicalism, observed that the provision of counselors, as well as the prayer groups, proved a great blessing in revitalizing parishes.[45]

Graham arrived in England on February 23, 1954. Perhaps because of the notoriety gained through the *Daily Herald*, as well as his youthful good looks, his arrival in London proved a magnet for those who had been praying for him. He was greeted at Waterloo Station by the largest crowd (about 4,000) since Rudolph Valentino visited England in 1926 (or possibly since Mary Pickford and Douglas Fairbanks visited in 1924).[46] He was accompanied by a number of fellow evangelists and was feted in much the same way as a minor royal or film star. He dined, for instance, with 800 clergy and ministers from across the denominations at the Café Royal. Soon after his arrival five members of parliament from different parties took him to the House of Commons, and over the course of the crusade, some 250 MPs were eventually introduced to him.

The crusade was based in an indoor arena in the unlikely venue of Harringay in North London, next to a greyhound racing track. After some trepidation on the part of the organizers, the opening night on March 1 saw all 11,400 seats occupied.[47] Accompanied by massed choirs of 2,000, who were partly responsible for popularizing a number of hymns and tunes including "Blessed Assurance" and "And Can It Be,"[48] Graham preached his usual message of repentance and certainty: "God loves you, whoever you are and wherever you are; whatever your past may have been, you cannot go out of this hall without the assurance of that pursuing love."[49] The climax of the first evening saw 150 people coming forward to make a commitment.

On the following day (March 2, 1954) the *Times* tried to explain the success. Again, what came over was Graham's "sincerity" rather than the power of his preaching. He was "a likeable man with whom it would be eminently easy to talk without too much English reserve." The *Manchester Guardian* claimed that he "lacks oratorical gift" but welcomed the "quiet beginning after so much beating of the big drum."[50] One leading evangelical, Canon Bryan Green of St. Martin's, Birmingham, even found Graham's success difficult to explain (except as the work of the Holy Spirit). He wrote in the *Birmingham Gazette* on March 25 that Graham was "absolutely sincere and genuinely humble. . . . Frankly, there did not seem to me to be any explanation on a purely human level of oratorical tricks or demagogic suggestion that would account for British people coming forward openly and so earnestly." What Hugh Gough had predicted in one of the publicity leaflets proved true: "I am convinced that many of the misgivings people seem to have concerning Dr. Graham would immediately be removed if they could see him and hear him as I did. His sincerity and humility are beyond question."[51] The Billy Graham religion was thus something personal and deeply moving, rather than something shocking or disturbing.[52]

Various other events were organized as part of the crusade. These included a testimony for 40,000 children and 10,000 adults by Roy Rogers (who had brought Trigger and his wife, Dale Evans) in the Harringay Stadium. Even on his day off (Sunday), Graham continued his punishing schedule, including an open-air rally on Streatham Common attended by the Anglican bishop of Southwark, Bertram Simpson, who gave the blessing.[53] Once again, he expressed a message appropriate to the Cold War, offering his usual rather simplistic solution: "There are still some people all over the world working for world peace, and this is the concern of you all. I am convinced that the only way for the world to have peace is through a great spiritual awakening in which we turn back to God, to Christ, to the Bible, and to the Church."[54] Twelve thousand attended the mass rally at Trafalgar Square in central London on April 3 (the largest gathering since the victory parades at the end of the war),[55] and over 40,000 gathered at Hyde Park on Good Friday.

Having gained such notoriety, Graham was received by a number of important churchmen and public figures, including the bishop of London and the archbishop of Canterbury. He even had a personal audience with Prime Minister Winston Churchill.[56] Graham also appeared on television on *In Town Tonight*, interviewed by Malcolm Muggeridge, and was halftime entertainment during the Chelsea versus Newcastle soccer match at Stamford Bridge on April 25.[57]

Throughout the crusade, Harringay continued to be filled to capacity. In the four weeks of the rallies 383,400 people attended, and 8,813 went forward to the inquiring room at the rallies, with 38,447 having gone forward for counseling. In addition, a large number (reportedly 1,770) made their commitment after hearing the relays of services that were broadcast to various venues across the country.[58] Those coming forward to the inquiring room were asked to make a short declaration—"I take Christ as my personal saviour"—after a short prayer had been said. This was followed up by taking name, address, age, and nature of decision (first-time decision, assurance of salvation, reaffirmation of faith, dedication of life to the service of God), as well as church connection or denominational preference.[59] Of those going forward, 75 percent were making a first-time decision, 40 percent indicated some degree of membership of a church (usually nominal), and 60 percent were under 18 (the majority were between 15 and 18).[60]

The final gatherings were held in bad weather on May 22 at Wembley Stadium, which was filled to more than capacity, with 22,000 sitting on the grass, followed by a second rally at the White City Stadium, which seated about 65,000. In all, some 185,000 people attended, with 2,184 going forward.[61] Part of the service was broadcast on the BBC Light Programme from 6:30 to 7:00 p.m. The Wembley service was attended by a large number of dignitaries, including Viscount Lambton and Lord Hore-Belisha, as well as Francis House of the BBC. Graham's challenge was to the churches: "Fill your churches and if they are not all they should be, go and make them so. Ask God to send a spiritual awakening throughout the churches of England." The archbishop of Canterbury concurred: "You have done your task superbly," he said to Graham. "It is now up to us; and if we fail it is our fault."[62]

The impact of the Greater London crusade is hard to measure, but what seems to be of central importance was the effect that the experience had on the internal lives of prominent churches. The clearest example is All Souls', Langham Place, where John Stott, then the rising star of English evangelicalism, was rector and where Graham had attended the morning service on his free Sundays in England.[63] Although Stott had been a successful evangelist before the crusade, particularly at Cambridge,[64] he was able to capitalize on the experience of Harringay. Stott himself attended most nights and organized buses to the arena. Afterward, large numbers of inquirers were referred to All Souls': "If I remember rightly," he said in an interview with Robert Ferm, "2000 of them had given the name of All Souls and 300 were assigned to us."[65] "For me," he added, "one of the great effects of the crusade was not just in winning people to Christ, but in giving Christians . . . church members . . . a taste through counseling of the joys of witness and service." The following year ninety people were trained and commissioned as pastoral assistants at the church.

More generally, according to the *British Weekly*, 64.03 percent of new converts were still attending church a year later. Only two years after the crusade, twenty-three of the thirty-three men ordained in London were evangelicals,[66] and a few years later, Maurice Wood, who had become principal of the evangelical Anglican Oak Hill Theological College, noted that most of his ordinands had been Billy Graham counselors or had been convert-inquirers from the 1954 crusade.[67] A form of evangelicalism that eventually became one of the dominant Christian subcultures in the mainline English churches was given a huge boost through the 1954 crusade.[68]

CONCLUSION

Billy Graham's 1954 crusade succeeded in pushing a distinct form of simple, enthusiastic, and nonintellectual religion into the center of English religious life. For the first time in a long period, religion had become an acceptable topic of conversation. What was revealed, according to the *Sunday Times*, was

> a longing in the heart of man, a sense of hunger for something he hardly knows what, a reaching out for that which can satisfy those hitherto unspoken yearnings deep within him. Moreover, Dr. Graham claims that thousands of such people have now found their hunger satisfied by their personal receiving of the presence of Christ into their hearts. . . . Will the churches be humble enough to learn the lessons of this crusade and be willing to apply them to themselves?[69]

The growth in the evangelical churches functioned in part as a warning sign to mainstream churches to get their own houses in order. Indeed, many from all traditions felt compelled not merely to tolerate but even cautiously to embrace Graham's particular form of evangelism and its concomitant straight-forward religion of sincerity, assurance, and enthusiasm. Hugh Gough expressed something of this feeling in the *Sunday Chronicle* of June 13, 1954:

> What an unspeakable tragedy if the Church should fail in this hour of opportunity! She has been shown that underneath the outward veneer of indifference and materialism people are hungry for that peace of heart and mind which only God can give. She has been shown that authoritative declaration of the simple facts of the Gospel of Christ meets with immediate response. She has been shown that men want to know what the Bible teaches. Billy Graham has pointed the way to revival. His farewell message to the churches now is: "Over to you." This may be the time of the Church's greatest opportunity in all her long history. It *can* be the church's "finest hour," for she has a message that can save the world. Will she proclaim it with the conviction of Billy Graham? What destiny depends on the answer![70]

The archbishop of Canterbury issued his own not dissimilar challenge to "begin again at the beginning in our Evangelism and speak by the power of the Holy Spirit of sin and righteousness and judgement."[71] Bryan Green was also aware of the importance and power of Graham's evangelistic techniques. The simplicity of the message was crucial:

> There is little full explanation of the Gospel. This, I believe, is a lesson for many of us, and I myself have found it extremely helpful. . . . Are we perhaps not proclaiming and explaining the Gospel of the redeeming love of Christ too soon? Should we not perhaps concentrate on what I might call the John the Baptist message of Billy Graham, and then explain the Gospel to those who turn to repentance?[72]

Although the evangelical journalist Edward O. England recorded many typical narratives of conversion of dreadful sinners and communists, he also noted the longer term consequences of the crusade that resulted in pan-evangelical cooperation and a renewed sense of purpose:

> Everywhere I was told and saw evidence of a new spirit of cooperation between churches of different denominations. Many of these had banded themselves into associations for the purpose of promoting evangelism in their locality, including the organizing of Saturday night youth rallies, after-church squashes and open-air services. . . . It is doubtful if any Gospel Crusades have made a more *lasting* impact than those held in Britain in 1954 and 1955.[73]

The Greater London crusade consolidated Graham's position as an unrivaled global evangelist. But it also made far more acceptable, especially in the Church of England, a form of religion that was quite different from the prevalent secular liberal Anglicanism of the interwar years. Rather than functioning as part of a moral consensus in a benign and supportive state, religion provided a certain and secure support for the individual facing a hostile world.[74] The success of Billy Graham's English mission, perhaps ironically, helped push Christianity further from the center of British public life by reinforcing a particular subculture. Christianity was understood primarily in terms of personal liberation from a collapsing public sphere. In Graham's own words, it was a form of "escapism." Pollock notes that "frequently converts would say, 'I felt as if I was the only person in the arena, and that every word was meant for me.'"[75]

Consequently, the crusade marked a critical stage in the decline of intellectual English public Christianity and its replacement with a view of religion as an experiential answer to the perceived breakdown of the moral sphere. The intellectually simplistic religion of personal "authenticity,"[76] which was (misleadingly) dubbed by Michael Ramsey, at the time bishop of Durham, as "fundamentalism," and which made such an impact on English church life after the crusade, left little space for political reflection, and to many was theologically suspect. As Ramsey put it, "The act of decision and conversion may involve the stifling of the mind instead of its liberation into the service of God and man."[77] This view of religion as escape from both the intellect and the world did not augur well for the survival of Christianity as a potent force in English public discourse.[78] In the end, the decline of the church's influence over society might have little direct correlation with the numbers attending church.[79]

NOTES

1. This unlikely event does not even merit a passing mention in Fisher's biography: Edward Carpenter, *Archbishop Fisher—His Life and Times* (Norwich: Canterbury Press, 1991).
2. Graham described the archbishop as a "charming and delightful man, wholly without pretense" (Billy Graham, *Just as I Am* [San Francisco: HarperSanFrancisco, 1997], 227).
3. John Pollock, *Billy Graham: The Authorized Biography* (New York: McGraw-Hill, 1966), 130.
4. The most comprehensive accounts of the Greater London crusade can be found in Frank Colquhoun, *Harringay Story: The Official Record of the Billy Graham Greater London Crusade 1954* (London: Hodder & Stoughton, 1955); Charles T. Cook, *London Hears Billy Graham: The Greater London Crusade* (London: Marshall, Morgan & Scott, 1954); Pollock, *Billy Graham*, 120–35; William Martin, *A Prophet with Honor: The Billy Graham Story* (New York: William Morrow, 1991), chap. 11; Graham, *Just as I Am*, chap. 13; and John Pollock, *Crusades: 20 Years with Billy Graham* (Minneapolis: World Wide Publications, 1966), 121–43. I am grateful to Martyn Percy, Martin Spence, and Wendy Dackson for their helpful comments on an earlier draft.

5. Martin, *Prophet with Honor*, 173.

6. Ibid., 175–76; Colquhoun, *Harringay Story*, 73.

7. Martin, *Prophet with Honor*, 176.

8. Hannen Swaffer, "Apologize, Billy—or Stay Away!" *Daily Herald*, February 20, 1954, 3. This controversy found its way into the American press. See "Bishop Defends Graham," *New York Times*, February 22, 1954, 3. A full report of the London crusade was published on March 7. See Peter O. Whitney, "Evangelist Billy Graham London's Top Attraction," *New York Times*, March 7, 1954, 66.

9. Colquhoun, *Harringay Story*, 44. See Graham, *Just as I Am*, 208–9.

10. Martin, *Prophet with Honor*, 177.

11. Graham, *Just as I Am*, 212.

12. See *London Crusade News* 1 (October 1953): "I am absolutely convinced that unless Britain has a spiritual revival, the entire Western world is in peril. Only a religious revival can give the English people the moral integrity and stability to stand with us in days to come. . . . The destinies of America and Britain are inseparably linked. We have been, and must continue to be allies in war and in peace. . . . Many British leaders are convinced that if we see a religious awakening in London, it could well change the course of world history."

13. Charles T. Cook, *The Billy Graham Story* (London: Marshall, Morgan & Scott, 1954), 12.

14. Martin, *Prophet with Honor*, 181. George MacCleod also criticized Graham for what he considered his lack of a political message and a refusal to express an opinion about Senator McCarthy (Cook, *London Hears Billy Graham*, 123).

15. Quoted in Colquhoun, *Harringay Story*, 175.

16. Quoted in Cook, *London Hears Billy Graham*, 90.

17. Hugh Gough, preface to Cook, *London Hears Billy Graham*, v.

18. Geoffrey Fisher, "The Archbishop's Letter," *Canterbury Diocesan Notes* 300 (June 1954), 1 (reprinted in Cook, *London Hears Billy Graham*, vii–ix; and Colquhoun, *Harringay Story*, 188–90).

19. Green, quoted in Cook, *London Hears Billy Graham*, 91.

20. In the *Sunday Chronicle*, Beverley Nichols wrote that Graham was "blazingly sincere. He sweats sincerity" (quoted in Colquhoun, *Harringay Story*, 176–77). Bishop Wand of London described Graham as "charming, sincere, and deeply religious" (89). Canon A. St. John Thorpe, vicar of Watford, spoke of the "unobtrusiveness of the speaker and his obvious sincerity" (92). The *Daily Telegraph* of May 19 commented that he had "charm, sincerity and simplicity, bound together by a deep Christian charity" (180). Even the liberal *Manchester Guardian* remarked, "He seems to be a man of great sincerity, very impressed by the importance of his work, but not greatly concerned with the heights of rational argument or spiritual adventure" (80–81).

21. Colquhoun, *Harringay Story*, 21.

22. Ibid., 158.

23. Pollock, *Billy Graham*, 127.

24. Quoted in Colquhoun, *Harringay Story*, 176–77. The H-bomb happened to have been tested in the Pacific on the very same day as the opening of the crusade.

25. Quoted in ibid., 177–78.

26. D. J. Wilson-Haffenden, preface to Colquhoun, *Harringay Story*, vii.

27. Colquhoun, *Harringay Story*, 182.

28. On evangelicalism in England (and the rest of Britain) see Daniel Bebbington, *Evangelicalism in Modern Britain: A History from the 1730s to the 1980s* (London: Unwin Hyman, 1989).

29. Quoted in Cook, *London Hears Billy Graham*, 93.
30. Robertson, in *British Weekly*, quoted in Cook, *London Hears Billy Graham*, 126.
31. It is not clear to me that Callum Brown (in *The Death of Christian Britain: Understanding Secularization 1800–2000* [London: Routledge, 2001]) is accurate in his view that British public discourse was dominated by an evangelical narrative before the 1950s. At least in England religious discourse might be better understood as characterized by an optimistic liberal Anglicanism that tended to give a far more positive value to the world. The rise of an evangelical narrative in the mainstream churches was boosted by the 1954 crusade. This may well have contributed to the loss of the public influence of Christianity in the 1960s. See also Matthew Grimley, *Citizenship, Community, and the Church of England: Liberal Anglican Theories of the State between the Wars* (Oxford: Clarendon Press, 2004).
32. "What Mr. Graham Has Proved," *Manchester Guardian*, May 24, 1954, 6.
33. Quoted in Cook, *London Hears Billy Graham*, 98.
34. Quoted in Colquhoun, *Harringay Story*, 191.
35. Quoted in ibid., 194–95.
36. Quoted in ibid., 195–96.
37. "New Crusade in Europe," *US News and World Report*, August 27, 1954, 87.
38. Bebbington, *Evangelicalism in Modern Britain*, 258.
39. Graham, *Just as I Am*, 209.
40. John Betjemen in *The Spectator*, quoted in Colquhoun, *Harringay Story*, 177–78.
41. Cook, *London Hears Billy Graham*, 90.
42. The organizers overspent by about £48,000, with the Billy Graham Evangelistic Association clearing most of the deficit (£40,729).
43. Cook, *London Hears Billy Graham*, chap. 2.
44. The film was shown in fifteen venues; see *London Crusade News* 3 (December 1953).
45. Cook, *London Hears Billy Graham*, 118.
46. Graham, *Just as I Am*, 217.
47. On this first day of the crusade, see Colquhoun, *Harringay Story*, 96–105.
48. Music proved important throughout the crusade, with a number of reports of the highly unusual activity of spontaneous singing on Underground trains and on buses. The *Crusade Song Book* (which had a picture of a horse guardsman on the cover and contained one hundred gospel songs) was put together by Cliff Barrows, who discarded his trombone, which was regarded as too brash for the English audience, during the crusade, and Frank Colquhoun (*London Crusade News* 5 [February 1954]).
49. Cook, *London Hears Billy Graham*, 41.
50. Quoted in Colquhoun, *Harringay Story*, 91.
51. *London Crusade News* 2 (November 1953).
52. Pathé news recorded a number of Graham addresses that illustrate his modest style. These are available at http://www.britishpathe.com.
53. See Cook, *London Hears Billy Graham*, chap. 9.
54. Quoted in Colquhoun, *Harringay Story*, 139.
55. See *London Crusade News* 7 (April 1954). See also "New Crusade in Europe," 84. In this interview for an American audience Graham was prepared to reflect far more on the Cold War than in England.
56. Graham, *Just as I Am*, 235–37.
57. "Mr. Graham Invites Football Crowd," *Manchester Guardian*, April 26, 1954, 7.

58. See Cook, *London Hears Billy Graham*, chap. 7; and Colquhoun, *Harringay Story*, 127–38.

59. Colquhoun, *Harringay Story*, 119.

60. Cook, *London Hears Billy Graham*, 109. On the work of the counselors, see Colquhoun, *Harringay Story*, 117–26.

61. *London Crusade News* 8 (July 1954).

62. Both quotes in Cook, *London Hears Billy Graham*, 63.

63. Graham, *Just as I Am*, 220.

64. Adrian Hastings regarded Stott as of at least equal importance to Graham in the revitalization of conservative evangelicalism (see *A History of English Christianity: 1920–2000* [London: SCM Press, 2001], 455).

65. Timothy Dudley-Smith, *John Stott: The Making of a Leader* (Leicester: Inter-Varsity Press, 1999), 296. See also Curtis Mitchell, *Those Who Came Forward: An Account of Those Whose Lives Were Changed by the Ministry of Billy Graham* (Kingswood, Surrey: World's Work, 1966), 67–74.

66. Martin, *Prophet with Honor*, 185.

67. Graham, *Just as I Am*, 237. See also J. C. Pollock, "England Four Years after Graham," *Christianity Today*, April 28, 1958, 10–12.

68. This marked a major development of what Paul Heelas and Linda Woodhead call "congregations of experiential difference" (*The Spiritual Revolution: Why Religion Is Giving Way to Spirituality* [Oxford: Blackwell, 2005], 18–19).

69. Quoted in Colquhoun, *Harringay Story*, 185.

70. Quoted in ibid., 196–97.

71. "Archbishop's Letter," *Canterbury Diocesan Notes* 300 (June 1954), 1.

72. Quoted in Cook, *London Hears Billy Graham*, 91.

73. Edward O. England, *Afterwards: A Journalist Sets Out to Discover What Happened to Some of Those Who Made a Decision for Christ during the Billy Graham Crusades in Britain in 1954 and 1955* (London: Victory Press, 1957), 149, 153. England also wrote a novel telling of the conversion of a journalist at Harringay, narrating the typical story of genuine religion superseding the stale and moribund: "'London needs God,' someone said behind him. 'The people have had enough of religion, dead, cold and formal, but now Christ is being presented to them. Eyes are being turned from stained glass windows to the Resurrected Christ.' The journalist was puzzled" (Edward O. England, *Hallowed Harringay* [London: Victory Press, 1955], 18; see also Curtis Mitchell, *Those Who Came Forward*; and Deborah Hart Strober and Gerald S. Strober, *Billy Graham: An Oral and Narrative Biography* [San Francisco: Jossey-Bass, 2006]).

74. See Joe E. Barnhart, *The Billy Graham Religion* (London: Mowbray, 1972), 82.

75. Pollock, *Billy Graham*, 125.

76. This understanding of the nature of modern evangelicalism owes something to the idea of a "subjective turn" noted by Charles Taylor, *The Ethics of Authenticity* (Cambridge, MA: Harvard University Press, 1991), 26. Indeed, the personalization and privatization of religion may even have contributed to the "spiritual revolution" discussed in Heelas and Woodhead, *Spiritual Revolution*, 2. I am indebted for these insights to Alana Harris and Martin Spence. See their article: "'Disturbing the Complacency of Religion?' The Evangelical Crusades of Dr. Billy Graham and Father Patrick Peyton in England, 1951–54," *Twentieth Century British History*, forthcoming.

77. Michael Ramsey, "The Menace of Fundamentalism," quoted in Paul A. Welsby, *A History of the Church of England: 1945–1980* (Oxford: Oxford University Press, 1984), 59–60.

78. This is not to imply that evangelicals lacked social commitment or that there was no little communal dimension to "individual" religion. What is central, however, is that public theology was no longer the predominant discourse. The social aspects of Billy Graham's message have been underexplored. See Ronald J. Sider, "Evangelism, Salvation, and Social Justice: Definitions and Interrelationships," *International Review of Mission* 64 (2006): 251–67; and Richard V. Pierard, "From Evangelical Exclusivism to Ecumenical Openness: Billy Graham and Sociopolitical Issues," *Journal of Ecumenical Studies* 20 (1983): 425–66.

79. This would mean that Steve Bruce's popular accounts of secularization (in, for instance, *God Is Dead: Secularization in the West* [Oxford: Blackwell, 2002]) need a degree of careful nuancing. See also Heelas and Woodhead, *Spiritual Revolution*, 9.

10

Niebuhr and Graham

Modernity, Complexity, White Supremacism,
Justice, Ambiguity

The image of Billy Graham that prevails in theology is the one that Reinhold Niebuhr painted of him: a throwback to pietistic fundamentalism who over-simplified "every issue of life." In 1956, while Graham's fame soared to heights that Niebuhr found incredible, not to mention embarrassing for American Christianity, Niebuhr panned that apparently there was still an ample market in American religion for simplistic preaching that reduced complex problems to pious slogans.[1]

Theologically, Niebuhr argued, Graham simply recycled the catchphrases of an outmoded Protestant individualism and literalism. His spectacular success in attracting an audience brought to mind the nearly forgotten reasons why liberal theology had been necessary. Niebuhr observed that liberalism was a needed improvement on the old evangelical religion, because it engaged modern criticism and had a sociological consciousness. Of course, the liberal Social Gospel was disastrously idealistic; Niebuhr had not spent twenty-five years attacking it for nothing.

But the masses had not flocked to Niebuhrian realism, and now that the old pietistic literalism was packing football stadiums, he commented ruefully, "Many of us, in our strictures against the Social Gospel, have forgotten the religious irrelevancies from which it saved us." Amazingly, the old nonsense about hellfire, biblical inerrancy, and the second coming was back with a vengeance.[2]

Niebuhr was appalled that American Protestantism had come to this. As an apologist for Christianity to its cultured despisers, he was also embarrassed.

Graham pronounced on theological and moral issues as though the past generation of theology did not exist. He simply ignored the tradition of social ethical analysis in which Niebuhr specialized, and Niebuhr reacted sarcastically: "He thinks the problem of the atom bomb could be solved by converting the people to Christ."[3] How could modern people take that seriously? For Graham, Niebuhr objected, every problem and story was a setup for an altar call. "Come to Jesus" was the answer to everything.

Niebuhr acknowledged that Graham had considerable virtues. He was obviously personable; by all evidence he was sincere in his faith and evangelistic calling; he mentioned social issues in his sermons; and he was not bad on the race issue. The latter point raised a possibility that maybe something good could be wrung from Graham's fame. Niebuhr remarked, "Though a Southerner, he has been rigorous on the race issue." Elsewhere he elaborated, "Though a Southerner, he is 'enlightened' on the race issue. He does not condone racial prejudice."[4]

In this context, "rigorous" meant merely that Graham was personally opposed to racial bigotry. Niebuhr observed that Graham did not preach against racism and that he treated the problem of racial justice with the same superficiality with which he handled other complex theological and ethical issues. Graham did not tell his audiences that racial prejudice was incompatible with the gospel or an evil standing in need of repentance and redemption. He did not preach that white Americans needed to give "the Negro neighbor his full due as a man and brother." On racism, as on the atom bomb, Graham was oblivious to the "serious perplexities of guilt and responsibility, and of guilt associated with responsibility, which Christians must face."[5]

Niebuhr specialized in the serious perplexities, fashioning a modern, Christian, ethical-realist dialectic that drew on Paul, Augustine, Luther, Calvin, Machiavelli, Hobbes, Marx, Weber, William James, and Ernst Troeltsch. To Graham, the devil was a literal agent of a literal hell; to Niebuhr these notions were symbols conveying true mythic import. Graham dichotomized between good and evil, while Niebuhr contended that evil was always constitutive in the good. To Niebuhr no human act, no matter how loving or seemingly innocent, was devoid of egotism. Purity of any kind was an illusion. Good and evil were always part of each other, not only as forces locked in dialectical tension but as interpenetrating realities. In the political sphere, Niebuhr taught, every gain toward a good end created new opportunities for evil. Every movement for democracy, equality, freedom, or community engendered new opportunities to create tyranny, squalor, or anarchy. Democratic gains increased the possibilities for greater numbers of people to do evil things.

At the same time, Niebuhr roared for democracy and social justice reforms, because democracy was indispensable as a brake on human greed and the will-to-power of elites, and justice was the ultimate end of Christian love in the social sphere. In Niebuhr's rendering, the love ethic of Jesus was an impossible ideal. It was relevant as a reminder that an ideal existed, even though sin made the ideal unattainable. The cross was the ultimate symbol of this fundamental Christian truth. Religiously, the cross was the means by which God established God's mercy and judgment on human sin; ethically, it was the ultimate symbol of the importance and unattainability of the law of love.

Niebuhr's dialectic of divine justice and mercy combined elements of the Anselmic idea of atonement with an overriding Abelardian doctrine of the spiritual effect of Christ's sacrifice. The heart of Christianity was the promise of salvation from humanity's enslaving egotism through divine grace. This was not a promise of deliverance or regeneration, Niebuhr cautioned. The redemptive work of God's gift of grace was to enable egotists to surrender their prideful attempts to master their existence. God's redeeming love in the cross of Christ reconciled human beings to their finitude, weakness, abasement, and dependency.[6]

Niebuhr wanted Graham to draw from deeper wells of Christian orthodoxy than modern fundamentalism. Even if Graham had to have an inerrant Bible, he could at least allow Augustine, Luther, Calvin, and perhaps modern neo-orthodoxy to chasten his superficial revivalism and perfectionism. The South had been rife with revivals, which did not stop the slavemasters from treating black Americans as chattel. How could Graham claim that the answer to every social evil was to accept Jesus as your Savior? For Niebuhr it was galling to have fought against liberal perfectionism for decades, only to witness the resurrection of an older, backward, reactionary version.

Some of Niebuhr's friends counseled him to lighten up on Graham; Union Seminary president Henry Van Dusen was one of them. In June 1957 Graham conducted a crusade at Madison Square Garden in New York, under the cosponsorship of the New York City Protestant Council of Churches, and Van Dusen was a key supporter, writing in the *Christian Century* that Graham offered "the pure milk of the Gospel in more readily digestible form" than Niebuhr's dialectics. Most people needed the pure milk before they could handle Niebuhr, Van Dusen admonished; moreover, many of Niebuhr's readers had entered the orbit of theology and the church through the evangelism of Billy Sunday, the Billy Graham of the previous generation. Van Dusen was one of them. Niebuhr summarized the appeal of Van Dusen and others to him: "Billy will bring people into the Christian church, and then the rest of us will have the opportunity to reveal all the duties and possibilities that a Christian commitment implies."[7]

He didn't buy it. For Niebuhr it was obviously disastrous that millions of people regarded Billy Graham as the exemplar of Christianity. Something terribly worrisome was happening in American Christianity if Graham was its leading voice.

Graham tried to meet with Niebuhr personally during the run up to the New York crusade, but Niebuhr refused. Graham's friend George Champion, vice president of the Chase Manhattan Bank and chair of the Protestant Council of New York's evangelism department, made a power move, appealing to the chair of Union's board, also a leading banker, who assured him that he would get Niebuhr to comply. Niebuhr still refused. He knew that Graham was good at defusing criticism with personal charm and took no interest in being charmed.

When the crusade took place, Niebuhr blasted it mercilessly, charging that Graham employed "all the high pressure techniques of modern salesmanship," selling Jesus in pretty much the same way that Madison Avenue sold soap and televisions. Watching the spectacle on television, Niebuhr was embarrassed for local pastors; in his telling they were reduced to carnival barkers to swell Graham's crowds.[8]

For Niebuhr, there were four main problems with the ascension of Graham-style evangelicalism in American life. First, pietistic revivalism was not an improvement on the faith of the Reformation but a degeneration of it that led to sectarian enthusiasms, rank subjectivism, dumbed-down theologies, and a variety of perfectionisms. Niebuhr's favorite epithet was "stupid," followed closely by "naive." He found a great deal of both in the pietistic strain of American Protestantism that fueled the fundamentalist and holiness movements, the Social Gospel movement, and then a rebirth of evangelical revivalism.

Second, modern liberalism, though wrong about certain things, had been right to take the Enlightenment seriously. Christian theology had no credibility if it contradicted modern science or denied the legitimacy of higher critical approaches to the Bible. To Niebuhr it was simply incredible that Graham, a college graduate living in the twentieth century, claimed to stand on the authority of an infallible, verbally inspired Scripture. Fundamentalism and conservative evangelicalism ignored critical problems on every page of the Bible, exposing Christianity to ridicule.

Graham told his audiences that God did not inspire falsehoods. Thus, there were no real contradictions in the Bible, only apparent ones, and every factual statement in the Bible was factually true. It was absurd to believe modern Bible scholars instead of God's word.

Graham had flirted with that absurdity just before his famous 1949 revival in Los Angeles. In a story he retold for the rest of his life, he had read enough of Niebuhr and Karl Barth to doubt the evangelical orthodoxy of his youth: "The new meanings they put into some of the old theological terms confused me terribly. I never doubted the Gospel itself, or the deity of Christ on which it depended, but other major issues were called into question." If Niebuhr and Barth believed that the Bible contained contradictions and factual errors, was he really so certain that the Bible was inerrant? If they believed that an errant Bible could still be the word of God, could he preach it that way?[9]

A close friend of Graham's, Chuck Templeton, had recently taken the latter path. For weeks Graham agonized over the trustworthiness of the Bible. Preaching an errant Bible was not an option for him, he realized. If he did not believe in the Bible's absolute trustworthiness, he was still young enough—at thirty—to opt for dairy farming.

Graham's crisis of faith climaxed while he attended a conference at Forest Home, California, a retreat center east of Los Angeles. Taking an evening walk in the woods, he laid his Bible on a tree stump, tearfully confessed to God that the Bible was filled with problems that he did not understand, and vowed in prayer to accept, by faith, the entire Bible as God's very word. After that, in his telling, the matter was settled: "In my heart and mind, I knew a spiritual battle in my soul had been fought and won."[10]

Niebuhr thought he had witnessed the irrevocable downfall of fundamentalism in the 1920s. After Clarence Darrow had humiliated William Jennings Bryan at the evolution trial in Dayton, Tennessee, it seemed obvious that fundamentalist inerrancy doctrine and premillennial eschatology were on the downward path, to be claimed only by reactionary sects. Fundamentalists built a vast network of Bible institutes, radio programs, new denominations, and parachurch ministries in the 1930s and 1940s, but all of it was off the map, largely out of view to Niebuhr and his colleagues. Nothing in the preaching or infrastructure of a defeated fundamentalism smacked of anything to be taken seriously. Thus, for Niebuhr, Graham's stadium spectacles were hard to take, even if Graham and the new evangelicals avoided fractious debates over evolution.

Graham seemed to have come from nowhere, making a national sensation at the 1949 Los Angeles revival. He had caught the attention of newspaper tycoon William Randolph Hearst, who decided to make him famous, probably because of Graham's fervent anticommunism. Afterward Graham routinely drew enormous crowds, curried favor with presidents, dispensed political advice, and explained to millions the meaning of Christianity.

Niebuhr's annoyance and embarrassment showed through whenever he wrote about Graham. Always he conveyed snobbish disdain, even when enjoining Graham to preach against racism. Secularism was a powerful opponent, Roman Catholicism had to be taken seriously as a rival, and Niebuhr fought hard for a realistic mainline Protestantism. But to his mind, fundamentalism should have passed away.

Though Niebuhr rejected liberal idealism and rationalism, he took for granted the liberal principle that truth questions cannot be settled by the word of an outside authority. In *An Interpretation of Christian Ethics* he declared that the old orthodoxies were no longer believable because they refused to acknowledge that Christian myths were myths. Instead of embarrassing Christianity by retaining "the dogmatisms of another day," conservatives needed to let the dogmas of verbal inspiration and infallibility, and the legalism of dogmatic morality, fall prey to "the beneficent dissolutions of the processes of nature and history."[11]

The third problem, closely related to the second, was that Graham-style evangelicalism was intolerant and theologically arrogant. It was one thing to say that the gospel is a source of grace and truth to all people, Niebuhr argued; it was something else to proclaim that one had to be a certain kind of Christian to avert eternal damnation in hell. Niebuhr pleaded for a Christianity with a more sensitive ethical spirit: "We must also have a decent modesty and humility about the righteousness of those whose common decencies contribute to our security, whether or not they have solved the ultimate mystery through faith or have made an ultimate commitment to Christ." The mystery of divine salvation transcended every theology, especially those that reduced God to provincial categories. Niebuhr allowed that Graham had more modesty than the average evangelist, but the practice of harping on "saved" versus "nonsaved" persons was morally repugnant, no matter how politely it was expressed. Niebuhr asked: What of the person who declined the altar call but outdid white Christians in accepting racial equality? What sort of Christianity ignored or dismissed the moral difference? Instead of dwelling on the "unregenerate" status of unbelievers, American Christians needed to ask themselves whether they were good coworkers with the "decent secularists" in their midst.[12]

"Whatever the church may do to spread the gospel," Niebuhr added, "it must resist the temptation of simplifying it in either literalistic or individualistic terms, thus playing truant to positions hard-won in the course of Christian history." Graham had caught the public eye, but at serious cost to American Protestantism's moral and intellectual image. Surging crowds of converts were not worth the loss of the church's soul: "We cannot afford to retrogress in regard to the truth for the sake of a seeming advance."[13]

Niebuhr urged that it was still possible, in 1956, to combine the good parts of liberalism with the biblical message of redemption recovered by the Reformation. Unlike modern Pietism, the Reformers did not dwell on saved versus unsaved; they stressed that all people needed divine forgiveness equally. Neither did they give simplistic answers to complex problems. They recognized the limits of human knowledge and virtue, spurning easy answers and quack cures. They understood that "the ultimate dilemmas are universal" and the word of Christ applied to all without exception. Claiming Luther and Calvin for his side, Niebuhr let Graham have the Awakening revivalists.[14]

But Graham did not burn for racial justice as the abolitionist revivalists had, which was the fourth problem (though Niebuhr did not mention the abolitionists). Graham's simplistic mentality was a stumbling block on other issues, Niebuhr judged, but the race issue was "fairly simple" on a moral level. It came down to the biblical principle that one cannot love God and hate one's brother. The moral root of the matter was as personal and individual as a typical Graham sermon. It should have suited revival preaching perfectly (as it did for abolitionists Charles Finney and Theodore Weld). So why did Graham's call to repentance not feature a condemnation of race prejudice?[15]

Niebuhr surmised that the question exposed a core weakness of conservative evangelicalism, which used a simplistic reading of select issues to pose a "crisis" that led to repentance and conversion. If Niebuhr had mentioned the abolitionists, he would have had to explain why their conversion preaching worked differently. As it was, he judged that contemporary evangelists went for obvious things that worked, like adultery and drunkenness. The most effective way to induce the crisis was to convict persons of sins that they and their peers regarded as sins. Race prejudice was a different kind of sin, Niebuhr reasoned, because its social basis was more important than its individual instantiation. Racism was embedded in the customs and social structures of communities. It was not a private sin committed one by one but something taught and approved by communities. Thus, adultery worked better at evangelistic rallies than racial sinning, which induced no emotional crisis among its perpetrators.

Niebuhr had little hope for evangelicalism in this area, noting that the most violently racist regions of the United States had the most revivals. On the other hand, he saw something hopeful in Graham, who was well traveled and had a sense of justice. It was not impossible to imagine Graham taking up the cause of racial justice as an evangelistic priority. If he did so, he had a chance to become "a vital force in the nation's moral and spiritual life." Of course, Graham was already a vital force in American life; Niebuhr really meant "a vital force for good."[16]

UNCLAIMED AMBIGUITY:
GRAHAM ON RACIAL JUSTICE

For the most part Graham went on to the career that Niebuhr expected of him, lifting evangelicalism out of its sectarian ghetto, reducing social problems to matters of personal piety and morality, avoiding conservative debates over the extent of biblical inerrancy, and treading carefully on racial justice. Graham left it to his scholarly friends at Fuller Theological Seminary, Carl F. H. Henry and E. J. Carnell, to decide what inerrancy meant, staying above the fray of a draining, fractious, never-ending battle.

On the necessity of de-ghettoizing fundamentalism, his guide was Henry's *The Uneasy Conscience of Modern Fundamentalism*, which made the case for a new evangelicalism just before Fuller Seminary opened its doors in 1947. Henry depicted American fundamentalism as a sectarian retreat from the gospel mission to spread righteousness throughout the world. Fundamentalists hardly ever preached against "such social evils as aggressive warfare, racial hatred and intolerance, the liquor traffic, exploitation of labor or management, or the like," he observed. Ignoring centuries of Christian theology, biblical scholarship, and spiritual practice, they replaced the great hymns of the past with "a barn-dance variety of semi-religious choruses" and turned the world-changing gospel of Christ into "a world-resisting message" of apocalyptic deliverance.[17]

Henry called for a different kind of fundamentalism, one that reclaimed the social mission of the gospel and discarded shibboleths that "cut the nerve of world compassion." J. N. Darby-style apocalypticism, which ruled most of the fundamentalist movement, was a chief cause of the shibboleths. Darby's dispensational scheme turned the Bible into a strange guidebook of signs foretelling God's "rapture" of Christians out of the world and inauguration of Christ's millennial kingdom on earth. Henry treaded lightly in this area, describing his position as "broadly premillennial," which placed him with the Puritans, not the sectarian dispensationalists. Moreover, he respected the sober amillennialism of Reformed and Lutheran orthodoxy.[18]

Henry simply wanted fundamentalists to stop obsessing about signs of the end time. What mattered was to allow a certain range of views on this issue, he argued, proposing a truce between premillennialists and amillennialists that ruled out the postmillennial fantasy of a Christianized world. The parties of orthodoxy needed to make room for each other on eschatology. They also needed to acknowledge that the postmillennial tradition was right about one thing: the church had a mission to transform society. That was a gospel theme, Henry urged, even though postmillennialists misconstrued it. The gospel was relevant to every world problem while the Lord tarried: "The main difference between the kingdom of God now and the kingdom of God then is that the future kingdom will center all of its activities in the redemptive King because all government and dominion will be subjected to Him. This difference overshadows the question, however important, whether the future kingdom involves an earthly reign or not."[19]

Graham drank more deeply than Henry from the dispensationalist well, avidly promoting Wilbur Smith's updated dispensational interpretations of biblical prophecy, which painted the threat of world communism in lurid colors. However, the fundamentalists who launched Fuller Theological Seminary and the "neo-evangelical" movement in the late 1940s—Henry, Smith, Carnell, Harold J. Ockenga, Harold Lindsell, and Everett F. Harrison—agreed with Henry not to fight over eschatology, at least not immediately. In its early years Fuller Seminary took a strict line on biblical inerrancy and basked in its association with the increasingly famous Graham. It also did little to break the mold of fundamentalist conservatism in the political arena.

For years Henry was consumed with building up the seminary, and afterward he steered the movement's flagship magazine, *Christianity Today*, which took conservative positions on social issues closely resembling Graham's. Henry was the movement's leading thinker, but to the general public, Graham was the symbol of whatever difference there was between the old fundamentalism and the new evangelicalism.

As the public face of this transition, Graham had to figure out what it meant for evangelicalism to have a social mission, especially in dealing with America's original sin of racism. Here the ironies were thick. In writings and interviews scattered through his later life, Graham claimed to have supported the civil rights movement consistently. In reality, in the name of Christian morality and his imagined "voluntary integration," he blasted the movement's troublemaking demonstrations and condemned its advocacy of coerced integration.[20]

Though accused of simplemindedness, Graham's record in this area approached Niebuhrian levels of ironic complexity and strategic ambiguity. Keenly attuned to the white supremacist anxiety of his white conservative base, though of course he never called it that, Graham played a careful hand. He understood that his group had a very limited capacity to acknowledge wrongdoing against African Americans, and on many occasions he showed that his own capacity was similarly limited. On the whole Graham played a role in the struggle for racial justice that redeemed some of Niebuhr's hope for him, even using arguments that sounded like Niebuhr. But both of them fell short of giving racial justice the high priority it deserved, and Graham never accepted that the "race problem" was a white problem.

Niebuhr's appeal to Graham on racism might have had some of the effect that he sought. Years later Graham told his friend and biographer John Pollock, "I thought about it a great deal. He influenced me and I began to take a stronger stand." Graham might well have struggled internally with Niebuhr's critique and proposal, and he might have resolved to preach more directly about racism. But he never had a moment or phase of conversion on race equality, and the only event marking a clear change in his behavior was a Supreme Court decision. Recalling his upbringing in the rural South, Graham's autobiography disposed of a large topic in one sentence, remarking that, having grown up in the rural South, "I had adopted the attitudes of that region without much reflection." Elsewhere he recalled, "If there were Negroes who chafed in their status as second-class citizens, I was not aware of them."[21]

Biographer Marshall Frady filled part of the gap, reporting Graham's boyhood use of racial epithets and his everyday support of Jim Crow. When Graham brushed near this subject, he emphasized his boyhood respect for the black foreman on the Graham dairy farm, Reese Brown, and recalled that he never liked the white supremacist theme of his favorite books, the Tarzan stories of Edgar Rice Burroughs. At the age of sixteen Graham had a born-again experience at a segregated revival. Years later, as a professional evangelist, he often claimed that after his conversion he found American segregation incomprehensible, especially in the church. He could not treat blacks as inferior after he had come to Jesus. In 1960, however, Graham remembered his past more accurately: "Even after my conversion, I felt no guilt in thinking of my dark-skinned brothers in the usual patronizing and paternalistic way."[22]

Implicitly, that remembrance undermined Graham's self-image as an agent of racial reconciliation and his vocational assurance that born-again conversion was the answer; thus, he rarely verbalized it. But it fit Graham's personal trajectory, which included studying briefly at Bob Jones University, joining the staunchly segregationist Southern Baptist Convention, preaching at countless segregated Youth for Christ meetings, and, in the late 1940s, conducting numerous segregated crusades throughout the South. As a student at Wheaton College in the early 1940s, Graham was influenced by classmate Carl Henry's advocacy of racial integration, and he discovered the possibility of friendship with blacks.

By 1949, when the Hearst papers made him a media star, Graham was a veteran evangelist with a record of ignoring racial injustice. In his telling, no one challenged segregation in the South before 1950, and he gave no thought to doing so. In the early 1950s, however, the media spotlight on Graham and the early rumblings of what became the civil rights movement raised the moral issue in his consciousness; Graham also wanted to reach black audiences.

For two years he zigged and zagged on segregation, sometimes refusing to address segregated audiences, other times backsliding. In his memoir he retold a favorite story about tearing down the dividing ropes at a 1953 crusade in Chattanooga, Tennessee. He did not, however, mention backsliding subsequently in Dallas, Texas, and Asheville, North Carolina. Michael Long aptly remarks that courageous antisegregationist leaders were rare in the South, and Billy Graham, "for all his stunning progress, was not that rare."[23]

In 1954, twenty years after his conversion, the Supreme Court settled the matter, for Graham, in *Brown v. Board of Education*. Before the Supreme Court outlawed public school segregation, Graham had assured his segregated audiences that the Bible had nothing to say about the segregation issue. After the court ruled, Graham had the basis that he needed to get on the right side of the civil rights movement. He spoke only to integrated audiences, reminded them that Jesus identified with the marginalized and segregated people of his time, and drew the connection to twentieth-century African Americans. Later he spoke against the stupidity of racist Christianity, admonishing white suprema-cists that Jesus was a Mediterranean Jew with a "swarthy" complexion. He also stressed that America's mistreatment of its black population handed the com-munists easy propaganda victories in their drive to conquer the world.[24]

By the 1960s Graham found it difficult to remember his early career cor-rectly, sometimes claiming, laughably, that only two or three of his crusades had been segregated. By the 1970s he had similar difficulties remembering his actual relation to the civil rights movement, which was equally ambiguous. Graham's version of his civil rights ministry featured an approving quote by Martin Luther King Jr. and a carefully vague self-placement between "extreme conservatives" and "extreme liberals." In his telling, King told him "early on" that he would best serve the cause of racial equality by preaching integrated crusades, not by joining King in the streets: "'You stay in the stadiums, Billy,' he said, 'because you will have far more impact on the white establishment there than you would if you marched in the streets. Besides that, you have a constituency that will listen to you, especially among white people, who may not listen so much to me. But if a leader gets too far in front of his people, they will lose sight of him and not follow him any longer.'" As Graham told it, he followed King's advice, which placed him "under fire from both sides" as extreme conservatives condemned his support of integration and "extreme lib-erals" found him too moralistic and solicitous of the establishment.[25]

That made Graham sound remarkably like King. At times he merited this self-description as the King figure in the white evangelical community. Gra-ham added a black evangelist, Howard Jones, to his team in 1957; he invited King to pray at the 1957 New York crusade, introducing King as the leader of "a great social revolution"; he conducted an integrated crusade in Birming-ham, Alabama, a few months after the 1963 church bombing that killed four black girls; he served on a national citizens committee to help implement the Civil Rights Act of 1964; and in 1965 he made his strongest statement of sup-port for King's nonviolent demonstrations, observing that they "brought about new, strong, tough laws that were needed many years ago."[26]

But King had ample reason to judge, as he did, that Graham was nowhere near the white evangelical leader that was needed. At the time that King made his "you stay in the stadiums" statement to Graham, at a planning meeting for the 1957 New York crusade, King dreamed of a Graham/King crusade that would preach to integrated audiences in the North, proceed to border states, and culminate in the Deep South. That dream foundered on Graham's anxi-eties about publicly cooperating with King and on his unwillingness to address the politics of racism. Graham never invited King to appear with him again, and within a year of the New York crusade, King had to plead with Graham to stop allowing segregationists on the platform of his Southern crusades.[27]

In public, and with King, Graham claimed to avoid politics, but he was a font of political advice to a succession of presidents. Unknown to King, Graham advised President Dwight Eisenhower in 1956 not to risk his reelection by appealing to northern blacks, which would hurt him politically in the South. Besides watching out for Eisenhower's interests in the South, Graham repeatedly objected to civil rights campaigns there. King, realizing that he had very limited means of attacking a national and global problem, sought to dramatize the ravages of racism by conducting manageable campaigns in selected cities. Graham protested that this strategy stirred up racial animosity and scapegoated selected southern communities. When King marched in Selma, Alabama, for instance, Graham decried singling out Selma; it was wrong to divert attention from a national problem by stigmatizing one particular community, he declared.[28]

These were exactly the high-minded arguments favored by moderate white ministers who opposed the marches and sit-ins of the civil rights movement while claiming to support its ultimate objective. King's "Letter from Birmingham Jail" responded directly to eight local ministers making that case. On the one hand, Graham's team helped King orchestrate the timing and release of King's famous letter against going slow; on the other hand, temporizing ministers across the nation took comfort that Billy Graham was on their side. Graham legitimized the very reaction that King viewed as the greatest threat to the movement. Overall his record during the King years was only slightly more progressive than *Christianity Today*, which defended voluntary segregation, opposed coercive integration, and denounced the demonstrations and sit-ins of the civil rights movement.[29]

At times Graham not only legitimized clerical opposition but heightened its rhetorical ante. In 1958 he thundered in Charlotte, North Carolina, that Satan was the instigator of the current unrest over racial inequality: "We see the forces of evil stirring up racial tensions all over America. . . . It seems as if the whole world is a pot and the devil has a big stick stirring everybody up. Why, he has even got the church stirred up."[30]

There were plenty of equally low points registering Graham's defensiveness as a white Southerner. He speculated that the Birmingham girls were killed by outside professionals to fan the flames of racial tension; he took offense at the civil rights movement's emphasis on white racism; most of his stories illustrating racial prejudice illustrated black racism; he warned repeatedly that "forced integration" would never work; right up to the Civil Rights Act of 1964 he protested that integrationists were pushing "too far too fast." Of course, the *Brown* decision had legalized and required forced integration. Graham never quite explained how he could accept *Brown* and adamantly reject forced integration.

By the late 1960s all was forgotten, and in his later remembrances, Graham had supported all the civil rights legislation of the King years. Michael Long gets it right: "No matter what he said in later years, Graham was no integrationist, at least in the sense that King and others in the civil rights movement were integrationists."[31]

The movement's short-term goal was government-enforced integration, but Graham supported only voluntary integration, which required nothing of whites and allowed them to feel righteous for whatever allowances they dispensed to blacks. Graham's sermons were long on the latter theme. In his telling, the moral revolution of the King years was mostly a white phenomenon. It was a story of whites letting go of customs that soiled their own virtue and of opening their institutions to blacks despite encountering so many ungrateful blacks. Graham might have struggled inwardly with the moral pitfall that disturbed Niebuhr—that of proudly holding oneself above the prejudices of one's group—but there is little evidence of it. On the other hand, Niebuhr's anxiety about the latter species of moral pride inhibited him from following completely his own advice to Graham.

THE PRIORITY OF RACIAL JUSTICE

Niebuhr was better than most theologians about racism. He cared deeply about racial justice and wrote nearly a dozen articles about it, usually describing racism as a transcendently evil form of self-worship. But he never featured this subject in his major works or gave high priority to it in his activism. In his early career Niebuhr was devoted to pacifism and making a name for himself; in his middle career he burned for socialism and religious realism; in his later career he gave priority to antifascism, anticommunism, and vital center realism.

Niebuhr was sincere in challenging Graham to devote his crusades to racial equality; he was not just seeking another way to put down Graham. But the problem of liberal righteousness is a slippery, confounding one that has a way of turning on itself, as in Niebuhr's case. Uncharacteristically he failed to acknowledge the irony of his challenge to Graham. Niebuhr urged Graham to an extraordinarily difficult task, one entailing dangers and burdens from which Niebuhr was far removed. He had no contact with Graham's audiences, and by the 1950s he faced little prospect of confronting angry crowds of any kind. Yet even in Niebuhr's rarefied world of prestige lectureships and publishers, he did not take the risk that he asked of Graham—telling his group to interrogate its white supremacism.

Asking white liberals in the 1950s to interrogate their casual racism would not have gone well. It would have evoked, for Niebuhr, the kind of hostility that Graham confronted constantly in the South, even as Graham tried not to offend the moral pride of his audience. Liberals took pride in having no racial biases; that was what made them liberals.

For all of his railing against liberal illusions, Niebuhr did not regard this as one of them. He took for granted that the problem was to eliminate racial bias, not to dismantle an entire national culture of white supremacism. He believed that liberals were closer than others to it and that America as a whole was moving, albeit belatedly, to the goal of a society without racial discrimination. On the way to that goal, he fretted more about the sin of liberal false righteousness than about liberals being too easy on themselves.

Niebuhr worried that when liberal white Christians apologized to blacks or Jews for the sins of white America, they won moral points for humility and contrition, but wrongly. Confessions of this sort were dictated by pride; thus, they carried a whiff of hypocrisy. Instead of expressing a real confession, the penitent communicated his or her moral superiority. That scruple, plus the social punishments that would have fallen, impeded Niebuhr from saying as much as he should have about white racism. It also troubled him that, in his experience, victims of racial discrimination rarely confessed their own shortcomings, though he allowed that this appearance could be a defensive reaction to the insincerity of white Americans' contrition for racism.[32]

Racism ignored the conditioned character of one's life and culture, Niebuhr stressed. It fed on the false pretense that one's color, creed, or culture represented the final good: "This is a pathetic and dangerous fallacy, but it is one in which almost all men are involved in varying degrees." Unlike Graham, Niebuhr took for granted during the King years that coercive government policies to prohibit racial discrimination and promote racial justice were necessary. Graham's lip service to the ideal might have paid some practical dividends, but it was better not to have any illusions about the near-term possibility of integration without government coercion.[33]

When Niebuhr talked about racism beyond the level of politics, however, he sounded more like Graham than his withering rebukes of Graham. Niebuhr argued that the problem of racial bigotry was ultimately a spiritual issue; thus, it could not be cured by social engineering: "The mitigation of racial and cultural pride is finally a religious problem in the sense that each man, and each race and culture, must become religiously aware of the sin of self-worship, which is the final form of human evil and of which racial self-worship is the most vivid example." Racism was like every other form of evil in its egotistical presumption: "Religious humility, as well as rational enlightenment, must contribute to the elimination of this terrible evil of racial pride."[34]

In 1957, three years before Niebuhr retired from Union Seminary and shortly after he got heartburn from Graham's New York crusade, Niebuhr judged that his country was correcting its only serious social problem. The United States had solved the problems of liberty and equality "beyond the dreams of any European nation," he opined. The New Deal had been so successful that even Republicans accepted it. In domestic politics and society, there was only one major problem left to solve in American life: "We failed catastrophically only on one point—in our relation to the Negro race." Niebuhr believed, however, that even America's racial pathology was "on the way of being resolved." The Supreme Court finally recognized equality as a criterion of justice, and the *Brown* decision redeemed the promise of America for black Americans: "At last the seeming sentimentality of the preamble of our Declaration of Independence—the declaration that 'all men are created equal'—has assumed political reality and relevance."[35]

That is a measure of the bland optimism of the 1950s, that even Reinhold Niebuhr could be naive in celebrating America the good, even on the politics of the color line. When Niebuhr died in 1971 the Protestant mainline was still at the center of American culture, but there were signs of an impending downturn. The mainline churches never outgrew their ethnic families of origin; demographically they failed even to reproduce themselves, and they did a tepid job of raising their children in the faith. By the end of Niebuhr's life, the college chapel circuit that made his fame possible no longer existed. He died barely in time not to witness the eclipse of his group by one that he disdained, never imagining that the National Association of Evangelicals (NAE) would become a juggernaut. In Niebuhr's time the NAE was a decidedly marginal outfit; by 1980 it was a powerhouse that capitalized on Graham's fame and the success of *Christianity Today*.

THE "RIGHTNESS" OF GRAHAM?

The verdict on Graham's "rightness" must refer to different things. As the herald of a new evangelicalism he was phenomenally successful. As a temporizing advocate of racial integration he helped white evangelicals break free of segregation and, to some extent, white supremacism, although he felt compelled in later life to whitewash his record. It was not enough to say that his approach had worked; to feel good about it, Graham needed to revise what had happened, taking positions retroactively that he never quite managed when it mattered.

As a theologian, however, he rested entirely on what had worked for him, which made his position intellectually impossible. Instead of struggling honestly with intellectual problems, Graham told the story of his 1949 walk in the woods. He preached and lived with winning conviction after vowing in faith to believe that the Bible contains no contradictions or factual errors.

Believing in unbelievable things had worked for him; however, that strategy identified evangelicalism with fideistic escape.

The larger verdict rests on an outcome not yet known. From the beginning of the organized Christian Right in 1977, Graham has had an ambivalent relationship with it. Christian Right leaders are too nakedly partisan for him, and often too mean-spirited. He takes pride in the evangelical boon but steps back when evangelical leaders equate Christian faith with right-wing politics or make obnoxious pronouncements that embarrass him. Bailey Smith announced that God does not hear the prayers of Jews. Pat Robertson and Jerry Falwell opined that the fiendish attacks of September 11, 2001, were God's retribution for moral perfidy. Robertson added that God struck down Israeli president Ariel Sharon for giving back the Gaza Strip. Today, Franklin Graham insists that Islamic terrorism is the essence of Islam, not a perversion of it.[36]

If evangelicalism of that sort prevails, it will be pointless to make a case for Billy Graham. But a great deal of American evangelicalism is temperamentally moderate, and there is such a thing as progressive evangelicalism. For the past thirty years, *Sojourners* magazine has embraced progressive concerns and claimed its kinship with the antislavery, feminist, temperance, black church, and Social Gospel evangelicalisms of the nineteenth century. To the extent that progressives such as Jim Wallis, Tony Campolo, and Eugene Rivers have made inroads within evangelicalism, the reactionary spirit of evangelical fundamentalism has given way to the discourse of a generous orthodoxy, one that lives more peaceably and graciously within a religiously plural world. It speaks to the sensibility of young evangelicals who yearn for gospel-centered teaching that does not violate their own experience of living in a pluralistic, multicultural, postmodern society.

On these points contemporary evangelicals have reason to say, "It started with Billy Graham." Besides conducting racially integrated crusades, Graham broadened the ecumenical common ground within evangelicalism and sustained respectful relationships with Catholics, liberal Protestants, and Jews, which made him an object of loathing to fundamentalist leaders. He was a close friend of Rabbi Marc Tanenbaum, and in 1977 Graham won the American Jewish Committee's National Interreligious Award for his efforts to strengthen mutual respect between evangelicals and Jews. In later life Graham surprised interviewers by calling himself a theological conservative and social liberal.[37]

But most of Graham's movement never shared much of his social conscience; his own was repeatedly compromised by his intimate access to power and lust for political influence, and today much of the evangelical movement is stridently dogmatic and mean-spirited. Graham's son Franklin preaches fundamentalist hellfire evangelism, disdaining ecumenical niceness: Jesus is the only way to salvation; every knee shall bow; most knees will bow in hell, where it will be too late. The elder Graham preached the same theology—but with better manners. That was the real difference between Graham-style evangelicalism and old-style fundamentalism: civility and the rejection of separatism, which led to the development of ecumenical and public skills. If Billy Graham is to be vindicated historically, evangelicalism must combine the liberationist spirit of its abolitionist past with Graham's ecumenical temperament.

NOTES

1. Reinhold Niebuhr, "A Theologian Says Evangelist Is Oversimplifying the Issues of Life," *Life*, July 1, 1957, 92.
2. Reinhold Niebuhr, "Literalism, Individualism, and Billy Graham," *Christian Century*, May 23, 1956, 64, reprinted in Niebuhr, *Essays in Applied Christianity*, ed. D. B. Robertson (New York: Meridian Books, 1959), 127.
3. Ibid., 128.
4. Ibid.; Reinhold Niebuhr, "Proposal to Billy Graham," *Christian Century*, August 8, 1956, reprinted in Niebuhr, *Love and Justice*, ed. D. B. Robertson (Philadelphia: Westminster Press, 1957), 155.
5. Niebuhr, "Proposal to Billy Graham," 155; Niebuhr, "Literalism, Individualism, and Billy Graham," 128.
6. See Reinhold Niebuhr, *An Interpretation of Christian Ethics* (New York: Harper & Brothers, 1935); Niebuhr, *The Nature and Destiny of Man*, 2 vols. (New York: Charles Scribner's Sons, 1941, 1943).
7. Henry Van Dusen, "Billy Graham," *Christian Century*, April 2, 1956, 40; Niebuhr, "Proposal to Billy Graham," 156.
8. Reinhold Niebuhr, "The Billy Graham Campaign," *Messenger*, June 4, 1957, 5; Niebuhr, "Graham Sermon in Garden on TV," *New York Times*, June 2, 1957, 38; Billy Graham, *Just as I Am: The Autobiography of Billy Graham* (San Francisco: HarperSanFrancisco, 1997), 301; Richard Wightman Fox, *Reinhold Niebuhr: A Biography* (Ithaca, NY: Cornell University Press, 1996), 266.
9. Graham, *Just as I Am*, 135.
10. Ibid., 136–40, quote at 139; Graham, *The Journey: How to Live by Faith in an Uncertain World* (Carmel, NY: Guideposts, 2006), 108–9; Graham, *How to Be Born Again*, in Graham, *The Collected Works of Billy Graham*, one-volume ed. (New York: Inspirational Press, 1993), 188.
11. Niebuhr, *Interpretation of Christian Ethics*, 2.
12. Niebuhr, "Literalism, Individualism, and Billy Graham," 130.
13. Ibid.
14. Ibid., 131.
15. Niebuhr, "Proposal to Billy Graham," 156.
16. Niebuhr, "Proposal to Billy Graham," 156, 158.
17. Carl F. H. Henry, *The Uneasy Conscience of Modern Fundamentalism* (Grand Rapids: Eerdmans, 1947), 18–19, 29–30.
18. Ibid., 29.
19. Ibid., 29–34, 52–57, quote at 54.
20. See Gary Dorrien, *The Remaking of Evangelical Theology* (Louisville, KY: Westminster John Knox Press, 1998), 49–123; George M. Marsden, *Reforming*

Fundamentalism: Fuller Seminary and the New Evangelicalism (Grand Rapids: Eerdmans, 1987); Daniel P. Fuller, *Give the Wind a Mighty Voice: The Story of Charles E. Fuller* (Waco, TX: Word Books, 1972), 189–227; Wilbur Smith, *The Atomic Age and the Word of God* (Boston: W. A. Wilde, 1948); Smith, *World Crises and the Prophetic Scriptures* (Chicago: Moody Press, 1951).

21. John Pollock, *Billy Graham: Evangelist to the World* (San Francisco: Harper & Row, 1979), 157; Graham, *Just as I Am*, 425; Billy Graham, "Why Don't Churches Practice Brotherhood?" *Reader's Digest*, August 1960, 55. See John Oliver, "A Failure of Evangelical Conscience," *Post-American*, May 1975, 26–30; Donald W. Dayton, *Discovering an Evangelical Heritage* (New York: Harper & Row, 1976), 2–3.

22. Marshall Frady, *Billy Graham: A Parable of American Righteousness* (Boston: Little, Brown, 1979), 67–69; Graham, *Just as I Am*, 425–26; Graham, "Why Don't Churches Practice Brotherhood?" 55.

23. Graham, *Just as I Am*, 426; Michael G. Long, *Billy Graham and the Beloved Community: America's Evangelist and the Dream of Martin Luther King, Jr.* (New York: Palgrave Macmillan, 2006), 80–83, quote at 83.

24. See Long, *Billy Graham and the Beloved Community*, 83–101; William Martin, *A Prophet with Honor: The Billy Graham Story* (New York: William Morrow, 1991), 255–67; Jerry Beryl Hopkins, "Billy Graham and the Race Problem, 1949–1969," PhD diss., University of Kentucky, 1986.

25. Graham, *Just as I Am*, 426. In the recollection of Howard Jones, King made this statement at a planning meeting for the 1957 New York crusade; see Martin, *Prophet with Honor*, 235.

26. Long, *Billy Graham and the Beloved Community*, 99–107, quotes at 105, 102.

27. Taylor Branch, *Parting the Waters: America in the King Years, 1954–63* (New York: Simon & Schuster, 1988), 227–28.

28. Billy Graham to President Dwight D. Eisenhower, March 27, 1956, and Graham to Eisenhower, June 4, 1956, cited in Long, *Billy Graham and the Beloved Community*, 112. On the Selma campaign, see ibid., 113; and Hopkins, "Billy Graham and the Race Problem," 41–42.

29. Martin Luther King Jr., "Letter from a Birmingham Jail" (1963), *A Testament of Hope: The Essential Writings and Speeches of Martin Luther King, Jr.*, ed. James W. Washington (San Francisco: HarperSanFrancisco, 1986), 289–302. The eight white ministers had published an open letter in January urging King to wait for decisions in the local and federal courts.

30. Long, *Billy Graham and the Beloved Community*, 114.

31. Ibid., 125, 121; Billy Graham, "No Solution to Race Problem 'at the Point of Bayonets,'" *U.S. News and World Report*, April 25, 1960, 94–95.

32. Reinhold Niebuhr, "The Confession of a Tired Radical," *Christian Century*, August 30, 1928, reprinted in Niebuhr, *Love and Justice*, 120–24.

33. Reinhold Niebuhr, "The Sin of Racial Prejudice," *The Messenger*, February 3, 1948, reprinted in *A Reinhold Niebuhr Reader: Selected Essays, Articles, and Book Reviews*, ed. Charles C. Brown (Philadelphia: Trinity Press International, 1992), 70–71.

34. See Niebuhr, "Sin of Racial Prejudice," 70–71; Niebuhr, "Christian Faith and the Race Problem," *Christianity and Society*, spring 1945; and Niebuhr, "The Race Problem," *Christianity and Society*, summer 1942, reprinted in Niebuhr, *Love and Justice*, 125–132.

35. Reinhold Niebuhr, *Pious and Secular America* (New York: Charles Scribner's Sons, 1958), 76.
36. See Peter J. Boyer, "The Big Tent: Billy Graham, Franklin Graham, and the Transformation of American Evangelicalism," *New Yorker*, August 22, 2005, 42–55.
37. See David Rausch, "Chosen People: Christian Views of Judaism Are Changing," *Christianity Today*, October 7, 1988, 53–59; "CT News," *Christianity Today*, November 18, 1977, 57; David Blewett, "What the Protestant Churches Are Saying about Jews and Judaism," a lecture presented at the University of St. Thomas, Center for Jewish-Christian Learning, April 11, 1994, http://www.nclci.org/Articles/art-blewett-whatthe.htm; Boyer, "Big Tent."

11

Graham, King, and
the Beloved Community

RUFUS BURROW JR.

Until very recently Billy Graham did not figure prominently in my thought and work, since I always believed him to be solely concerned about saving individual souls, without challenging converts to take seriously the prophetic tradition of the Jewish and Christian faiths. In addition, I knew little of his acquaintance with Martin Luther King Jr. However, I knew enough to realize that they were quite different personalities and that they thought differently about the relation of the Christian gospel to the problems of social injustice and, more particularly, the method of addressing and eradicating such problems.

A SOCIAL CONSCIENCE WITH PROBLEMS

Although he is clearly in the tradition of nineteenth-century revivalism and pietistic evangelism, Graham has for many years exhibited a social conscience and a sense that the gospel is relevant to major social issues. By 1952 he even "said a few kind words about the social gospel movement" and rejected the charge that he was fundamentalist in the traditional meaning of the term. He was not, he said, the type of fundamentalist who was "narrow," "bigoted," "prejudiced," "extremist," "emotional," a "snake-handler," or "without social conscience."[1] Given his own words, then, the present reflections assume that Billy Graham had a social conscience from the beginning of his evangelistic career.

The content of Graham's social conscience is not without its problems, however, and the issues are twofold. First, Graham's idea about how social problems are best solved is problematic for those who believe, as King did, that God not only expects us to witness to injustice in the world but to do all in our power to work cooperatively toward its eradication. Second, there is no convincing evidence that Graham ever possessed a real sense that the kingdom of God, or some approximation of it, can be achieved in history and that human beings will help to bring it about. Rather, more often he has focused on the kingdom that will be ushered in by some dramatic or cataclysmic intervention by Jesus Christ, who will then rule a perfect social order free of all social problems and injustice for a thousand years.

From the beginning to the end of his career, Graham's conscience has seemed most influenced by the static values and stances of the powerful and privileged rather than by those forced to the margins—all of whom cry out for human liberation in the here and now. Indeed, there is no sense in which it can be rightly said that Graham's was a liberation social ethic.

In this regard he differs significantly from the liberationist King, who was likely first introduced to the notion of the beloved community in his graduate studies under Edgar S. Brightman and L. Harold DeWolf at Boston University, and who later carried this vision of liberation into his public ministry. Not long after the Montgomery bus boycott, for example, King declared that the purpose of the newly formed Southern Christian Leadership Conference was to save the soul of America and to contribute to establishing the beloved community, a thoroughly integrated community in which the dignity and human rights of every person would be acknowledged and respected.

NO ETHICAL PROPHET

King frequently used the beloved community as a prophetic tool when he opposed the powers that oppressed him and his people. By contrast, Graham never assumed the role of an ethical prophet—the type found in the tradition of the Hebrew prophets of the eighth century BCE, such as Amos, Isaiah, Hosea, and Micah, who prophesied against their respective nations, national leaders, and ruling classes, declaring "thus says the LORD" about the absence of justice among the poor and the weak. Contrary to priests who merely bowed their heads in prayer, these prophets courageously declared exactly what God required of the privileged and powerful—that justice be done in righteous ways, that they love kindness, and that they walk humbly with the God of Israel (Mic. 6:8).[2] This message, pointed and critical, required that the prophet retain a sense of autonomy—a sufficient distance from governing rulers and other power holders—so that he or she could freely oppose individuals and practices deemed to be contrary to God's expectations.

Graham, of course, did not always keep such distance from U.S. presidents, especially Lyndon Johnson and Richard Nixon, and other governing officials, including congressional and Pentagon leaders. Because of his failure in this regard, as well as his disdain for confrontation initiated by the disadvantaged— for example, African Americans during the civil rights struggle—Graham was too often on the wrong side of the prophetic fence. The two most dramatic instances of this were his responses to King's method of seeking to overcome racism in its interpersonal and systemic manifestations and his response to King's linkage of the civil rights and peace movements.

Nevertheless, not a few have sought to place Graham next to King in the category of prophet, as if they were of the same genre. Former Texas governor John Connally, for example, characterized Graham as the conscience of the nation, and Marshall Frady, in *Billy Graham: A Parable of American Righteousness*, contends that King *shares* this distinction with Graham. They "were like the antipodal prophets of that continuing duality in the American nature between the Plymouth asperities and the readiness for spiritual adventure, between the authoritarian and the visionary."[3]

But surely this is a mistaken notion of social prophecy. It would be much more accurate to say that Graham has been the conscience of individuals, since his appeal, consistent with the old-time revivalist tradition of Finney, Moody, and Sunday, has always been to the individual—to changing and saving souls, one individual at a time. Indeed, nowhere do we get a sense that Graham consistently challenged crusade converts to live their lives in accordance with ethical prophecy's demand that justice be done.

The absence of this challenge is perhaps what is most striking about Graham's social ethics, especially during the civil rights and Vietnam eras, when Will Campbell, a nontraditional southern white pastor during the civil rights movement, accurately described Graham as "a false court prophet who tells Nixon and the Pentagon what they want to hear."[4] This was particularly true regarding the war in Vietnam, when Graham had early reservations but chose not to criticize the Johnson and Nixon administrations.

King, on the other hand, literally sought to arouse, alter, and save the conscience and soul of the entire nation, indeed the world, and this all-inclusive, prophetic goal was consistent with his conviction that nonviolence is not merely a strategy for social change but a way of life. Not long after the Montgomery bus boycott, he declared that only through nonviolence is there hope of achieving reconciliation between the races and establishing the beloved community. Nonviolence seeks to save and enhance human life rather than to destroy it. In his view, the community of love had no chance of being achieved apart from nonviolence as a strategy as well as an attitude or disposition.

Living out his own principles, King sought to save the soul of the nation not merely by preaching to the souls of individuals but especially by putting his very life on the line in protest demonstrations, as well as witnessing and calling others to join him in nonviolent protest. Not unlike the Hebrew prophets, he risked his very life by daring to tell the powers that God required that justice be done to the least, and that judgment would be the consequence of failing to comply.

Graham remained a dissident from ethical prophecy. Even after King was assassinated, the evangelist was not persuaded to engage in more daring action to achieve human rights and justice for all. While rejecting King's prophetic tactics as a means to challenge the unjust and callous policies and practices of the powerful, Graham always chose a safer path.

CHANGING SOCIETY ONE SOUL AT A TIME

The beloved community, King believed, is achievable in history through the mutual cooperation of human beings and the God of the Hebrew prophets and Jesus Christ. From the beginning to the end of his ministry, King lived by the conviction that to the extent that the community of love could be achieved in history, it would be done through cooperative human and divine efforts—collective efforts that would include using the resources of social institutions and organizations.

But the same cannot be said of Graham, whose primary emphasis has always been on the conversion of individuals, even though he has acknowledged that faith without works is dead. We may accept Graham's self-estimate that he has always possessed a social conscience, but not before pointing out that he has exhibited simplistic thinking about social issues and their possible solutions.

Graham has come dangerously close to saying that the solution to social problems is found in born-again individuals alone—a claim based on the "perfectionistic illusion" that once one is converted, she or he is free from sin and enjoys the assurance that there will be divine assistance to overcome future temptation to sin. Coupled with individualism, the perfectionist illusion also holds that it is the newly converted person who is the real hope for improving social conditions. If the world is to be a better place, it is the converted individual alone who will make it so. Indeed, as William McLoughlin notes, the individualistic logic of this revivalist theology "disparaged and even deplored collective efforts at reform."[5]

Like his revivalist ancestors, Graham maintains that sin is personal and that social reform must therefore be personal or individual. While conceding the importance of the social implications of the gospel, Graham believes that at the end of the day "we must change men before we can change society."[6] Protest marches and civil disobedience cannot change the human heart, he argues, subordinating everything, including radical social transformation, to conversion and soul winning.

Graham therefore claims that a racism-free society will emerge only when God has eradicated personal sins. "The one great answer to our racial problem in America," he declared back in 1957, "is for men and women to be converted to Christ."[7] Only spiritual regeneration can change the human heart, and only the human heart can ultimately eliminate racism. Until our hearts are converted to Christ, social action and social reform are baseless and useless.

Graham has thus had difficulty seeing the sociological evidence that substantial social reform, indeed the enhancement of the quality of life for millions, can occur through various types of social activism long before individual souls are transformed. He has also had problems seeing that social, political, and economic structures themselves are immoral and not merely because they are composed of immoral individuals. Indeed, Graham's individualistic approach has been blind to the social dimension of problems and their real solutions. As McLoughlin noted long ago of Graham's individualistic ethics, "It was escapist because it ignored the social complexity of evil. It was shallowly optimistic because it assumed that evangelization was the simple cure for all contemporary problems."[8] With his belief that converted Christians would automatically form their organizations in accord with Christian principles, Graham revealed a naiveté that was uncharacteristic of Martin Luther King Jr.

SERIOUS ABOUT RACISM?

Graham, who was not seminary trained (and in later years said this was "one great failure"),[9] rose to evangelistic fame while King was in seminary and graduate school from the late 1940s to the mid-1950s. Although they were from different traditions—Graham was a Southern Baptist, and King was a member of the National Baptist Convention—the two recognized that they were yoked together as fellow Baptists, and the evangelist invited King to give the opening prayer at the 1957 Madison Square Garden crusade, introducing him with the words, "A great social revolution is going on in the United States today. Dr. King is one of its leaders, and we appreciate his taking time out of his busy schedule to come and share this service with us tonight."[10]

Of course, Graham was neither condoning the revolution nor King's involvement in it. Nor did King say anything in his prayer that might have implied Graham's commitment to the revolution as such. The closest that King came to this was when he urged the renewed and vigorous cooperative endeavor between God and human beings to achieve "a warless world and for a brotherhood that transcends race or color."[11]

Already having tested the use of organized confrontation to achieve a modicum of social justice by this time, King knew that prayer and evangelism alone were not sufficient to the task of moving toward the community of love. But he did recognize that prayer and evangelism were indispensable tools for his constructive work. A preacher by calling, he never undermined the importance of prayer and preaching in evangelistic outreach that had a strong social justice component, and he remained ever mindful that the potential changes brought about by protest demonstration, legislative change, and judicial enforcement would not be lasting if there were not corresponding changes in people's hearts, souls, and attitudes. Consequently, King blended his more vigorous confrontation tactics with preaching to the souls of people for the purpose of effecting inward transformation as well.

A similar blending was not characteristic of Billy Graham's ministry. Although he would come to some sense of appreciation for nonviolent action, his sermons usually neglected to charge individuals with the responsibility of applying Christian principles to social issues such as racism and war. Nevertheless, even though their styles of ministry differed dramatically, the two leaders were far from hostile to each other.

After King delivered the invocation at the Madison Square Garden service, for example, Graham invited him to educate his crusade team about the race situation in the United States. Although Graham was the one to extend the invitation, the suggestion was actually made by two distinguished black preachers and close friends of King, Gardner Taylor and Thomas Kilgore, both members of Graham's crusade committee for the Harlem rallies that took place during this period.[12] No matter where it originated, however, Graham's invitation communicated a willingness to identify himself with the black struggle and with its leader. And King's acceptance essentially assured blacks that Graham was—or at least could be—an ally in the struggle.

There is no doubt that King was attracted to Graham and the worldwide success of his crusades, even considering them a potential model for his own work as a civil rights leader. On a much smaller scale he had utilized the mass rally technique with much success during the Montgomery bus boycott, and this "revival-style format," writes Taylor Branch, "held great promise for King, who, like Graham, was still above all else a proselytizer."[13] In fact, both men were mutually optimistic about the evangelistic possibilities of mass crusades.

King, in particular, was excited about the prospect of a joint crusade whose purpose would be to convert racially mixed audiences, beginning in the North and eventually moving through the Deep South.

But this turned out to be only a dream, for King's advisers soon discovered that Graham resisted serious conversations about day-to-day race relations and specific steps for addressing the matter.[14] Beyond this, Graham also took actions that called into question his apparently moderate stance on race relations. Not unlike most southern white moderates of the day, Graham was being forced at the time to show more of his hand in the cause of ending racial injustice, and in part because of the increased protest demonstrations and the heightened sense of self-affirmation experienced among larger numbers of blacks after the Montgomery struggle, especially throughout the South, it was increasingly difficult for white moderates like Graham to find a comfortable position on the fence. At times Graham fell off, and King noticed.

Within a year of the Madison Square Garden crusade, King found himself writing to Graham, pleading that he uninvite segregationist Texas governor Price Daniel to accept an honored role at the 1958 San Antonio crusade. Black pastors in San Antonio had informed King that such support for Daniel would be a great detriment to race relations in Texas and throughout the South.

The invitation for Daniel to introduce Graham at the rally was both strategic and a matter of grave concern among blacks, primarily because it was to occur on the eve of the Democratic primary, in which Daniel was seeking reelection as governor. In his letter, King wrote that this could be interpreted as Graham's "endorsement of racial segregation and discrimination."[15] It would be better, King added, if Daniel did not appear on the platform with Graham at all. But if the show were to go on as planned, Graham should at least publicly clarify his stance on segregation and his position on Daniel's possible reelection, for even an implied endorsement of the racist governor would have damaging effects on blacks' struggle for justice and human dignity and would diminish the importance of Graham's message to blacks about race relations.[16]

King surmised that if Graham mishandled the Daniel situation, it potentially would no longer matter, at least to many blacks, that Graham had early on rejected segregation and racism in the crusades. Solely on Graham's initiative, the first fully desegregated crusade in the South had been held in Chattanooga, Tennessee, in 1953, nearly a year before the landmark Supreme Court decision in *Brown v. Board of Education of Topeka, Kansas.*[17] Several years later, in 1957, Graham also desegregated his team by hiring Howard Jones, then a Cleveland pastor. King recognized these acts as groundbreaking but warned Graham that their significance would be vastly diminished for many blacks if he mishandled the situation at San Antonio.

Graham balked, and his lieutenant, Grady Wilson, a friend since childhood, penned King a patronizing reply, suggesting that the civil rights leader had been misinformed by black pastors in San Antonio. Graham had never taken sides in politics, Wilson wrote, and Daniel's invitation to introduce Graham was made at the request of San Antonio ministers. This was simply policy, Wilson suggested. As guests in the cities where crusades were held, the Graham team had no say about which personalities local ministers invited.

As if to discipline King, Wilson then wrote, "We were surprised to receive your telegram and learn of your feeling toward the Governor of the Sovereign State of Texas. Even though we do not see eye to eye with him on every issue, we still love him in Christ, and frankly, I think that should be your position not only as a Christian but as a minister of the Gospel of our risen Lord."[18] And turning even more personal, he added, "We received scores of letters and telegrams concerning your coming to our meeting in New York, and yet Mr. Graham was happy to have you come as a fellow minister in Christ."[19]

Wilson's letter ignored and distorted a few key facts. He totally glossed over the obvious point that King was not a racist like Daniel and that Graham himself had invited King to give the opening prayer at the 1957 crusade at Madison Square Garden. This latter point indicated that the Graham team had considerable say in who appeared on the dais. Interestingly, during that very year liberal pastor George C. Bonnell complained in a letter to the *Christian Century* that even on the local scene the Graham team actually ran the show and that others were mere figureheads. "Once the churches promise to cooperate with the crusade," Bonnell penned, "they find it necessary to rubber-stamp every effort of the Billy Graham Team."[20] Wilson also conveniently ignored Graham's political acts prior to the San Antonio crusade, such as his intentional efforts to prop up the Eisenhower presidential campaign and administration. The defense that Graham "never engaged in politics on one side or the other" was simply not true. At best, Wilson's letter was an example of disinformation—a flimsy defense for his boss, who, for whatever reason, was unwilling to clarify his position on segregation and discrimination during the San Antonio crusade.

One wonders what King thought about Wilson's response, especially since King had been so appreciative of having been invited by Graham to give the opening prayer at one of the Madison Square Garden services. In a letter to Graham after that event, King complimented him on his stance in race relations. Then, giving him more praise than he actually deserved, King wrote, "You have courageously brought the Christian gospel to bear on the question of race in all of its urgen [*sic*] dimensions. I am sure you will continue this emphasis in all of your preaching, for you, above any other preacher in America can open the eyes of many persons on this question."[21]

But Graham failed in the eyes of King's advisers, who eventually concluded that Graham was increasingly unwilling to discuss race and racism in its more concrete, day-to-day aspects—a conclusion that was strengthened all the more by Graham's unwillingness to distance himself from the segregationist Texas governor, even in light of King's prophetic advice.[22] The most that Graham was willing to do, and then only through his associate, was to express—naively— the need to love others, regardless of their beliefs and behavior, and to continue associating with them. But King was right: Graham's decision called his credibility into question, and it leaves me wondering just how serious his stance against racism really was.

LAW AND ORDER

The Daniel incident did not drive Graham and King completely apart, and in 1960 their paths crossed again, this time at the Miami airport, from which they flew together to the Baptist World Alliance meeting in Rio de Janeiro. The two leaders engaged in lengthy conversation during the trip and learned more about each other's works and goals. According to Graham, it was during this time that King invited him to call him by his birth name, Mike. Only his close friends could call him this, of course, and Graham became one of the very few whites invited to do so.

At the Rio meeting King urged his fellow Baptist ministers to take more seriously "the religious context of political freedom," and although King's equating of the Christian faith with the struggle for civil rights earned him few supporters among his white Baptist brethren from the southern United States, Graham showed his support for King by hosting a banquet in his honor. This itself caused a clamor, since some of the white southern ministers, long accustomed to segregated facilities, were uncomfortable eating with King in a restaurant.

More telling, however, is the direct exchange that took place between Graham and King about their respective work. According to Graham's authorized biographer, the evangelist told King, "I'm holding integrated 'demonstrations' in the big stadiums of America. You feel that you must march and even go to prison. I respect your views."[23]

Clearly, this was far from an admission of support, either for King's views or for his methods in the social struggle. The problem for Graham was not the adherence to nonviolence—since he would have it no other way within the boundaries of the United States—but rather the fact that the method was confrontational and even permitted civil disobedience of laws perceived to be unjust. This was simply too radical for the law-and-order evangelist.

According to Graham, King acknowledged in reply that his work in street demonstrations was only part of what needed to be done, and that it was also necessary for the hearts of people to be changed. Demonstrations, congressional legislation, and judicial enforcement could change behavior and practice but not hearts and attitudes. This, King reportedly said, is the reason that Graham's crusades were so important, that it was so necessary for Graham to remain in the stadiums rather than join him in the streets.[24]

Curiously, the content of King's reply, as reported by Graham, seems fitting, if not perfectly convenient, for one whose temperament, theology, and ideology were aligned against the tactics and goals of civil disobedience. And this gets to an important point. At the very least, it is problematic for Graham to claim that he was merely following King's advice to keep preaching the gospel to desegregated groups in the stadiums, for the reason that he could have had greater influence "on the white establishment" than he would have had by marching.[25] The implication, after all, is that Graham would have joined the street demonstrations if only King had advised him to do so. But this is certainly far-fetched, for all the evidence suggests that it would have been highly unlikely for Graham ever to have locked elbows with King in a march through any part of the segregated South.

In any case, King paid tribute to Graham's crusades, allegedly claiming that without them his own work in the civil rights struggle "would be much harder."[26] There was truth in this claim, of course, and one cannot help but wonder just how much Graham's crusades would have contributed to the goal of the direct action campaigns led by King had the evangelist consistently and publicly offered them his endorsement, as well as actually participated in some of them, such as the march on Washington in 1963 and the march from Selma to Montgomery in 1965.

But this was not to be the case. Graham's legalistic approach to social problems simply would not allow for it. Although he slowly came to see that preaching alone was not adequate and that one had to do something to witness to love, as King had done during the Montgomery boycott, Graham could muster no appreciation at all for civil disobedience that included breaking laws—even unjust laws. Throughout the civil rights movement, Graham continued to oppose civil disobedience, standing firm on the principle that citizens should obey all laws, just and unjust. He conceded that protest marches and civil disobedience aroused the conscience of the nation, but his main point of emphasis was that there must be law and order in society.

The potential for anarchy was always the greater evil for Graham—far greater than the unjust laws of discrimination and segregation—and it is difficult not to wonder whether this legalism was merely the result of his privileged location. Would Graham have been so adamant and consistent in holding this legalistic stance had he been among the socially, economically, and politically oppressed who were being victimized by violence every day of their existence? Whatever the case may be, Graham consistently rejected civil disobedience. Like most white moderates, he was for law and order, first, foremost, and last, no matter what.

Fascinatingly, Graham coupled this legalist approach with his revivalist theology and a strategy of diffusion. During the Selma crisis in 1965, for example, he reiterated his disdain for civil disobedience, even to attain civil and human rights, and in the same breath sought to shift the focus—and blame—away from the brutal actions of the whites of Alabama. William Martin makes this point when he writes that Graham's

> observations were of the nonconfrontational, blame-diffusing sort that black and white civil rights activists so resented. Alabama had its problems, he conceded, but so did other parts of the country, and using Alabama as a whipping boy diverted attention "from other areas where the problem is just as acute." Further, as he had been saying all along, only "a spiritual and moral awakening" could solve such problems. In the meantime, all parties should obey all laws, "no matter how much we may dislike them."[27]

A CRITICAL FRIENDSHIP

Graham's response to the Selma campaign was a classic case of his wanting to befriend, at the same time, his white racist southern brothers and sisters as well as African Americans who were the recipients of white supremacist antics. There is no evidence that he saw clearly enough the inconsistency in this stance to modify it, and here I cannot help but recall Malcolm X's declaration to white moderates and liberals that they could not simultaneously be friends of the likes of racist Mississippi senator James Eastland and the friends of black people.

As for their own relationship, Graham and King sought to remain on friendly terms with one another. Graham was a pietistic evangelist and King a social reformer, yet a quiet, albeit begrudging, respect and admiration seemed to exist between them throughout King's life. Helping the relationship along was a tacit agreement "to confine their cooperation to privacy."[28]

Of particular note, however, is that when one or the other was in disagreement, it was Graham who more often publicly named and criticized King, as he did in response to King's civil disobedience and his linking of the civil rights struggle with the war in Vietnam.

Although King most assuredly criticized Graham's ideas and stances, he seldom named him in public. Instead, aware that Graham was among the

leading white moderates in the South, he named and criticized the ideas and
practice of white moderates generally. In a number of instances King surely
had Graham in mind, but he declined to actually name him. For example,
when Graham called for a cooling-off period during the Birmingham sit-ins
in 1963 and asked for "a period of quietness in which moderation prevails,"
King did not name him in the famous "Letter from Birmingham Jail," in which
he criticized those white moderates and liberals who called for gradualism,
moderation, and avoidance of extremism.[29] In this regard King exhibited a
deeper sense of Christian humility than the great evangelist.

That Graham named King was also an issue of race privilege and not just
one of politeness. Still, there is one area that Graham did not address in public, and that involved the content of his confidential discussions with J. Edgar
Hoover. Looking back, Graham has said that he was pleased to count King a
friend.[30] He also admits, however, that the FBI director and some of the people around King later poisoned his thinking about him. Graham has not
revealed the content of these discussions, but it most certainly affected his
friendship with King. Indeed, Daddy King was probably close to the truth
when he said that Martin's and Graham's was "a distant" friendship.[31]

SERIOUS ABOUT PEACE?

Another apparent strain on their friendship centered on their respective
stances on the Vietnam War and Graham's public criticism of King's pacifist
position. Opposed to pacifism, Christian or otherwise, Graham consistently
placed himself within the just war tradition,[32] believing that there will be war
as long as there are sinful hearts in the world, and that, until Jesus comes again
to establish peace on earth, nations sometimes have an obligation to conduct
war in order to restrain sin.

Coupled with this was Graham's high sense of the status and destiny of the
United States. In 1956, for example, his unabashed Americanism led him to claim
that the United States is "the key nation of the world" and "truly the last bulwark
of Christian civilization."[33] Believing the United States to be superior to other
nations—morally, spiritually, and physically—the evangelist stated that while the
United States had a "God-appointed mission" to save the world, it was essentially
a peaceful nation and did not uncritically or maliciously seek to instigate war.[34]

With his just war stance and abiding Americanism, Graham simply could
not tolerate either King's pacifism or his identification of the United States as
the most violent nation in the world, and in spite of their private cooperation
at times, the evangelist was sharply critical of King's anti–Vietnam War sentiments. Although he would eventually question the war in Vietnam, wondering

how the United States ever got involved in it in the first place, Graham publicly lambasted King when he came out against the war in the famous Riverside Church address on April 4, 1967. Graham's public criticism, which quickly found its way into national publications, suggested that King's anti–Vietnam War stance harmed the civil rights movement and served to rebuke black soldiers fighting honorably for their country in Vietnam.

At the time, Graham himself claimed not to take sides as to whether the United States should be involved in Vietnam, although he did believe that inasmuch as the United States was already there, it would be irresponsible to leave before there was a successful outcome.[35]

Determining Graham's position on the Vietnam War is not easy, because to this point it is not exactly clear what he actually said to Presidents Kennedy, Johnson, and Nixon, in part because of his insistence on disagreeing or being adversarial with such persons only in private. To have publicized his disagreements, he maintained, would only have meant that he would not be sought out for advice again.[36] This is understandable, but it is not the stance of one who does ministry in accordance with ethical prophecy.

ETHICAL PROPHECY, THE CHURCH, AND HUMAN EXPERIENCE

We have thus far seen that while safeguarding his relationships with the powers that be, Graham has not been an ethical prophet when dealing with matters of race and war, and he has never exhibited the level of enthusiasm and the sense of urgency about the beloved community that King had.

The ethical prophet is not concerned about achieving justice either in an abstract sense or in some distant kingdom. Rather, the ethical prophet always has a sense of dire urgency about justice here on earth, believing that persons generally, and oppressed poor persons in particular, are so utterly precious that God demands justice right now, not tomorrow, next week, or some other more acceptable time for the privileged and powerful. And the ethical prophet is not persuaded by arguments that only the miraculous intervention of divine forces can establish justice on earth. On the contrary, the ethical prophet is always convinced that humans have the ability, right here and now, to work with God in establishing a community of love and that such work can and will succeed.

This is the type of prophet that King was. From the time he was in seminary, he believed that the kingdom of God—a society in which persons will be ruled supremely by love and the will of God—demands that people cooperate with God right now in establishing justice here on earth. Precisely because Jesus taught his disciples to pray "thy will be done, on earth as it is in heaven," King believed that no matter how bad things appear on earth at any given time, the faithful must not lose hope that human and divine cooperation can bring about God's purpose in the world. God will not do for human beings what they can do for themselves through cooperative endeavor, faith, and relentless struggle. "Rather," King stated, "both man and God, made one in a marvelous unity of purpose through an overflowing love as the free gift of himself on the part of God and by perfect obedience and receptivity on the part of man, can transform the old into the new and drive out the deadly cancer of sin."[37] Since God is always faithful and present in the world, it is up to human beings to choose to cooperate with one another and God to eradicate social injustice of all kinds—especially segregation and unjust wars. "God has promised to cooperate with us," King rightly noted, "when we seek to cast evil from our lives and become true children of his divine will."[38]

This is what Graham and so many others under the influence of white revivalist Christianity fail to see. Refusing the mantle of ethical prophecy, they fail to see that social evil can be removed not by merely proclaiming the gospel, accepting Jesus, or calling on God to remove it, but only when the faithful surrender their safety and choose to work cooperatively with God—in prayer, evangelism, and social action—right here on earth.

It is this core message of ethical prophecy that King hoped the church would take up and live out. King clearly did not see the church as a feel-good institution whose ministry is divorced from the devastating social occurrences of the day. While he understood the need for the church to perform the function of comfort both for its members and for the beaten and crushed of society, he was also quite explicit about reminding the church of its prophetic function amid social injustice. "If the church does not recapture its prophetic zeal," he said, "it will become an irrelevant social club without moral or spiritual authority."[39] The church is called to be an active participant in the struggle for peace and justice, which means that it must "free itself from the shackles of a deadening status quo."[40]

King had a sense of urgency about ethical prophecy—about achieving the beloved community—that Graham and most otherwise well-meaning whites clearly lacked, and perhaps this was partly because of their different experiences. Take racism alone. Unlike Graham, King experienced racism—despite his middle-class status in the South—from the time he was a child and into adulthood. Every day of his life he saw the effects of racism and discrimination on his people throughout the South and the rest of the nation. He personally knew what it felt like when others denied him basic respect and dignity because of the color of his skin, and he knew what it felt like to see others deny those same things to those he loved. For example, he witnessed the adverse effects of cramped, low-income ghetto housing on his children when he and

Mrs. King decided to move them to Chicago during the campaign there in the mid-1960s. The conditions had such a devastating effect on the psyche and behavior of their children that they decided to send them back to Atlanta. And while King could not do the same with the other children of the ghetto, he felt that the quality of their lives demanded his efforts, right here and now, to make their world a better place.

If only Graham had experienced the same, things might have been different. Things could have been different, for the promise was always there, and sometimes the promise became real. In 1965, for example, Graham took constructive action in response to the brutal murder of the Rev. James Reeb, a white Unitarian pastor from Boston who offered his help in Selma in 1965. While in a Honolulu hospital, the evangelist heard about Reeb's murder and immediately scaled back on other obligations and instructed his associates to organize meetings for him in several cities in Alabama.[41]

But contrast this with the senseless murder of Jimmy Lee Jackson by a white policeman near Selma only weeks before Reeb's death. The youthful Jackson was a farm laborer, church deacon, and civil rights activist—and the color of his skin was black. And, given the harsh reality of race politics, this meant that Jackson was not the type of person whose murder would provoke national outrage or direct presidential action. (After learning about Reeb, President Johnson expressed his shock, sent flowers to Reeb's widow, and arranged for her to fly to Alabama, among other things.)

King lamented and grieved over the difference in reactions to the two deaths, no doubt believing that had people like Johnson and Graham taken just a bit of Jimmy Lee Jackson into their personal realm of experiences, as they had with Reeb, things could have been much better.

Perhaps Graham's reaction to Reeb's murder suggests that had he had experiences similar to King's, he might have had a sense of dire urgency about achieving the beloved community and that he would have been much more open to direct confrontation against racism and injustice, to preaching about the importance of such a method and, when possible, even to participating in some of the protest marches.

Or perhaps this, too, is just a dream.

Although in recent years Graham has named racism as "the biggest social problem" in the nation and the world, he continues to believe that the social system and society are evil because of the evil in the hearts of individuals.[42] Unfortunately, Graham's view continues to be simplistic because of the absence of power analysis and his continued naive perfectionist belief that converted individuals are the hope of society.

Whether Graham agreed with King's vision of the beloved community or not, there is no question that he disagreed with his method for achieving it. As the end of his evangelistic career approaches, one can only hope that on reflection he can now see that God has always needed us humans to help achieve God's purpose in the world.

NOTES

1. Quoted in William McLoughlin, *Modern Revivalism: Charles Grandison Finney to Billy Graham* (New York: Ronald Press, 1959), 500. While separating himself from apolitical fundamentalists, Graham nevertheless claimed strict adherence to the authority of the Bible and accepted the virgin birth of Jesus, his atoning death and bodily resurrection, salvation by grace through faith, and the second coming.
2. See Mary Alice Mulligan and Rufus Burrow Jr., *Daring to Speak in God's Name: Ethical Prophecy in Ministry* (Cleveland: Pilgrim Press, 2002).
3. Marshall Frady, *Billy Graham: A Parable of American Righteousness* (Boston: Little, Brown, 1979), 412.
4. Quoted in William Martin, *A Prophet with Honor: The Billy Graham Story* (New York: William Morrow, 1991), 361.
5. McLoughlin, *Modern Revivalism*, 526.
6. Billy Graham, "What Ten Years Have Taught Me," *Christian Century*, February 17, 1960, 188.
7. Quoted in McLoughlin, *Modern Revivalism*, 505.
8. McLoughlin, *Modern Revivalism*, 527.
9. David Frost, *Billy Graham: Personal Thoughts of a Public Man* (Colorado Springs, CO: Victor Books, 1997), 63.
10. Quoted in Martin, *Prophet with Honor*, 235.
11. *The Papers of Martin Luther King, Jr.*, ed. Susan Carson et al. (Berkeley: University of California Press, 2000), 4:238.
12. Billy Graham, *Just as I Am: The Autobiography of Billy Graham* (San Francisco: HarperSanFrancisco, 1997), 314; Taylor Branch, *Parting the Waters: America in the King Years, 1954–63* (New York: Simon & Schuster, 1988), 227.
13. Branch, *Parting the Waters*, 227.
14. For details on this subject, see ibid., 228.
15. *Papers*, 4:457.
16. Ibid., 4:457–58.
17. McLoughlin, *Modern Revivalism*, 526. McLoughlin made the erroneous claim in 1957 that Graham began to oppose desegregation only *after* the *Brown* decision.
18. *Papers*, 4:458.
19. Ibid.
20. Quoted in McLoughlin, *Modern Revivalism*, 502.
21. *Papers*, 4:265.
22. See Branch, *Parting the Waters*, 228.
23. Quoted in John Pollock, *Billy Graham: Evangelist to the World* (New York: Harper & Row, 1979), 127.
24. Graham, *Just as I Am*, 426.
25. Ibid.
26. Quoted in Pollock, *Billy Graham*, 127.
27. Martin, *A Prophet with Honor*, 314.

28. Branch, *Parting the Waters*, 228, 594.

29. "Billy Graham Urges Restraint in Sit-Ins," *New York Times*, April 18, 1963, 21; King, *Why We Can't Wait* (New York: Harper & Row, 1963), 82–83.

30. Frady, *Billy Graham*, 416; Graham, *Just as I Am*, 314.

31. Edward L. Moore, "Billy Graham and Martin Luther King, Jr.: An Inquiry into White and Black Revivalistic Tradition," PhD diss., Vanderbilt University, May 1979, 453.

32. Billy Graham, *Answers to Life's Problems* (New York: W Publishing Group, 2003), 258, 259.

33. Quoted in McLoughlin, *Modern Revivalism*, 508.

34. Graham, *Answers to Life's Problems*, 258.

35. Martin, *Prophet with Honor*, 345.

36. Frost, *Billy Graham*, 51.

37. Martin Luther King Jr., "Answer to a Perplexing Question," in *Strength to Love* (New York: Harper & Row, 1963), 124.

38. Ibid., 125–26.

39. King, "A Knock at Midnight," in *Strength to Love*, 47.

40. Ibid.

41. Moore, "Billy Graham and Martin Luther King, Jr.," 460.

42. See "Billy Graham: Racism Remains a Problem of Society," Glasgow.Daily Times.com.

12

Above Politics? Graham
after Watergate

STEVEN P. MILLER

By the early 1980s, Billy Graham had safely entered his third and final stage as an American public figure. His initial, fundamentalist phase lasted only as long as he remained a sociopolitical outsider—a firebrand novelty or a saw-dusted throwback. The 1952 election of President Dwight Eisenhower then helped to thrust Graham forward as a spokesperson and symbol for a resurgent public evangelicalism seeking to rescue the United States from atheistic communism abroad and morally acquiescent liberalism at home. Two decades later, the Nixon presidency seemingly mocked the ideal of Christian statesmanship upon which so much of Graham's political ethic rested. In the years following Watergate, the evangelist cultivated a noticeably more moderate image. He reconsidered his dalliances with partisan politics (after partly acknowledging them) and surprised critics with his newfound support for nuclear disarmament. The new Graham drew sustenance from his increasingly international and inclusive ministry. He stood as an elder statesman—an icon beyond partisanship and, by the 1990s, beyond the culture wars as well.

The familiar narrative of a postpolitical Graham, however, does justice neither to the full breadth of his legacy nor to his ongoing comfort with the powers that be. The journalistic tale of Graham's self-described "pilgrimage" toward moderation has highlighted certain changes at the expense of other telling continuities. Popular portraits of Graham have exaggerated the nature of his depoliticization. Specifically, they have elided his social ties with the emerging Christian Right, underestimated his presence in the Reagan and George H. W.

179

Bush White Houses, exaggerated his defense of Bill Clinton, and not connected the dots between the motif of Christian statesmanship and the faith narrative of George W. Bush. In short, Graham never completely abandoned the world of politics.

With time, Graham's post-Watergate claim that "everybody knows I've become politically neutral" grew in credibility.[1] His increasingly nonpartisan identity benefited greatly from his public distance from the Christian Right, the new standard against which the media and many Americans measured Christian political involvement. While Graham criticized Jerry Falwell and the larger Christian Right out of principle, he also knew that even a partial association with such a controversial movement could severely hamper his evangelistic outreach. His exact relationship to the Christian Right thus remains unclear or oversimplified.

In key respects, Graham helped to construct the political and religious culture that made the Christian Right possible. He gave public expression to the shift among many post–World War II evangelicals away from separatist fundamentalism and toward greater social and political engagement. During the 1950s, he helped to make evangelicalism a vital component of anticommunist discourse. He was the best-known, if hardly the noisiest, postwar exponent of "Christian Americanism," bluntly upholding an "American way of life" that could survive the challenge of atheistic communism only through "an old-fashioned, heaven-sent revival."[2] Even after Graham toned down his Cold War jeremiads, he continued to view patriotism as a normative manifestation of piety. His feelings were prominently on display during the 1970 Honor America Day in Washington, DC. Graham delivered a rousing defense of American pride and patriotism from the steps of the Lincoln Memorial. Paraphrasing Winston Churchill, he implored his audience to "Pursue the vision, reach the goal, fulfill the American dream—and as you move to do it, never give in! Never give in! Never! Never! Never!"[3]

Graham had forever urged God-fearing Americans to express their values through political involvement. One year before the 1952 presidential election, he predicted that the "Christian people of America are going to vote as a bloc for the man with the strongest moral and spiritual platform, regardless of his views on other matters."[4] His repeated calls during the 1960s for alternative Christian "demonstrations" implied openness to forming a faith-based political movement. Moreover, his evangelistic efforts modeled the type of conservative ecumenism necessary to create such a bloc. His subsequent advice to Presidents Nixon and Carter that they take note of conservative Protestants as an electoral group derived in part from a long-voiced desire for greater evangelical influence on policy making.

During the 1950s and 1960s, however, Graham and his fellow neo-evangelicals (that is, moderate fundamentalists who refashioned themselves as evangelicals) remained most interested in electing "Christian statesmen," leaders who shared their faith perspective or who recognized the integral contribution of evangelical Christianity to the nation's health. Graham regularly urged Christians to run for office and had at least pondered doing so himself. Postwar evangelicals assumed, in the words of historian D. G. Hart, that "being born again results in holy instincts about the way societies should be ordered and governments run."[5] They saw no inherent conflict between Christian statesmanship and the Establishment Clause. Christian principles, they believed, had always informed the American political tradition, while the true threat to church-state separation, many of them still suspected, came from Roman Catholicism. "We believe in separation of Church and State in this land," said Texas governor Price Daniel in *Christianity Today*, "but never have we believed in separation of Church and statesmen."[6]

Graham never departed from his preference for Christian statesmanship, and this consistency eventually helped to distinguish him from the more activist Christian Right. The Watergate affair only reinforced his belief that the political realm was in dire need of more committed Christians.[7] He hoped his crusades would result in "spiritual growth in the political arena. We want to see the finest of people entering politics at the local, state, and national level."[8] However, Graham hesitated to link Christianity with specific platforms that might commit believers to positions not explicitly spiritual in nature. He and many fellow evangelicals continued to draw a distinction between the unassailable good of Christians in office and the more ambiguous status of Christianity as a political movement. Doing so, of course, allowed him to deny that his spiritual message sometimes had political implications—a move that became particularly important following the Watergate crisis. Just as Graham was trying to cleanse himself from the stain of partisan politics, though, a vocal group of conservative evangelicals and fundamentalists started challenging the distinction between Christian statesmanship and faith-based political activism.

Graham possessed obvious and sometimes close ties with many of the founding fathers of the Christian Right. For example, Bill Bright, the influential Campus Crusade for Christ leader who flirted with politics in the mid-1970s, had worked closely with Graham during the previous two decades. Graham was involved in early discussions about the Christian Embassy, an outreach to Washington, DC, politicos that Bright helped to found (and from which Graham eventually distanced himself).[9] In 1976, Graham publicly supported the Senate bid of Arizona Congressman John Conlan, a strongly conservative Republican who had long sought to mobilize evangelical voters.[10] Graham's ties also extended to several ministers-cum-evangelists who mobilized their empires in support of the Christian Right later in the decade. Graham gave early encouragement to the ministry of Fort Worth televangelist James Robison and later spoke at the dedications for both D. James Kennedy's Coral Ridge Presbyterian and Pat Robertson's Christian Broadcasting Network headquarters.[11]

Moreover, Graham appeared to sympathize with important facets of the Christian Right agenda. That platform owed much to the emergence during the 1970s of a new set of social issues—including sex education, women's liberation, homosexuality, and with time, abortion—that generally revolved around gender norms and familial authority. To be sure, Graham did not directly link these matters with electoral discontentedness (as he had with law-and-order themes a decade earlier). He took no formal stance on the Equal Rights Amendment, distanced himself from the prolife movement before abortion became a partisan issue, and even conceded the possibility that a gay person could be a Christian.[12] On the other hand, he politely dismissed women's liberation, professed admiration for the anti–gay rights work of Anita Bryant, and helped to found a pioneering Protestant antiabortion organization, the Christian Action Council.[13] On a fundamental level, then, Graham shared the Christian Right's sense of national decline. He theorized a forty-year moral slippage that coincided with forty years of liberal rule (along with, of course, the Israelites' time in the wilderness).[14]

Other than not formally aligning himself with the Christian Right, Graham did little to arrest its germination. Indeed, he was something of an early shadow presence within a movement he would eventually criticize. In 1979, Graham attended a foundational meeting of the Christian Right, a two-day prayer and strategy session held to address the nation's moral decline. The participants at the Dallas gathering included Robison, Bright, and Robertson. Robison recalled that Graham declared himself in sympathy with the attendees, but stressed that his past experiences with politics precluded any public association with their efforts.[15] The following year, Graham offered only faint support for another Christian Right milestone, the Washington for Jesus rally.[16] More importantly, he claimed to have turned down an offer to speak at a more famous gathering, the August 1980 National Affairs Briefing, at which GOP presidential candidate Ronald Reagan endorsed the Christian Right.[17]

Graham is better remembered, however, for his subsequent chiding of the Christian Right. His first move in this direction actually came in 1976, long before the Christian Right had formally coalesced. During that first presidential election after Watergate, when Graham placed a premium on asserting his political neutrality, he declared himself "opposed to organizing Christians into a political bloc."[18] The evangelist also canceled an engagement at a 1976 Bright-sponsored prayer rally in Dallas, deeming the election-eve event too political.[19] Graham's public censure of the Christian Right proper began immediately after the 1980 election, during which the movement had played a prominent role. Jerry Falwell's Moral Majority "is not my cup of tea," Graham declared. "I do not intend to use what little moral influence I may have on secular, nonmoral issues like [opposing] the Panama Canal [treaty]," he added, referring to a major shibboleth of many conservatives. In a "Dear Jerry" letter, Graham politely, but firmly, admonished Falwell for failing to address arms control and other social justice issues. Falwell, an avowed fundamentalist with whom the evangelist possessed only minimal social ties, risked "los[ing] sight of the priority of the Gospel."[20]

Graham's critique of the Christian Right represented a consistent application of his theological values as a neo-evangelical. His behavior suggested that he drew a parallel between the "political bloc" of the Christian Right and the hard-core fundamentalist separatism that his brand of evangelicals had long repudiated. Such an association, while seemingly ironic, made genealogical sense. Even back in the 1940s, when Graham still had the support of the Bob Jones community, Graham had chided "ultra-Fundamentalism" for its obsession with theological purity.[21] As Graham's evangelistic inclusiveness became more apparent, fundamentalist organs, including *Bible Baptist Tribune* (the flagship publication of Jerry Falwell's home denomination), attacked Graham for his ecumenism and moderate support for social causes like desegregation. In the 1970s, Falwell and a number of other fundamentalists starkly reversed course and embraced political activism. Going far beyond the neo-evangelical focus on Christian statesmanship (which, to be sure, entailed a general political conservatism), Falwell and his peers employed the divisive language they had previously applied to sectarian squabbles. Graham could have affirmed many of the basic principles of the Moral Majority. Still, he could not support an organization led by someone who, as late as 1981, declared himself "a Fundamentalist—big F!" and urged Graham-style evangelicals to "reacknowledge your fundamentalist roots" and cease "trying to accommodate the Gospel to the pitiful philosophies of unregenerate humankind."[22] In response, Graham voiced legitimate skepticism "that the Moral Majority would represent more than 10 percent of the evangelicals in America."[23] The evangelist, then, continued a decades-long pattern by chiding this latest group of fundamentalists for prioritizing ideological trees over the evangelistic forest.

In the area of foreign policy, however, Graham did differ explicitly with the Christian Right. Starting in 1979 (the same year Falwell founded Moral Majority), Graham surprised observers by announcing his conversion to the cause of disarmament and nuclear abolition. In a CBS news interview, the former anticommunist militant lamented the development of the atomic bomb, as well as President Harry Truman's decision to use it.[24] Elsewhere, Graham called for "SALT X," by which he meant "total destruction of nuclear arms."[25]

He consistently stressed, though, that he was neither a pacifist nor a unilateral-ist.[26] Still, his comments drew praise from heretofore critics, such as Southern Baptist rebel Will D. Campbell.[27]

By washing his hands of the Christian Right, of course, Graham also pro-tected his image. In particular, he sought to conserve his appeal to broad audi-ences, his ties to leading public figures, and, more than ever, his possible access to prospective new crusade locations, including the Eastern Bloc and China. Never one to court controversy, Graham apparently viewed disarmament as a less contentious issue than abortion and "some of the other issues that evoke so much emotion."[28] He likely also had in mind his legacy. The Nixon era, he claimed, had taught him the danger of playing God. "I learned my lesson the hard way," he said.[29] Part of that lesson involved recognizing the perils of Chris-tian Americanism. Now, he said, "I no longer think we are a Christian nation."[30]

Graham's neo-evangelicalism and his impulse to preserve his status did not lend themselves to the formation of a partisan political movement. Yet neither of those characteristics precluded his support for Christian-friendly leaders who also happened to share his general political outlook. Two such persons, Richard Nixon and George H. W. Bush, appreciated this distinction. A postpresidential Nixon advised the evangelist to steer clear of the Christian Right, while Vice President Bush privately differentiated Graham's kind of Christian conservative from those "flamboyant money-mad, teary temple builders."[31] The continuing attachment of Graham to the Christian statesman trope did not sustain a story line during the era of the Christian Right. His post-Watergate style differed so notably from the headline-grabbing pronouncements of Falwell and Robertson that few observers perceived it as a type of political behavior.

The 1980 election of Ronald Reagan promised Graham the kind of access to the White House he had lacked since the Ford administration. Reagan and Graham first met during the early 1950s, and their acquaintanceship deepened after Reagan won the 1966 California gubernatorial race as a law-and-order Republican. Their relationship, though, never entailed the frankly political tone that had been a reflex to President Nixon. Reagan lacked the utilitarian calculation Nixon brought to religious matters. While neither an especially pious nor doctrinaire Christian, Reagan did possess an abiding interest in spir-itual matters, especially biblical prophecy, a topic Graham addressed during a 1971 appearance before the California legislature.[32]

Although Graham declined to describe the contents of the absentee ballot he cast in the 1980 election, Reagan was undoubtedly his candidate of choice (especially after two closer friends, John Connally and George H. W. Bush, had ended their efforts to gain the GOP nomination).[33] Graham played noth-ing resembling a direct role in the Reagan campaign, yet he was not a complete stranger to it. During the height of primary season, he met with Reagan and campaign director Ed Meese for a publicized breakfast in Indianapolis, where the evangelist was holding a crusade. Graham declined a casual request from Reagan to put in a good word for him in North Carolina, where the candidate faced a tight primary race.[34] Footage from the meeting, including the congratulations Graham offered Reagan for his victory in the Texas primary, made the national news feed.[35] Later in the campaign, Graham apparently did consent to serve as a liaison to the Christian Right. Following the 1980 Republican convention—the only convention Graham prayed at that year—he vacationed with vice presidential nominee Bush in Kennebunkport, Maine. A photograph of the visit appeared in the *Washington Post*.[36] At the time, Bush was seeking to amend his identity as a party moderate. According to Falwell, Graham called the Moral Majority head to gauge his reaction to Bush as a running mate. "Billy," Falwell recalled saying, "I'll just pray that God will give Ronald Reagan eight years of wonderful health."[37]

Graham possessed a discernible comfort level with the Reagan White House, where he spent a number of evenings, as well as a few mornings.[38] He welcomed the prospect of visible demonstrations of faith from the administration. He prayed at an inauguration-day church service attended by the Reagans, and hosted a breakfast for White House officials in 1985.[39] Graham corresponded with the president, Nancy Reagan, and staffers on numerous occasions and felt comfortable requesting favors. In 1987, for example, Reagan asked French president Francois Mitterand to meet with Graham during an upcoming crusade.[40] In most cases, Graham's communication with the White House lacked the political content of the evangelist's interactions with the Nixon administration. While Reagan knew he could expect "support and friendship" from the evangelist, he did not jump at staff advice that crusade appearances might boost his status among mainstream evangelicals or bolster his tax-cut proposals.[41]

On several occasions during Reagan's first term, Graham privately lobbied on behalf of particular causes. Even before the president took office, Graham put in a good word on behalf of Nixon-era acquaintance Alexander Haig, whom Reagan nominated as secretary of state.[42] The evangelist was particularly useful in Reagan's efforts to retain the support of the Christian Right without acting on its core agenda. One matter of concern involved a proposal to grant full diplomatic status to the Vatican, a matter that had riled conservative Protestants for several decades. In 1982 or 1983, Reagan staffer William Clark asked Graham to gauge the likely response of conservative evangelicals to a policy of recognition. Graham and an aide contacted prominent mainstream evangelicals, including the editor of *Christianity Today*, as well as Christian Right leaders such as Falwell and Robertson. In a detailed report, Graham hesitated to offer a formal policy recommendation, but noted a perceived decline in anti-Catholic sentiments among evangelicals.[43]

The evangelist served a similar liaison function in the area of weapons policy. Apparently, Graham's support for nuclear abolition did not entail opposition to the proliferation of antimissile technology. According to Falwell, Graham encouraged several senators to support Reagan's sale of AWACS defense planes to Saudi Arabia, a policy the Moral Majority rejected as a threat to Israel. A Reagan aide cited Graham's position when trying to change the mind of the Moral Majority leader.[44] Reagan informed Graham that his opposition to unilateral arms control "will be most useful in . . . anything from AWACS to our disarmament talks with the Soviets."[45]

Graham was not always on the same page with the Reagan administration, however. For example, Reagan higher-ups strongly opposed Graham's involvement in a 1982 disarmament conference held in Moscow for world religious leaders. They feared (correctly) that the Soviets would use Graham as a propaganda tool. The most intense opposition came from U.S. ambassador to the Soviet Union Arthur Hartman, along with members of the National Security Council (NSC), who fretted that "Billy has been had already" by the Soviets.[46] While Graham resisted administration appeals to reconsider his travel plans, he had no personal desire to hinder Reagan's foreign policy. He sent two aides to discuss the conference with an administration official, who promptly reported the details to Reagan.[47] Vice President Bush eventually assumed authority over the matter and chose to mediate, rather than resist, Graham's plans. Bush briefed a Graham assistant on arms control policy and facilitated a meeting between the evangelist and Soviet Pentecostals.[48] As Reagan shifted toward a policy of engagement with the Soviets, Graham encouraged the president's existing eschatological optimism concerning the fate of the communist nation. "There is no doubt in my mind that there is a quiet religious revival on throughout the Soviet Union, and in much of eastern Europe," Graham wrote to Reagan on the cusp of his critical December 1987 summit with Soviet president Mikhail Gorbachev. "I think this can be kept in the back of your mind at all times in your dealings with them."[49]

During the Reagan years, Graham maintained even closer ties to Vice President Bush, whom the evangelist had known and admired since the late 1960s. Graham was an overnight guest of the vice president two weeks into the Reagan administration.[50] During Bush's successful 1988 presidential campaign, the religiously demure candidate hesitated to play up his ties with Graham—a point a campaign biography ironically highlighted. Readers also learned from a prominent evangelical that Graham considered Bush "the best friend he has in the whole world outside his own immediate staff."[51] During the 1988 campaign, Graham prayed at both the Republican and Democratic conventions but attended the entire GOP meeting. He accepted an invitation from the Bush family to be present for the official nomination.[52] After Bush took office, Graham continued in his roles as friend and spiritual advisor. During the run-up to the 1991 Persian Gulf War, Graham privately and publicly blessed military intervention against Iraqi president Saddam Hussein.[53] The Bushes invited Graham to stay with them during their final night in the White House. The evangelist then prayed a new president, Bill Clinton, into the Oval Office.[54]

Graham's willingness to identify with President Clinton endures as evidence in favor of his bipartisanship. It also garnered no small amount of surprise and criticism from antiabortion activists and conservative pundits. The former protested Graham's acceptance of Clinton's invitation to pray at his first inaugural, an offer the president repeated four years later.[55] In contrast to most public evangelicals, Graham did not criticize the social policies of Clinton. He also hesitated to judge the president's personal transgressions. Appearing on the *Today Show* two months into the Monica Lewinsky scandal, Graham offered pastoral forgiveness to Clinton. Graham cited "the frailty of human nature," along with the fact that women "just go wild over" Clinton. The evangelist's remarks drew prompt retorts from conservative commentators Cal Thomas and Bill Bennett, who noted that Clinton had yet to acknowledge having had sexual relations with Lewinsky.[56]

Yet Graham did not grant Clinton a full pardon. Immediately following the *Today Show* flap, the evangelist adopted a significantly more circumspect tone in a *New York Times* op-ed piece, titled "The Moral Weight of Leadership." Graham sandwiched the heart of his message between warnings against reflexively judging his "personal friend" for still-alleged transgressions. Still, he did not wholly depoliticize the president's private life. "A leader's moral character . . . influences the way he or she does his or her job," Graham wrote. "There simply is no such thing as an impenetrable fire wall [*sic*] between what we do privately and what we do publicly." Indeed, he added, "the moral meltdown in our country in part results from a failure of leadership."[57] As the impeachment crisis wore on, Graham went no further than to say he was "very disappointed" in Clinton.[58] Already, though, the evangelist had highlighted an issue—character—that remained on the political front-burner throughout the 2000 presidential campaign.

During that campaign, an aging Graham supported the electoral beneficiary of the character issue, George W. Bush. The Bush team repeatedly highlighted the life-changing 1985 encounter between the candidate and Graham in Kennebunkport. During those summer weekends with the Bush family in the 1980s, Graham would preach and make himself available for questions about faith matters.[59] The first published account of Graham's influence on George W. Bush appeared in the aforementioned 1988 campaign biography of his father. The younger Bush recalled that one family session with Graham had particularly affected him. The following year, he said, Graham "made it a point to call me aside and ask how things were going. . . . It's an example of one man's impact on another person's life. And it was a very strong impact."[60] In George W. Bush's 1999 autobiography, the primary source for most subsequent descriptions of the weekend, the events occur during one visit, climaxing with a stroll at Walker's Point. Their conversation, Bush wrote, "planted a mustard seed in my soul. . . . It was the beginning of a new walk where I would commit my heart to Jesus Christ."[61] The encounter was likely one of the many friendly faith checkups the evangelist routinely administered.

Bush invoked Graham and the Kennebunkport story from the start of his two-year presidential campaign. On the same weekend when Bush launched his campaign exploratory committee, he delivered two identical sermons at a prominent Southern Baptist church in Houston. He noted how Graham had inspired him "to search my heart and recommit my life to Jesus Christ." The Houston sermons and subsequent addresses employed language that closely echoed Graham's belief that regenerated hearts, not the imposition of positive law, represented the ultimate answer to a myriad of social ills. "To truly change the culture, we must have a spiritual renewal in the United States," Bush claimed. "Faith is a powerful tool for change," he also argued, one that could solve problems immune to prescriptive government programs.[62] Bush tapped into the evolving social consciousness of a modern American evangelicalism now undertaking innovative forms of "social concern" in such areas as hunger relief and prisoner rehabilitation. The Bush team soon subsumed such efforts, sanitized of their evangelical exclusivity, under the banner of "compassionate conservatism."[63] The electoral usefulness of Bush's faith-based theory of social change, however, lay in its prescriptive repackaging of a familiarly conservative critique of the liberal state.

Graham received mention in many, if not most, election-year accounts of Bush's faith journey and outreach to conservative evangelical voters. A Bush intimate told a campaign biographer that Graham had personally encouraged Bush to seek higher office, "because of where America is today."[64] A campaign mass mailing included a letter in which Bush mentioned his lengthy friendship with Graham.[65] On at least one occasion, Graham publicly vouched for the politically inexperienced candidate's intellect, as well as his integrity in the face of investigations into his booze-filled early adulthood. "There's a depth to him that I think [journalists] overlook," the *New York Times* quoted him as saying. "They think he's a man of little substance, but that's not true. I think that he's a man of tremendous moral character to begin with, and what they have written about his earlier years could be true of nearly all of us."[66]

Two days before the 2000 election, Graham went a step further and voiced support for a Bush victory. The setting for what can only be called Graham's endorsement of Bush was Jacksonville, Florida, in a state where the evangelist was wrapping up a three-day crusade and where Bush had staked his electoral prospects. The candidate was fending off a slip in the polls following the disclosure of a previously unacknowledged 1976 arrest for drunk driving. A week earlier, an adviser had sent Bush a strangely worded memo urging him to contact Graham about attending the Jacksonville crusade. On Sunday, November 5, Graham met with George and Laura Bush for a private prayer breakfast. The gathering took place after Bush attended a worship service with prominent Florida evangelicals and before he commenced a whirlwind final tour of the state. Florida governor Jeb Bush mentioned the breakfast on the Sunday morning news show *Face the Nation*. "I'm confident that Dr. Graham will be able to purge all that evilness from my brother's soul," the candidate's brother quipped, referring to Democratic candidate Al Gore's usage of good-and-evil rhetoric. After the prayer meeting, Graham (accompanied by his son Franklin) and the Bushes posed for photographs and talked with reporters. "I don't endorse candidates. But I've come as close to it, I guess, now as any time in my life, because I think it's extremely important," said the aging evangelist. "It's comforting to be with a close friend," Bush noted, before briefly recalling that weekend in Kennebunkport. Graham further affirmed the character of Bush, who faced accusations of covering up his arrest. "I believe in the integrity of this man," Graham told reporters. "I'll just let you guess who I voted for," he added, making sure (as he had during the Nixon years) to reiterate his nominal status as a registered Democrat. Graham's remarks, which would have made headlines in earlier decades, received only modest coverage from a print media more attuned to last-minute poll data.[67] The national papers ignored the part of his comments that most resembled a traditional endorsement: "And we believe that there's going to be a tremendous victory and change by Tuesday night in the direction of the country—putting it in good hands. . . . And if [George and Laura], by God's will, win, I'm going to do everything in my power to help make it a successful presidency."[68] The prayer breakfast details (the timing of the arrest story excepted) received prominent play in a 2004 homage to Bush's piety.[69]

As Graham shed the political residue of the Nixon era, he walked an increasingly forgiving line between his reconstructed image and the fundamental endurance not only of his basic theological assumptions but of his political inclinations as well. Prodded by Graham, the mainstream American media correctly avoided classifying him with the Christian Right. Indeed, as the Christian Right grew in prominence, Graham sometimes hardly looked conservative at all. His intimacy with Reagan and both Bushes, however, begs the question of his perceived status as a counterweight to the Christian Right.

To what extent did Graham represent a sustainable alternative to Jerry Falwell, Pat Robertson, and their peers? Graham appears to have been more successful in distinguishing himself from the Christian Right than in checking its growth. Reagan and George H. W. Bush followed Nixon in viewing Graham as a potential liaison to Protestant conservatives, while George W. Bush invoked the evangelist in presenting himself as a Christian statesman.

Graham influenced and reflected the evolution not only of American evangelicalism but also of American conservatism. His post-Watergate pilgrimage resonated with an important yet underappreciated strand of American conservatism that began to speak a compassionate language of postracialism and international human rights without abandoning a profound wariness of the liberal state. Many American evangelicals have followed Graham's path toward a greater appreciation for such issues as racial justice, AIDS relief, and environmentalism. Yet the George W. Bush era has told another story as well. During the first six years of the Bush administration, issues such as terrorism and judicial appointments drove such certifiable evangelicals as Chuck Colson and Graham's heir, Franklin, toward an antisecular tone that differed little from the Christian Right proper. Indeed, the hyperpoliticization of conservative Protestantism under Bush undermined the very distinction between fundamentalism and conservative evangelicalism that Graham's ministry had helped to cultivate and upon which arguments for Graham as a counterpoint to the Christian Right have at some level relied. Graham may have denounced the tone of politicized conservative Christianity, yet he assisted the Christian statesmen who most benefited from that same phenomenon.

NOTES

1. Genevieve Stuttaford, "PW Interviews: Billy Graham," *Publishers Weekly*, June 20, 1977, 10.
2. Daniel Kenneth Williams, "From the Pews to the Polls: The Formation of a Southern Christian Right," PhD diss., Brown University, 2005, 74–85.
3. Quoted in Billy Graham, "The Unfinished Dream," *Christianity Today*, July 31, 1970, 21. See also *Washington Post*, July 5, 1970.
4. *Greensboro Daily News* (clipping), October 17, 1951, in Billy Graham Center Archives (BGCA), Collection (CN) 360, Reel (R) 4.
5. D. G. Hart, *That Old-Time Religion in Modern America: Evangelical Protestantism in the Twentieth Century* (Chicago: Ivan R. Dee, 2002), 146.
6. Price Daniel, "God and the American Vision," *Christianity Today*, June 23, 1958, 13.
7. Raleigh press conference transcript, September 21, 1973, BGCA, CN 24, 3–22.
8. Linda Thorsby, "Graham's Hope for Crusade—Spiritual Growth," *Jackson Clarion-Ledger*, May 16, 1975, 1. See also Jim Wallis and Wes Michaelson,

"The Plan to Save America: A Disclosure of an Alarming Initiative by the Evangelical Far Right," *Sojourners*, April 1, 1976, 4–12.

9. Williams, "From the Pews to the Polls," 148–53; Rolfe H. McCollister interview, July 24, 1977, BGCA, CN 141, 13–32; Kenneth L. Woodward, "Politics from the Pulpit," *Newsweek*, September 6, 1976, 50–51.

10. "Graham Opens a Southern Crusade," *Jackson Clarion-Ledger*, May 12, 1975, 1.

11. William Martin, *With God on Our Side: The Rise of the Religious Right in America* (New York: Broadway Books, 1996), 198; *Fort Lauderdale News* (clipping), February 1, 1974, in BGCA, CN 360, R35; Dedication of Christian Broadcasting Network building, October 6, 1979, BGCA, CN 240, Video 1.

12. Graham allowed for health and rape exceptions on the matter of abortion. Marjorie Hyer, "Billy Graham Favors Law Requiring Church Finances to Be Made Public," *Washington Post*, March 24, 1979, B7; Ann Rodgers-Melnick, "Graham Quietly Wrought Changes," *Pittsburgh Post-Gazette*, May 31, 1993, 1; "Graham's Views," *Charlotte Observer*, February 7, 1976, 9.

13. Billy Graham, "Jesus and the Liberated Woman," *Ladies' Home Journal*, December 1970, 40–44, 115; *Louisville Courier-Journal* (clipping), June 17, 1977, in BGCA, CN 544, 37–3; Martin, *With God on Our Side*, 156, 193–94; Religious News Service (clipping), July 31, 1976, in BGCA, CN 345, 68; and *Sherman (Texas) Democrat* (UPI) (clipping), November 27, 1975, in BGCA, CN 360, R36.

14. Address to the Southern Newspaper Publishers Association, September 16, 1974, BGCA, CN 26, T55; Black Mountain, NC, press conference transcript, October 13, 1970, BGCA, CN 24, 1–26.

15. Martin, *With God on Our Side*, 205–6.

16. Carol Flake, *Redemptorama: Culture, Politics, and the New Evangelicalism* (New York: Anchor, 1984), 210.

17. Megan Rosenfield, "Billy Graham, Preacher to the Mighty," *Washington Post*, January 29, 1981, B1. On the Dallas meeting, see Martin, *With God on Our Side*, 214–18.

18. Woodward, "Politics from the Pulpit," 49.

19. Marjorie Hyer, "Evangelist to Launch $1 Billion World Crusade," *Washington Post*, November 18, 1977, C14.

20. Michael Reese, "Jerry Falwell's Troubles," *Newsweek*, February 23, 1981, 23; Kenneth L. Woodward, "The Split-Up Evangelicals," *Newsweek*, April 26, 1982, 91.

21. Billy Graham, "America's Hope," in Joel Carpenter, ed., *The Early Billy Graham: Sermon and Revival Accounts* (New York: Garland, 1988), 23.

22. Jerry Falwell, "Future-Ward: An Agenda for the Eighties," in Jerry Falwell, ed., *The Fundamentalist Phenomenon: The Resurgence of Conservative Christianity* (Garden City, NJ: Doubleday, 1981), 219, 222–23.

23. Woodward, "Split-up Evangelicals," 89, 91.

24. *CBS Evening News*, March 29, 1979, in BGCA, CN 74, V1; Colman McCarthy, "The Converter Appears to Be a Convert," *Washington Post*, June 29, 1979, C14.

25. Richard V. Pierard, "Billy Graham and Vietnam: From Cold Warrior to Peacemaker," *Christian Scholar's Review* 10 (1980): 38.

26. Graham address, John F. Kennedy Jr. Forum, April 20, 1982, http://ksgaccman .harvard.edu/iop/events_forum_video.asp?ID=770 (accessed October 16, 2006); "Press Statement by Dr. Billy Graham," May 19, 1982, Richard Nixon Library (RNL), Post Presidential Correspondence (PPC), 1–6.

27. Frye Gaillard, "The Conversion of Billy Graham: How the Presidents' Preacher Learned to Start Worrying and Loath the Bomb," *Progressive*, August 1982, 30.
28. Ari L. Goldman, "Graham Says Political Clerics 'Went Too Far,'" *New York Times*, January 3, 1985, B7.
29. Quoted in Woodward, "Politics from the Pulpit," 49.
30. Quoted in James Michael Beam, "'I Can't Play God Anymore,'" *McCall's*, January 1978, 154, 156.
31. Richard Nixon, *In the Arena: A Memoir of Victory, Defeat, and Renewal* (New York: Simon & Schuster, 1990), 90–91; Billy Graham, *Just as I Am: The Autobiography of Billy Graham* (San Francisco: HarperSanFrancisco, 1997), 453. George H. W. Bush, *All the Best, George Bush: My Life in Letters and Other Writings* (New York: Scribner, 1999), 320.
32. Richard V. Pierard and Robert D. Linder, *Civil Religion and the Presidency* (Grand Rapids: Zondervan, 1988), 271.
33. Rosenfield, "Billy Graham, Preacher to the Mighty," B1.
34. Graham, *Just as I Am*, 529–30.
35. *ABC Evening News*, May 4, 1980, in BGCA, CN 345, V9; WNBC newscast, May 4, 1980, in BGCA, CN 345, V10.
36. AP photograph, *Washington Post*, August 4, 1980, 4. Graham received an invitation to pray at the 1980 Democratic convention, but said a scheduling conflict with a crusade in Alberta prevented his doing so ("Graham Rejects Bid from Democrats," *Washington Post*, August 1, 1980, 29).
37. Deborah Hart Strober and Gerald S. Strober, *Billy Graham: An Oral and Narrative Biography* (San Francisco: Jossey-Bass, 2006), 99.
38. See Graham to Reagan, July 23, 1981, National Archives and Records Administration (NARA), Ronald Reagan Library (RRL), WHORM: Subject File (WHORM: SF), ME001-03, ID #042394; Graham to Nancy Reagan, August 20, 1982, NARA, RRL, WHORM: SF, CO125, ID #097558; Graham to Reagan, December 26, 1983, NARA, RRL, WHORM: SF, CO034–02, ID #193966SS; Graham to Reagan, December 17, 1987, NARA, RRL, WHORM: SF, SO002, ID #537376; and Graham to Reagan, February 8, 1988, NARA, RRL, WHORM: SF, RE010, ID #563448.
39. Rosenfield, "Billy Graham, Preacher to the Mighty," B1; Graham to Ed Meese, February 23, 1985, NARA, RRL, WHORM: SF, FG006–01, ID #297854.
40. Reagan to Francois Mitterand, July 7, 1986, NARA, RRL, WHORM: SF, TR163, ID #430849.
41. Reagan to Graham, February 17, 1981, NARA, RRL, WHORM: SF, FG001-03, ID #004680; Frederick J. Ryan to Faith Whittlesey and Ed Rollins, June 27, 1983, NARA, RRL, WHORM: SF, IV083, ID #139625; Ryan to Linda Chavez, July 2, 1985, and Ann Brock to Fred Ryan, June 28, 1985, both in NARA, RRL, WHORM: SF, IV085, ID #304533.
42. Graham to Nixon, December 15, 1980, RNL, PPC, 1-6.
43. Graham to William Clark, April 25, 1983, NARA, RRL, Executive Secretariat, National Security Council: Records, System File, System II NSC casefile 8391492.
44. Strober and Strober, *Billy Graham*, 98.
45. Reagan to Graham, October 5, 1981, NARA, RRL, WHORM: SF, ME001-03, ID #042394.

46. William L. Stearman to William P. Clark, February 10, 1982, NARA, RRL, WHORM: SF, FO008, ID #048718SS.
47. James W. Nance to Reagan, February 4, 1982, NARA, RRL, WHORM: SF, FO008, ID #048718SS.
48. Note dated February 16, 1982, NARA, RRL, WHORM: SF, FO008, ID #048718SS; correspondence tracking paper, March 24, 1982, WHORM: SF, FO008, ID #071277; Bush to Ambassador Arthur Hartman [April 1983], NARA, RRL, WHORM: SF, FO008, ID #075190.
49. Graham to Reagan, November 23, 1987, NARA, RRL, WHORM: SF, CO165, ID #601483. On the disarmament treaty, see James T. Patterson, *Restless Giant: The United States from Watergate to Bush v. Gore* (New York: Oxford University Press, 2005), 215.
50. Rosenfield, "Billy Graham, Preacher to the Mighty," B1.
51. George Bush (with Doug Wead), *Man of Integrity* (Eugene, OR: Harvest House Publishers, 1988), 44–45.
52. Kim A. Lawson, "Republicans or Reaganites?" *Christianity Today*, September 16, 1988, 38–39.
53. Graham, *Just as I Am*, 584–87; Jim McGrath, ed., *Heartbeat: George Bush in His Own Words* (New York: Scribner, 2001), 134–35; Graham to Nixon, December 21, 1989, NPL, PPC, 1–4.
54. "Graham's Inaugural Role Opposed," *Christian Century*, January 20, 1993, 48–49.
55. Ibid., 49; Billy Graham, "The Moral Weight of Leadership," *New York Times*, March 17, 1998, A25.
56. Cal Thomas, "It's Not Graham's Place to Forgive Clinton," *Buffalo News*, March 11, 1998, 11; "He's Not Ready to Forgive Bill," *New York Daily News*, March 7, 1998, 8.
57. Graham, "The Moral Weight of Leadership," A25.
58. Bill Coles, "Even Billy Graham Loses Faith in Clinton," *London Sun*, September 9, 1998, 7.
59. Graham to Nixon, August 18, 1986, RNL, PPSP, 1–5.
60. Bush, *Man of Integrity*, 45–46; Bill Minutaglio, *First Son: George W. Bush and the Bush Family Dynasty* (New York: Times Books, 1999), 220.
61. George W. Bush, *A Charge to Keep* (New York: William Morrow, 1999), 136.
62. Quoted in Fred Barnes, "The Gospel according to Billy Graham," *Weekly Standard*, March 22, 1999, accessed from Lexis Nexis Academic database, October 11, 2006. See also R. G. Ratcliffe, "Faithful Have a Place in Politics, Says Bush," *Houston Chronicle*, March 7, 1999, 1.
63. See Marvin N. Olasky, *Compassionate Conservatism: What It Is, What It Does, and How It Can Transform America* (New York: Free Press, 2000).
64. Quoted in Elizabeth Mitchell, *W: Revenge of the Bush Dynasty* (New York: Hyperion, 2000), 331.
65. Gustav Niebuhr, "Evangelicals Found a Believer in Bush," *New York Times*, February 21, 2000, 13.
66. Laurie Goodstein, "Conservative Church Leaders Find a Pillar in Bush," *New York Times*, January 23, 2000, 16.
67. Memo in Nancy Gibbs and Michael Duffy, *The Preacher and the Presidents: Billy Graham in the White House* (New York: Center Street, 2007), 335–36. Prayer breakfast details in Ken Herman, *Atlanta Constitution*, November 6, 2000, 11

(accessed in Proquest database, October 20, 2005); Matthew I. Pinzur, "Graham Worships in Jacksonville," *Florida Times-Union*, November 6, 2000, 1; and Andre Miga and Joe Battenfeld, "Bush Arrest Stirs Up Race," *Boston Herald*, November 6, 2000, 3. Background details in Paul Pinkham, "City Comes Together for Crusade," *Florida Times-Union*, November 3, 2000, 1; Pinzur, "Bush to Return Briefly on a State Drive," *Florida Times-Union*, November 4, 2000, 5; Pinzur, "Bush Kicks Off Day of Florida Rallies with Church Visit," *Florida Times-Union*, November 5, 2000, 1; Ed Vulliamy and Peter Preston, "Bush's Drink Crime Helps Gore," *The Observer*, November 5, 2000, 1; and Tim Nickens, "Staying Positive as Judgment Nears," *St. Petersburg (FL) Times*, November 6, 2000, 1.

68. "Statement by the Rev. Billy Graham Supporting George W. Bush," November 6, 2000, http://www.cnsnews.com/Politics/Archive/200011/POL20001106c.html.

69. Paul Kengor, *God and George W. Bush: A Spiritual Life* (New York: ReganBooks, 2004), 78–79.

A Question of Legacy

13

U.S. Evangelicals

Recovering a Post-9/11 Prophetic Spirit

Mark Lewis Taylor

In the present period of crisis, what hope is there that U.S. evangelicals will find a prophetic voice and, even more importantly, find their way into broader movements that can work prophetically today against the practices of war, torture, repression, and surveillance, all of which have become mainsprings of U.S. sovereignty in national and global contexts?[1] The legacy of Billy Graham need not follow in lockstep with the Christian Right's faith-based nationalism and fear-based reinforcement of quasi-fascist policies of U.S. governance.[2]

In the evangelical home of my childhood, two television events were required viewing by my parents: the New York Philharmonic Young People's Concerts with Leonard Bernstein, and Billy Graham's televised crusades. It was not a terribly strict ethos in my home. My anthropologist father, who though an evangelical himself taught with distinction in U.S. secular universities, exposed us to travel and living in Mesoamerica, and both of my parents supported in word and action the burgeoning civil rights movement of the time. Moreover, in my early teen years there were no objections to my keeping at bedside Bertrand Russell's *Why I Am Not a Christian*.

Over time, Leonard Bernstein's temper clearly won out, and perhaps a bit of Russell's. I long ago left behind the evangelicalism of Graham the crusader

The first version of this chapter was presented at the Billy Graham Center in Wheaton, Illinois, on March 24, 2006. I appreciated the invitation and register here my gratitude to the event organizers in Wheaton, Dr. Bruce Ellis Benson and Dr. Peter Heltzell.

and of my family, save perhaps the scars and some other vestiges. Graham unsettled my youthful heart with his portraits of horrible apocalyptic futures, which provoked fear even if they were accompanied by some teenage amusement and doubting puzzlement. Moreover, as I journeyed during my college and seminary years, struggling with and eventually beyond the evangelical theological and political paradigm, I also became increasingly critical of Graham's sacralizing of the United States, its presidents, and its generals and their missions—especially those that laid waste to Vietnam during the years of my youth. Nevertheless, the evangelicalism of Billy Graham and E. J. Carnell (former president of Fuller Seminary) are not the same, in moral temper or theological content, as the religiosity of the Christian Right today.[3] Graham, in fact, has distanced himself in recent years from fundamentalist views that see all "pagans" headed for hell, eschewed the word "inerrant" for biblical authority, forgiven Bill Clinton for the White House dalliances that led many Christians to press for his impeachment, and allowed that there are occasions when abortion is the only alternative. Even while continuing to claim that homosexuality is "a sin," Graham has criticized Christians who make of it "the overwhelming sin" above all others.[4]

I presume in this chapter, then, that there is at least some possibility that a U.S. evangelicalism that continues in the legacy of the Carnell/Graham temperament might be able to separate itself from the Christian Right of the twenty-first century and make some common cause with the religious, interreligious, and secular prophetic movements that we need in the present time of crisis.

The present crisis in the United States has a distinctive structure. Exploiting currents that long have been at work in history, U.S. power-holders today have aligned themselves at high levels of governance in a dramatic form of what I have termed an "imperial triumvirate." This is a three-way alignment of neoconservative war-planners with corporate commerce, and then both of these with the Christian Right.[5] It is a familiar structure of destruction. As philosopher Alain Badiou writes, "There has always been an imperial triad: first, the military that conquers; second, the commerce that opens the markets; and third, the proselytizing missionary."[6] Badiou's imperial "proselytizing missionary," reconstellated in the United States today as the Christian Right, is a particularly important element of the triad, not only because it recruits its faithful into the imperial project but also because its religious dynamics inject an intense sacral fervor and meaning into the political and economic agendas of imperial power. But as I have stressed in my book and elsewhere, mostly for my fellow leftist friends and coworkers, the Christian Right should not be confused with either all Christians, or even with all Christian theological conservatives. The "theocons" of today who make up the Christian Right are *theocratic* conservatives, not *theological* conservatives. They represent a more vigorous conservatism and one considerably more dangerous because of the patterns of domination—their word is "dominion"—they seek to enact for others in their vision of a divine political order.[7]

I have also argued that it is the distinctive task of the "prophetic spirit" to galvanize and sustain a prophetic tradition and community that erodes the power of the kind of structural triad that imperial power seeks to consolidate. That prophetic tradition emerges from great religious histories, such as those of Judaism, Christianity, and Islam, but also from many other religious and "secular" groups of persons and activists who find their suffering, belief, and conscience to mobilize resistance. This prophetic tradition is more like what historians Peter Linebaugh and Marcus Rediker term a "motley crew," a patchwork of hybrid, struggling communities in resistance.[8] It is made of many strands of Christianity, multiple forms of religiosity, and a teeming collection of secular spirits of conscience struggling for more justice and love in social life.

In this chapter I ask how U.S. evangelicals might participate in prophetic movements to challenge the theocratic Christian Right. How might U.S. evangelicals relate to the motley crew of prophetic movements? This is particularly important to do because U.S. evangelicals have had, and still have, a strong public impact and an extensive vital spiritual presence for so many residents of the United States.[9] Moreover, in the post-9/11 United States, evangelicals are an especially important group, because the Christian Right has harnessed so much of the language of evangelicalism for its participation in the imperial triumvirate with neocons and corporate powers. Even though I will not be discussing Billy Graham directly in this chapter, my comments may be taken as reflections on his legacy, that is, U.S. evangelicalism, forms of which, as Graham himself sometimes displayed, could depart from the moralistic and theocratic politics and the Armageddon apocalyptics of the Christian Right.

UNDERSTANDING "U.S. EVANGELICALS"

In spite of these areas of shared language between the "Christian Right" and "U.S. evangelicals," these terms should not be used interchangeably. Both are subsets of a larger phenomenon in the United States of conservative Protestants (but on various political issues some evangelicals are more progressive, even radical, than self-styled "progressives" or "liberals"). Scholars have debated how to distinguish evangelicals from other conservative Protestants. Sociologists Woodbury and Smith, for example, use "evangelicals" for the more moderate wing of conservative Protestants that emerged after World War II, and I will generally follow their lead.[10] What is more important is distinguishing today's Christian Right (what Carwardine terms "the new Christian Right"[11]) from today's evangelicals.

The Christian Right can generally be presented as unifying within its cultural practices three crucial dimensions: political proactivity, theocratic intention, and a piety fused with U.S. militaristic nationalism.[12] It is particularly the latter two dimensions that most distinguish the Christian Right from evangelicals. But how then shall we speak of evangelicals? Are there similar markings that we might propose for this group? I will use three other criteria developed in a remarkably even-handed, historical study by historian Anne Loveland.[13] She described her criteria as part of her research into U.S. evangelicals' post-1940s mission work in the U.S. armed forces. She has drawn from a wide array of sources and institutional centers, at evangelical institutions and many other academic centers, to provide her portrait of this important setting of evangelical growth and mission. She is careful to observe the heterogeneity of U.S. evangelicals, particularly the need not to identify them with the new Christian Right.[14]

What are the three criteria for identifying U.S. evangelicals? It is worth quoting Loveland's paragraph on this in full:

> Notwithstanding certain doctrinal differences, all of these members of the evangelical community affirm three principal religious beliefs. All regard the Bible as the inerrant authority on faith and life. All agree that one achieves salvation only through faith, by undergoing a conversion experience in which one gives up one's life to Jesus Christ as Lord and Savior. And finally, all are devoted to carrying out the Great Commission handed down by Jesus in Matthew 28:19 to "go . . . and teach all nations, baptizing them in the name of the Father, and of the Son, and of the Holy Ghost."[15]

If we take these three criteria—for brevity, let us refer to them as belief in biblical inerrancy, in salvation through being born again, and in Christian missions—two interesting questions arise. One, how might evangelicals maintain these beliefs in critical relation to the Christian Right today, with its three marks of political proactivity, theocratic intentions, and militarist, nationalist piety? Second, how might evangelicals not only differentiate themselves from the Christian Right but do so in ways that make common cause with prophetic movements that are resisting the imperial triumvirate at work today?

I will address these two questions together by discussing five features of U.S. evangelical belief that make positive contributions to the prophetic spirit. My discussion will not only identify these contributing features, though; it will also suggest that certain betrayals of the prophetic spirit by evangelicals (more cautiously termed "departures") can both work against the prophetic spirit and also accommodate, all too easily, the ways of the Christian Right. I will then risk suggesting, with respect to each of the five features, what evangelicals might do (and sometimes, in fact, are already doing) in order to remain contributors to the traditions of the prophetic spirit and resist co-optation by the Christian Right.

EVANGELICALISM IN THE HISTORY OF THE PROPHETIC SPIRIT

From a historical point of view, a case can be made that evangelicalism has been a proactive, contributing force in the formation of the prophetic spirit, a force at work in the very "motley crew" of people who have embodied the prophetic spirit's tradition. This is particularly true if we recall, as Glenn Stassen of Fuller Seminary has pointed out, that evangelicalism has long been at work from the time of the prophetic action of revolts by Levellers and Diggers against emergent capitalists during the English Revolution.[16] This is certainly correct, and in examining the documents of Christians in that period one can even find something we might call an "evangelical liberation theology." Richard Overton, a Leveller pamphleteer (1646, *A Remonstrance of Many-Thousand Citizens)*, drew connections between the brutal slavery of the "aged, sick and crippled, begging your halfe-penny Charities," those in the imperial navies' ships, the "poore; your hunger-starved brethren," and also "those whom your owne unjuste Lawes hold captive in your owne Prisons," and also the "Gally-slave in Turkie or Argiere."[17] Similarly, Gerard Stanley of the Diggers denounced the nobility and emergent capitalism in these terms: "The teeth of *all nations* have been set on edge by this sour grape, the covetous murdering sword." In *A Declaration from the Poor Oppressed People of England* (1649), his sermons preached God's glory as manifest in and arising "from among the poor common people."[18]

One might find something similar to this English evangelical "liberation theology" in U.S. history. As Sean Wilentz points out, in spite of American evangelicals' struggle with Whiggery, their overweening respect for standing orders, and at times an anti-immigrant nativism, their work in such areas as abolitionism was striking. As at Lane and Oberlin seminaries in Ohio, evangelical abolitionists helped spawn "a new kind of American political community" involving "no rote profession of faith" but "an act of defiance of widely and deeply held social conventions, placing oneself in a position that courted disapproval, ostracism, and even physical attack" due to their commitments to eradicate slavery.[19]

What needs to be added to all of this, however, is that this prophetic evangelical heritage was rooted in and suffused by the motley crew that also included slaves from Africa, indigenous peoples, pirates, indentured servants, men and women, young and old from the churched *and* nonchurched, resisters to exploitative labor and impressment into the imperial navies—all those ringing the rim of what Linebaugh and Rediker have called the Revolutionary Atlantic in the 1600s and 1700s. The prophetic spirit is not the special trait of evangelicalism—English or American. It is a current of struggle carried by a broader array of traditions, religious and secular. It is in this current of struggle that we wait to see U.S. evangelicals make entry in the present hour of crisis.

With this history of evangelicals' openness to the prophetic spirit, I return to the challenge of identifying the five contributing features of U.S. evangelicalism to the prophetic spirit, which, if nurtured and developed further, might continue to help catalyze the prophetic spirit today.

REINFORCING CHRISTIAN PROPHETIC IDENTITY

First, U.S evangelicals, particularly through their tendency to insist on notions of biblical authority, can help to ground a Christian prophetic identity. This orientation to biblical sources—even when emphasizing authoritarian modes of biblical inerrancy and infallibility—can have the effect of setting before Christian communities a narrative, a story, that has the function of centering and grounding the identity of its people. A text such as the Bible, unfolding a great saga from creation to future apocalypse, rife with adventures in nation building and almost every human vicissitude, is an especially powerful resource for shaping the character and identity of the community. Communities, Christian or otherwise, without such a narrative text are often left asking, "Who are we? What is our relation, our uniqueness, within the larger public with which we interact?"

A particular contribution of this emphasis on narrative Christian identity to the prophetic spirit is that it foregrounds the stories of the biblical prophets. The prophetic spirit may be extrabiblical, even extra-Christian and extrareligious,[20] but evangelicals' embrace of the Bible can contribute a storied concreteness about the prophetic function, telling of a Moses, a Joshua, certainly of Amos, Micah, Isaiah, Jeremiah, and the other Hebrew prophets. The biblical story lays out others, such as Jesus, perhaps even Paul, in relation to the biblical tradition of the prophets. Even if evangelicals insist that Jesus was "more than a prophet," his life in the New Testament again gives storied form to the prophetic function. This narrative concretizing of the prophetic function in the Bible is an important contribution of evangelicalism to the prophetic spirit.

Alas, evangelicals often subvert the power of their potential contribution here. In particular, the affirmations of the Bible as normative often come dangerously close to a form of textual fetishism. By this I mean that the Bible is often *de facto* (if not *de jure*) revered as a powerful object in itself. Perhaps this is what Graham sensed when he is reported to have cautioned in 1982, "I don't use the word 'inerrant' because it's become a brittle divisive word."[21] I know there are very complex and carefully qualified arguments for biblical inerrancy and biblical infallibility, but most of these still fail to admit the importance of contextual variables (particularly of race, gender, class, sexual orientation, national, political, cultural, and social location) in establishing the meanings of the narrative text. Again, evangelicals may often address matters of the contextual conditionedness of the biblical narrative, but if they also hold to inerrantist or infallibilist commitments to the text, they are disallowing our dissent to the Bible when we discern it to be in error or fallible on various matters.

When the biblical text is made a fetish in this way, protected from challenges to its error and fallibility, it often takes its place in regimes of discourse that undercut the prophetic function, working against the prophetic spirit. The prophetic spirit, as I have indicated, is marked by rigorous identification with and dissent in the name of those living at the edges and undersides of marginalizing and oppressive regimes of power. Those who situate the biblical text in regimes of power, allowing the text to sacralize a regime whose authority also usually is held to be beyond questioning, stifle their relation to the prophetic spirit. Given the Bible's usability for repression and oppression, not to mention its many unusable sections, dissent to the text is essential to the prophetic spirit's resistance and creative building.

What might be the remedy for this textual fetishism? How might the fruitful biblical tendency of evangelicalism to create Christian prophetic identity be preserved, reawakened, catalyzed? I suggest that the best way would be for evangelicals to reinscribe a vigorous political, social, and cultural contextualization into the study of biblical texts. In his book *Jesus and Empire*, Richard Horsley has shown that a comprehensive "de-politicizing of Jesus" has characterized biblical scholarship of both conservative and liberal exegetes. To "re-politicize Jesus" and the biblical traditions, but not in a politically reductionist way, would mean examining anew Jesus' context of ministry as occurring amid Roman empire and occupation, seeing Jesus' death by crucifixion as an imperial execution, and understanding Paul's ministry throughout Asia Minor as a comprehensive daily challenge to the politics of empire. The fruits of such reading will be strikingly biblical and evangelical, but hardly the politics of Jesus that we see emergent among the chrisotocrats and theocrats of the new Christian Right. Such a repoliticizing of the New Testament is just one example of how the evangelical contribution to the prophetic spirit might be catalyzed anew, by deploying a stronger contextual analysis vis-à-vis biblical materials.

RESISTING REDUCTIONISM

Evangelicalism, particularly because of its tradition of criticizing secularism, usually out of an interest to preserve a sense of the transcendence of God, offers, as a second contribution to prophetic spirit, a hedge against those theologies that would completely empty Christian experience of its mystery. In other terms, Christian evangelical discourse, in the United States and elsewhere, preserves what many Christians value in different ways, that is, a sense of "something more," or a mystery or otherness within life, often limned in symbolic discourses about "the holy," "the sacred," "God." There are theologies often styled as "incarnational" that speak of a radical kenosis of the divine in the realms of humanity and creation and that often stress this pouring out to the point of leaving in place only "creation" as natural and social order. While I have long appreciated such incarnational theology and even often self-identify as a "deeply spiritual secular humanist," I can appreciate the evangelical theologians and others who push more strongly than I do for the transcendent otherness of God. After all, without some gesture in that direction, what would my "deeply spiritual" qualifier of "secular humanist" mean? U.S. evangelicalism shares this emphasis on the transcendent—and hence a resistance to social, political, and any other cultural reductionism—with the Christian Right. The Christian Right declares outright war against reductionism (demonized as "secular humanism"), but evangelicalism is, at least, vigilant against reductionism too.

What I am underscoring here is that this resistance to reductionism can be an essential contribution to the prophetic spirit. It reminds those who embody the prophetic spirit, if they were inclined to forget it, that the prophetic is more than a political function. The prophetic may be extrabiblical, extra-Christian, and even extrareligious, but it is not without some spiritual dimension. This dimension may use God-language, or it may not. It usually does deploy some God-language, especially among Christians in the United States, but it may also utilize a more generalized discourse about spiritual meaningfulness (as in Michael Lerner's talk of the "politics of meaning") or speak of an ultimate concern with meaning and power, as in the writings of Paul Tillich. In these varied senses, the prophetic function usually entails a mystical politics, and thinking carefully about politics and some sense of openness toward transcendence (if only an "open immanence," or "transimmanence," as philosopher Jean-Luc Nancy puts it[22]) is a crucial part of the challenge for prophetic reflection. Here my major point is that evangelicalism's resistance to reductionism can have the positive fruit of helping to preserve a dimension of spirit or spirituality in prophetic work.

But this points to another way in which evangelicalism's valuable contribution to the prophetic spirit can morph into a theological sensibility that subverts its contribution. The resistance to reductionism can lead to a valuing of transcendence that directs faith concerns to a place of alien otherness, above and apart from the politics of earth and society, indeed, of all creation. The spirit of the prophetic function, in all its earthly, political, and cultural complexity, thus becomes something subordinated to an alien, higher spirit. God becomes so much the "Almighty Other," or the "Wholly Other," vis-à-vis "the world" that political action and thought are almost by definition consigned to an inferior, if not wholly other, lower sphere. Views of God as "wholly other" can easily spawn views of earth and politics as "wholly lower" in importance. The irony here is that the same insistence on transcendence that might preserve the mystery of the prophetic now drives transcendence out of the world, so to speak, leaving the the prophetic just as empty of its mystery as some secular reductionisms are. The spirit becomes "heteronomic" (having the character of an alien, "other law"), existing above and often outside the world of politics and culture, bodies and desire—these various human and earthly sites of the prophetic function.

What would be a better way, better from the perspective of making possible a stronger link between U.S. evangelicalism and the prophetic spirit? Evangelical sensibilities committed to the prophetic function will need to harness those more fully dialectical understandings of transcendence, which hold that it is of the mystery of God to be poured out in history and thus able to be met and known *within* that history. The remedy for alien, heteronomic transcendence, then, would be some version of a relational transcendence. There are many versions of this latter category. I am aware of them more in the neo-orthodox, liberal, and especially liberation and feminist theological traditions, but I am sure they could be—perhaps they have been—worked out in evangelical modalities. (I think here of some of the Quaker traditions.) The prophetic spirit thrives as a political mode of relational transcendence, and while evangelicals nurture transcendence (a valuable contribution to the prophetic spirit, I repeat), they also need to safeguard the relationality of divine transcendence—to and in humanity and earth—if the prophetic spirit is not to labor without evangelical support.

A marked example of relational transcendence in the biblical materials, which evangelicals might have a strong interest in accenting to support the prophetic spirit, can be found in the parable of the great judgment in Matthew 25:31–46. There the "Son of Man" is portrayed as full of transcendent power, sitting on a glorious throne, rendering judgments about what has been prepared "from the foundation of the world" and about what humans' "eternal" fates are to be. These transcendental judgments, however, are made on the basis of very earthy, political activity—giving drink to the thirsty, clothing the naked, and visiting the sick and the imprisoned. Moreover, in doing unto those with these concrete needs, which surely means more than just handing over a cup of water (it might mean fighting the Bechtel Corporation's privatization of water in Bolivia and elsewhere), the transcendent one says that the doing was, in fact, a doing unto him. This parable points to a profound case of "relational transcendence" in the mode of the prophetic spirit.

NURTURING COSMIC/SOCIAL ANTAGONISM

A third contribution of U.S. evangelicalism to the prophetic spirit is a spin-off from its commitment to transcendence. This is its tendency to nurture a sense of cosmic and social antagonism. There is, as I will argue, a problematic aspect to this, but I want to note the value of it. Concomitant with evangelicals' sense of God's transcendence is a sense that the world of that transcendence is not just different or "other" but also involves differences in tension, contestation, and conflict. In evangelicalism at its best, this is not to say that the divine other is good and the world bad, but that there are ways of the world that must be seen as radically evil and thus in conflict with the values of the divine character and will. The sense of cosmic antagonism suggests also a situation of conflict *within* the world, as the people of God, to various degrees and in various ways, see themselves in conflict with forces—among them, political formations—that are thought to be undesirable, distorted, oppressive, and, in short, "evil." The prevalence of references to Satan in evangelical discourses, whether from C. S. Lewis, other theologians, or any number of conservative believers, is further indication of the way a cosmic and generalized antagonism *between* the divine other and ways of the world entail also antagonism between forces *in* the world.

I myself have no personal belief in the literal reality of Satan, and I particularly have objected to the ways Billy Graham wielded the Satan label to demonize opponents of U.S. policies abroad and the peace and civil rights movements at home. Nevertheless, I certainly acknowledge the powerful function that a mythic and symbolic discourse of Satan has had, and still has, for opening up consciousness about the vitality and vigor of radical evil. I know of African American evangelicals who use the term "Satan" easily for naming the way white racism emerges continually in cultural practices and institutions as a veritable "power and principality" in the New Testament sense. I also know conservative Christians of Chiapas, Mexico, *los evangélicos*, who utilize the discourse of Satan for referring to the centuries of brutal and imperial policies of their northern nemesis, the United States, with its record of covert and overt military interventions in the history of Latin America. None of these are my preferred discourses for mobilizing liberating action, and there are numerous risks to one's own emancipatory practice in deploying them. Nevertheless, as with some

Nation of Islam adherents who speak of white racists as "blue eyed devils," this language can function as a way to mobilize antagonism and rage. It is not a fundamental obstacle to my seeking solidarity with them in emancipatory work.

This sense of antagonism is a contribution to the prophetic spirit, because a politics, especially one that functions as emancipatory for marginalized and oppressed groups, needs a sense of conflict and antagonism. Chantal Mouffe writes that an emancipatory politics will require, amid the most complex and pluralistic politics of difference, senses of antagonism, of agonistic striving, and of dealing with adversaries.[23] Similarly, French philosopher Alain Badiou, without sacrificing the complexity of political work, insists that emancipatory politics entails "militants" who make hazardous choices and who can set themselves "against" powerful forces, especially against the illusory false promises of parliamentary states, which he terms "capitalo-parliamentarism."[24]

Interestingly, even some secular theorists in political theory have recognized the importance of traditions of theological transcendence in nurturing this sense of agonistic striving in emancipatory politics. Political philosopher Ernesto Laclau, for example, has argued that, historically, strong senses of transcendence (as we see them in U.S. evangelicalism and elsewhere), which emphasize God's otherness as entailing a conflict with the world, have helped to produce a sense of antagonism within social and political life, which is necessary to any politics and prophetic movements of emancipatory import.[25]

Still to be worked out, of course, are other matters, such as evaluating the various modes of antagonism and agonistic striving, such as nonviolence, violence, parliamentary representation, and so on. My main point here, though, is that antagonism is essential to the political, especially to an emancipatory politics that is crucial to the prophetic spirit. Moreover, an evangelicalism whose sense of transcendence can contribute this sense of conflict in difference, of antagonism in social life, contributes something crucial to the prophetic spirit.

Again, there is a distortion near at hand, one that can shipwreck evangelical transcendence's contribution to the prophetic spirit at this point. It is closely connected to the problem noted in the previous section, about transcendent otherness becoming so other it becomes also alien and heteronomic vis-à-vis the world. Here the distortion of transcendence of concern is one that interprets divine antagonism as a license to rule from the position of otherness and in the way of conquering, overwhelming power. Theological transcendence is problematic, in other words, not just for becoming heteronomic but for becoming theocratic. Today's new Christian Right seizes upon evangelical notions of divine antagonism to radical evil in the world and transforms them into something they do not need to become, logically or politically. An antagonism between the world and God need not entail holding that God is related to the world as in a hierarchy. Similarly, on the level of politics, we can say that adversarial striving, even against radical evil, does not necessarily entail, as its primary modality, the use of coercion and overwhelming force by hierarchical powers. This does not mean a naive prohibition of all modes of coercion in striving with radical evil, but it refuses to grant coercion by authorities the primary power of eradicating radical evil.

The preventive course of action for theocratic transcendence, as for heteronomic transcendence, is to keep to the way of relational transcendence, as I have pointed out. In this case, transcendence that brings the fruit of antagonism is to be found within the relational, agonistic striving of those in need of emancipation. This agonistic striving has had to deploy—by necessity and as a gift—another mode of power to achieve enablement and emancipation. This power is creative, militant, nonviolent love. It is motivated by and expresses not almighty theocratic power but creative, risk-taking desire and organized politics of emancipation. Here the transcendent other is not the almighty theocratic one but the pouring out of the divine other's life into a flowing, empowering love, moving out into those places where the poor—the shepherd, the leper, the excluded, the foreigner, the crucified of every age—are groaning, searching, hungering for, desiring, working toward new relations of emancipatory community. This "transcendence of militant, nonviolent love" (even seeking ways of love for the enemy) is confrontive and agonistic, but it moves in an alternative mode, cutting against the "transcendence of command" that is so central to the Christian theocrats.

Can evangelicalism free its frequent discourse about "the Lord" (*kyrios*) from a "kyriarchal," theocratic paradigm? I think it can, and the resources for that freer discourse are to be found in those whose struggle has found that language oppressive and have turned to militant nonviolent direct action. Such resources are to be found in the Scriptures, which tell stories of the divine risk, the divine kenosis in the liberating struggles of enslaved peoples who had lifted their laments to God from the occupied territories of Egypt and Rome, where they were routinely dominated yet remembered and restored by the divine presence in their midst.[26] It would be a very biblical move, in short, for evangelicals to stress that the way this divine presence rivals and counters the lords and emperors of the world, the radical evil of whatever sort, is not by recycling the theocratic ways of caesars and some presidents who invoke "the Almighty" as their major term of reference for God (as does George W. Bush) but by exhibiting a more powerful, fundamentally different mode of lordship, one marked above all by the restless, desiring, working, agonistic life, wherein marginalized and oppressed groups take on the antagonism of the world's powers against them. Holding to this alternative mode of agonistic contestation would be a way for evangelicals to challenge the theocratic transcendence of command and so facilitate coalition between the prophetic spirit and evangelicalism.

FOSTERING A SENSE OF COUNTERVAILING
POWER AND HOPE

The strong discourses of transformation, salvation, and redemption in Christ, which characterize much of U.S. evangelicalism, make up a fourth contributing feature that is significant for the prophetic spirit. Provided that evangelicalism can keep its sense of transcendence from being distorted by heteronomic and theocratic formulations, that transcendental sense is important because it suggests the availability of a countervailing power. This countervailing power offers a specter of potentiality and being that helps build hope.

The prophetic spirit can derive a sense of hope from many sources (especially from art and celebration in struggle), but this spirit can be nurtured further with the help of those who are imbued with evangelical confidence in transcendent countervailing power. The prophetic spirit, as it surveys the full range of exclusions and oppressions meted out to so many, can easily crumple under the weight of so nefarious and tangled a web of political suffering. Burnout and fatigue, not to mention anxiety and despair, can easily and quickly eviscerate the powers of the prophetic spirit. Evangelicalism's countervailing transcendence, then, might yield for the prophetic spirit a confidence in overcoming that which seems too much to overcome. It can foster hope anew. That is no mean contribution. The prophetic spirit would do well to welcome it, and I dare say that historically, as in abolitionist struggles and in other social struggles as well, it has been the lively, hope-filled worship, prayer, and struggle of evangelical Christians that have helped keep the prophetic spirit alive in some contexts.

A real tragedy among U.S. evangelicals (as well as of other Christian traditions) is that the confidence and hope in countervailing power can deteriorate (historically and in the present) into a misplaced confidence in the powers of their nation. The hope offered by evangelicals in U.S. history has too often morphed into hope in the nation. The idolatry of nation is widely and frequently found in history, and not just in the United States. But when a nation has achieved the kinds of power that the United States has, and taken on new global and domestic powers as it has especially since the 9/11 attacks in New York and Washington, then the powers of nation are all the more easy to revere, especially in evangelical traditions so conditioned to honor governance and give respect to the United States, understood as an exceptionally guided nation. This is further compounded by Christian understandings of transcendence that stress a theocratic "transcendentalism of command." That kind of Christian transcendence has often been yoked with the imperial and colonizing apparatus of Western expansion in the name of "civilization" and of a U.S. mandate to pursue its "manifest destiny"—what John L. Sullivan called in the

1840s America's "gigantic boldness." Today the Christian Right's affirmations of that boldness merge with the neoconservative war-planning elites' affirmations of "American greatness." The tragedy is that a sense of overcoming, of divine countervailing power in history, is confused with the overweening power of a nation. Even if that nation is as powerful as the United States is today (and its powers may be waning), and even if it is believed to be as good as many citizens think it to be (alas, a grand illusion), the United States is but a part of the whole. The countervailing power needed by the prophetic spirit, and by a whole creation, cannot be served by looking to the powers of only one nation or one people.

What might be a corrective for an evangelicalism whose transcendent hope is prone to be misplaced onto a strong nation's destiny? The first answer is to remind itself, as all Christian traditions do well to remind themselves, that relational transcendence always points beyond any one entity, domain, or dynamic and to the whole set of relations we know as earth, world, creation. The domain of "nation" certainly cannot be a site complex enough to hold the transcendent that concerns all the relations of the whole of earth and humanity; it also does not bring into view a vision of earth and humanity that is usually taken as being of concern in the divine purview. If we are to trace the relationally transcendent in earth and humanity, it is better to seek it in relationalities that are as expansive and comprehensive as possible.

The earthen sites most fit to signal, represent, and symbolize the sacred as relational transcendence are not nations but transregional and international networks of coalitions and movements—for instance, the always unfolding, tested, and revised perspectives of international law, especially those newer forms that seek to break free from the mandates of Western legal traditions and typical nation-state categories for thinking about law. Indeed, international law, as any other historical social formation, can only approximate relational transcendence. But to the extent that the transcendent is signaled by a historical praxis, to the extent that it is embodied and poured out *within* history, it is the international and transregional loci, with their movements and organizations struggling toward ever new agreements, that will best serve and approximate the interests of divine relational transcendence. They certainly do so better than the one nation, the United States, with its increasingly global power and interests, seeking its own "full spectrum dominance" *over* earth and humanity.[27]

It is of the utmost urgency in the present climate that evangelicals and others break the tendency of so many today, especially among the Christian Right, to assume the congruence of divine power with U.S. power. Biblically and theologically, U.S. evangelicals and other Christians might emphasize ever anew that any experience of renewal in Jesus Christ is not a matter of becoming a citizen of the United States or any other nation. It is to be brought into a relation with one who is redeemer and also creator, one who has the whole of creation's peoples and nature systems in view. To be "in Christ" is to be loyal to the whole of creation, to have one's pulse, pleasure, praxis, and intellectual process attuned to the multitudes of peoples and the whole earth's ways. That takes precedence over loyalty to the "founding fathers," whose alleged Christianity is championed by the Christian Right even though many kept slaves in an age when others among their contemporaries called for abolition. This greater loyalty to the whole of God's creation, beyond the claims to power of any nation, especially those usurped by the United States today, can help to ground the dissenting postures so essential to the prophetic spirit.

OPENING A GLOBAL SCOPE
FOR PROPHETIC TRANSFORMATION

A final contributing feature is what I term U.S. evangelicalism's global scope of concern. Evangelicalism opens a global lens on questions of human transformation. Especially because of its commitment to evangelical missions—and recall the admonition of the Great Commission to "make disciples of *all nations*" (Matt. 28:19)—evangelicalism has global interests. This is again problematic, in ways that I will show, but it can be developed in some positive ways if certain key changes are made in evangelical understandings of "witness."

Religiously motivated human transformation—whether termed salvation, being "brought to the Lord," being converted, or being "born again"—is understood by evangelicals as a global concern. This has meant the placement of evangelicals and missionaries on almost every continent. They often serve for long periods of time and learn the languages and cultural ways of the people among whom they live. As I have documented in several of my writings on the interchange between missionaries and cultural anthropologists and ethnologists, this means that missionaries, through their linguistic and cultural studies (and especially if they left careful ethnographic records behind, as they sometimes did), provided valuable resources for understanding other societies.[28] Such contributions are still made by some missionaries today. Missionaries have also often combined their global interests in peoples' transformation with a host of practices for furthering the concrete betterment of the people with whom they work, seeking better conditions for them economically, politically, and medically. Recent concerns by mission workers and other evangelicals about the tragedy in Darfur are exemplary of the functioning of this global scope of concern, and evangelicals' work has been impressive as they continually lobby to turn a U.S. president toward the trauma of Darfur (and away from his millions-of-dollars-a-day investment in the travesty of Iraq).[29]

I suggest that the global scope of evangelical interest and concern can be a contribution to the prophetic spirit, since bearers of the prophetic spirit can also manifest various forms of ethnocentrism. There are a number of ways in which left-leaning prophetic critics can often manifest elitist, ethnocentric, and also nationalist orientations, even when criticizing their own context and nation. The left, for example, can exhibit the all-too-U.S. habit of aiming for the quick fix and the interventionist rescue operation. In the lead-up to the Iraq campaign, for example, a number of liberals got caught up with the political right in the rhetoric of a military intervention in Iraq that was promoted as necessary for national security.[30]

At their best, though, the bearers of the prophetic spirit stay steeped in the polycultural and international interests of the world, especially its multitudes who are forced to the edges and undersides of the global systems of control. Moreover, it is not *only* evangelicals who keep the prophetic spirit turned to a global, intercultural frame. The global labor movement and solidarity actions among socialist, student, and counterimperial groups also provide this global scope. But evangelicals, and well-funded U.S. evangelicals in particular, can play key roles in reinforcing the global, intercultural scope of the prophetic spirit's concern and action.

The contribution of evangelicals to reinforcing global scope and concern, nevertheless, also comes with some difficulties. Above all, the interpretation of the Great Commission as a call to conversion and propagation of Christianity, vis-à-vis other cultures and other religions, has been easily co-opted by the Christian Right for a religious imperialism that supports the current imperial agendas of the United States and other Western countries. The early attempts of Christian missionaries to make entry into Iraq after the 2003 invasion were not only another blatant reinforcement of U.S. imperial policies; they also issued in new patterns of violence, conflict, and intolerance between Christians and Muslims and others in Iraq. The security of Christians in Iraq, and their freedom of worship, is more in jeopardy now than before the U.S. invasion.

More generally, U.S. Christians' professed concern with the whole being of the world's peoples is constrained by its unidirectional understanding of Christian missionary work. This viewpoint usually sees the direction of missionary activity to be from cultures of powerful countries, especially from the United States, to other less-developed, non-Western, non-Christian worlds. I know there are exceptions, and there is much talk among missions theorists about missionaries coming from other cultural contexts to the United States and into other Western contexts. That might be welcomed as a way to challenge Euro-american ethnocentrism in Christian missions, but this needs to be combined with an explicit critique of the U.S. Christians' unidirectional model. This model all too easily morphs into a religious reinforcement of the political unipolar agenda of U.S. political power at work today in both Christian Right and neoconservative circles.[31] Evangelicals committed to missions have been interested in making this critique, and hence schools such as Fuller Theological Seminary and its School of World Missions, and others, have raised major questions about the unipolar model and combined it with critiques of U.S. imperialism.[32]

Beyond this critique of a unipolar model of missions is a greater need, something necessary for enabling and activating U.S. evangelicals' contribution to the prophetic spirit. This need is for a theological transformation of how divine transcendence is portrayed in relation to global cultures and peoples. A much more vigorous affirmation of the polycultural, multilocational presence of the divine life globally is required—prior to and apart from the organized activities of Christians who go to those many sites. This would also mean a reworking of notions of revelation, especially as they function in missions' societies and organizations, so that the adventure and work of missions would be understood more as an attunement of Christians to God's ongoing work in the world and less as a transporting of God's work and presence from one place to another, usually with a conversionist agenda.

Ultimately, I do not see how U.S. evangelicals, if they are really serious about completing this reformulation of transcendence and revelation in their mission work, can avoid renouncing conversionist intentions and agendas vis-à-vis peoples of other religions or no religions. There still may be a function and place for witness, as a clarifying of one's Christian beliefs in dialogical practice with others and seeking to embody those beliefs in action with and for a world whose inhabitants struggle with many common problems, above all to meet sustenance needs and needs for meaning. If in such a context of dialogue, sharing, and openness, others decide to cast their lot with Christian belief and community—to make a change, a "conversion"—that can be welcomed. The problem comes, though, with the cultural organizing of agendas to convert and transform others to one's faith. With institutional organizing of a conversionist intent and agenda, especially within the cultural worlds of the most powerful imperial nation, it is nearly automatic that receiving cultures (if they receive) will experience a unidirectionality of Christian mission fused with unipolar imperial projects. If U.S. evangelicals are to embrace the prophetic spirit and challenge the Christian Right's strong contribution to the rise of the imperial triumvirate in post-9/11 America, I suggest they renounce the organized intention to convert non-Christians. This need not mean renouncing all notions of the *missio Dei*, but it would be a view of mission as witness born on the other side of that renunciation.

What would that notion of witness look like? I suggest a vision of witness anchored in the Greek term *martyreo* (which combines both the ideas of giving testimony and suffering as a "martyr"). Evangelism, as bearing global witness, could mean giving testimony to one's faith and recording it in society and history, not to lengthen the list of others to be converted to Christianity but to take on the suffering and positive work of transformation that accompany standing with and for the world's poor. This is consonant with what I understand some of the best missionaries to say when pointing to Peruvian theologian Gustavo Gutiérrez, for example, who invited Christians from more powerful nations and classes to be "evangelized *by* the poor."[33] This is again consonant with the logic of "transimmanence" in Matthew 25, wherein to do and meet the Son of Man is to do unto "the least of these."

A U.S. evangelicalism that eschews U.S. societies, associations, and organizations with conversionist intent but that anchors its witness in organized movements and is "evangelized by" God at work within diverse struggles for justice and peace is the type of evangelicalism that might contribute mightily to the prophetic spirit. Moreover, this evangelicalism might issue in a veritable rebirth of what it means to be an evangelical, or even to be Christian.

In spite of his standard crusading practices, his programmatic prioritizing of individual conversions, his sacralization of war and denunciation of enemies as sponsored by Satan, as well as his fearmongering apocalypticism, Billy Graham nevertheless seems to have entertained some vision of a viable, alternative mode of witness vis-à-vis non-Christians and those of other religions. In a 1978 issue of *McCall's* magazine, for example, he reportedly infuriated fundamentalist Christians by saying, "I used to think that pagans in far-off countries were lost—were going to hell—if they did not have the Gospel of Jesus Christ preached to them. I no longer believe that. . . . I believe there are other ways of recognizing the existence of God—through nature, for instance—and plenty of other opportunities, therefore, of saying yes to God."[34] As wrong as I think Graham was on theological and political matters, it is heartening to see this openness.

HOPE FOR A NEW U.S. EVANGELICALISM

In sum, there is indeed a way forward for the prophetic spirit and U.S. evangelicalism together, and their cooperation and alliance is acutely needed in these truly perilous times of the rise of an imperial triumvirate in U.S. society. Again, while this chapter has not dealt directly with Billy Graham, his ability to distinguish himself on some points from certain fundamentalist postures that have generated the Christian Right of today is a sign that evangelicalism's prophetic spirit can come forth anew. Graham even challenged President Eisenhower and his secretary of state, John Foster Dulles, to "send tons of grain to feed the hungry" during a severe famine in India. Dulles—a Presby-terian and one of the great architects of mid-twentieth-century U.S. imperial policy, and much-loved by Graham—gave Graham a lesson on world trade and how such famine relief would damage the U.S. economy and its national sta-bility. Graham later observed, "We are followers of Jesus, who commanded that we feed the hungry, and if obeying that command causes prices to fall and profit margins to narrow, so be it."[35] This report from the Graham legacy offers U.S. evangelicals at least one exemplary vignette for their long journey toward more radical practices of emancipation, in more effective coalitions with formations of the prophetic spirit. One might hope that this vignette could be developed to point to a whole new evangelical prophetic politics that moves well beyond Graham's paradigm.

The major spiritual dynamic of transformation will come from a motley crew of religions and peoples, a global and diverse common folk at work in movements for justice and love. Evangelicals do well to accept being just one strand of that polycultural and multicoalitional, prophetic work. Nevertheless, the taking up by U.S. evangelicals of the mantle of the prophetic spirit, thus joining and rejoining the motley crew of today, may constitute one of the most important developments for unleashing the countervailing power that is needed. A U.S. evangelicalism that can rise to oppose the Christian Right *and* the imperial neocons and corporate elitism—and that is also willing to trans-form those planks of its tradition that the Christian Right has exploited toward empire's end—is an evangelicalism that the prophetic spirit most dearly needs.

NOTES

1. See Chalmers Johnson, *Nemesis: The Last Days of the American Republic* (New York: Metropolitan Press, 2007).
2. On the Christian Right and possibilities of current fascist tendencies, see Chris Hedges, *American Fascists: The Christian Right and the War on America* (New York: Free Press, 2007).
3. On E. J. Carnell's style of evangelicalism, especially evident in his critique of "rigid" and "doctrinaire" thinking, as he criticized it in *The Case for Orthodoxy* (1959), see Mel White, *Religion Gone Bad: The Hidden Dangers of the Christian Right* (New York: Tarcher/Penguin, 2006), 12–13.
4. White, *Religion Gone Bad*, 22–23.
5. Mark Lewis Taylor, "What's Going on in the USA: Rise of an Imperial Tri-umvirate," *The Ecumenist: A Journal of Theology, Culture, and Society* 43, no. 3 (summer 2006): 1–8. For background arguments and additional history, see Taylor, *Religion, Politics, and the Christian Right: Post-9/11 Powers and American Empire* (Minneapolis: Fortress Press, 2005).
6. Alain Badiou, *Polemics*, trans. Steve Corcoran (New York: Verso, 2006), 72.

7. For a history of these, see Hedges, *American Fascists*, and Sara Diamond, *Roads to Dominion: Right-Wing Movements and Political Power in the United States* (New York: Guilford Press, 1995).

8. Peter Linebaugh and Marcus Rediker, *The Many-Headed Hydra: The Hidden History of the Revolutionary Atlantic* (Boston: Beacon Press, 2001), 212–14.

9. See Richard J. Carwardine, *Evangelicals and Politics in Antebellum America* (Knoxville: University of Tennessee Press, 1997).

10. Robert D. Woodbury and Christian S. Smith, "Fundamentalism, Et Al: Conservative Protestants in America," *Annual Review of Sociology* 24 (1998): 26.

11. Carwardine, *Evangelicals and Politics*, ix.

12. See Taylor, "What's Going on in the USA," 3.

13. See Anne C. Loveland, *American Evangelicals and the U.S. Military* (Baton Rouge: Louisiana State University Press, 1996).

14. Ibid., 225.

15. Ibid., x.

16. See Glenn H. Stassen, "The Christian Origins of Human Rights," in *Just Peacemaking: Transforming Initiatives for Justice and Peace* (Louisville, KY: Westminster John Knox Press, 1992), 137–63. Cf. Christopher D. Marshall, *Crowned with Glory and Honor: Human Rights in the Biblical Tradition* (Scottdale, PA: Herald Press, 2002).

17. Quoted in Linebaugh and Rediker, *The Many-Headed Hydra*, 111.

18. For the full citation and further discussion, see Mark Lewis Taylor, "Spirit," in *The Blackwell Companion to Political Theology*, ed. William T. Cavenaugh and Peter Scott (London: Blackwell, 2004), 377–92.

19. Sean Wilentz, *The Rise of American Democracy: From Jefferson to Lincoln* (New York: W. W. Norton, 2005), 406.

20. Taylor, *Religion, Politics, and the Christian Right*, 10–12.

21. White, *Religion Gone Bad*, 23 and 337n15.

22. Jean-Luc Nancy, *The Muses*, trans. Peggy Kamuf (Stanford, CA: Stanford University Press, 1996), 69–72.

23. Chantal Mouffe, *The Return of the Political* (New York: Verso Books, 2005), 1, 4, and 8. Mouffe distinguishes contention with "adversaries" from the easy binarism that creates and demonizes "enemies."

24. On militants and militancy, see Alain Badiou, *Metapolitics*, trans. Jason Barker (New York: Verso Books, 2005), 23, 121–22; Badiou, *Being and Event*, trans. Oliver Feltham (New York: Continuum, 2005), xiii; and on "militants of emancipation," Badiou, *Polemics*, 81.

25. Ernesto Laclau, "Can Immanence Explain Social Struggles?" in Paul A. Passavant and Jodi Dean, *Empire's New Clothes: Reading Hardt and Negri* (New York: Routledge, 2004), 23–24.

26. Many of these dynamics, and this kind of interpretation of the divine life amid periods of New Testament formation, can be found in Mark Lewis Taylor, *The Executed God: The Way of the Cross in Lockdown America* (Minneapolis: Fortress Press, 2001).

27. See Andrew J. Bacevich, *American Empire: The Realities and Consequences of U.S. Diplomacy* (Cambridge, MA: Harvard University Press, 2002), 117–40.

28. See Mark Taylor, *Beyond Explanation: Religious Dimensions in Cultural Anthropology* (Macon, GA: Mercer University Press, 1985); and Mark Lewis Taylor, "On Spirit and the Researching of Cultural Worlds," in *Anthropology and The-*

ology: God, Icons, and God-Talk, ed. Walter Randolph Adams and Frank Salamone (Washington, DC: University Press of America, 2000).

29. For the National Association of Evangelicals' work on Darfur, see their Web site at http://www.nae.net. Here they lament the minimal response of the Bush administration to the NAE's call for action.

30. George Packer, "The Liberal Quandary over Iraq," *New York Times Magazine*, December 8, 2002, 103–7.

31. Gary Dorrien, *Imperial Designs: Neoconservatism and the New Pax Americana* (New York: Routledge Press, 2004), 111–14. Dorrien here treats explicitly the recent unipolarist affirmations by U.S. neocon leaders.

32. I am thinking of the critique of a unipolar model of missions that is implicit in Charles H. Kraft's notion of "receiver oriented communication" throughout his *Christianity in Culture: A Study in Dynamic Biblical Theologizing in Cross-Cultural Perspective* (Maryknoll, NY: Orbis Books, 1979).

33. Gustavo Gutiérrez, "The Evangelizing Potential of the Poor," in *Essential Writings*, by Gutiérrez, ed. James B. Nickoloff (Maryknoll, NY: Orbis Books, 1996), 111–15 (emphasis added).

34. Quoted in White, *Religion Gone Bad*, 22 and 337n14.

35. Quoted in ibid., 19.

14

The Lasting Imprint of Billy Graham

Recollections and Prognostications

Harvey Cox

Early in 2007 a student handed in to me an otherwise thoughtful paper that made reference to "the late Billy Graham." I speedily corrected her mistake, but this innocent blunder caused me to reminisce. My mind went back to the first time I met Graham in the flesh. Then, after a moment, I asked myself what his legacy might be when, sometime in the future, that student's premature obituary becomes fact.

I first met Billy Graham in New Delhi in 1962 during the Third Assembly of the World Council of Churches. I was present as a guest of the WCC, considering whether to accept a position on the staff (which I eventually declined). The meeting was not all business. The delegates, guests, and staff savored the raucous markets, exotic smells, and fiery food. And they trooped wearily from one reception to another. The one at which I met Graham was a gigantic spread on the lawn of the American embassy, complete with long tables piled with dal makhani, aloo gobhi, and saag paneer, and hosted by the ambassador, John Kenneth Galbraith. Later my colleague at Harvard, Galbraith had been appointed ambassador by John F. Kennedy, who thought his experience in economics might help a country that was struggling with poverty.

Galbraith was a famously tall man. He loomed over most of the guests. Graham, though in no way short, did not tower like the ambassador. Nonetheless, as soon as he appeared in the reception line, everyone's attention turned to him. In fact some people, including myself, stepped out of the formal reception line to walk over to meet the world-famous evangelist. He was smiling and shaking

219

hands with everyone, his blue eyes flashing, his brown hair combed in the familiar pompadour. When it was my turn to be grasped in his hearty grip I was a bit overwhelmed, but I managed to blurt out a question that, in retrospect, seems banal, one he had probably heard a dozen times that day. What, I asked, did he think of this WCC gathering?

He did not hesitate. "I love it—all these people!" he almost shouted with genuine enthusiasm. He swept his long arm—draped in a well-cut summer suit and just exposing sleeves with gleaming cuff links—around the crowd. "All these people here," he continued, "and all of them praising the name of Jesus Christ." This was 1962, and for most people Graham, even though he had played golf with Eisenhower, was still thought of as a somewhat rough-hewn southern preacher with a conservative evangelical's distrust of ecumenical organizations. But here he stood, under the blazing Indian sun, in the midst of the largest ecumenical organization of them all, and—by his own testimony—loving it.

The student's paper started me thinking about Billy Graham's legacy. What will it be? First, some full disclosure: I have often found myself on the opposite side from Graham on many issues. As an active member of Martin Luther King's Southern Christian Leadership Conference, who spent a few days in a southern jail, I was disappointed and angered, as were all the other members of SCLC, by Graham's lukewarm response to the civil rights movement. Not only did he never join any marches or speak at any of the many gatherings, at a time when segregationists were calling nonviolent demonstrators "lawless," but he publicly opposed any civil disobedience. "Only by maintaining law and order are we going to keep our democracy and our nation great," he said.[1] He maintained that only a widespread spiritual revival could possibly end racial bigotry in America. He never openly called for open housing or desegregated churches. *Christianity Today*, the magazine Graham founded, did not even give editorial support to the civil rights act sponsored by President Lyndon Johnson. Naturally, those of us who were marching and sometimes sitting in chilly cells for what we considered to be a self-evidently Christian cause were disappointed to the point of rage at Graham. With his national reputation, evangelical credentials, and southern roots he could have made a significant difference. He eventually changed his views and spoke out for civil rights, but he was late for the greatest moral movement of his time.

Those of us who, as Christians and ministers, involved ourselves in the effort to end the war in Vietnam were also sorely disappointed in Billy Graham's timidity on that vital front. "I have no sympathy," he announced to the Denver Press Club, "for those clergymen who [urge] the U.S. to get out of Vietnam. . . . Communism has to be stopped somewhere, whether it is in Hawaii or on the West Coast."[2] His position contrasted dramatically with that of King, who risked the backing of many supporters by mounting the pulpit of the Riverside Church to announce his opposition to the war. Little by little Graham began to understand the awful scope of the tragedy, but he continued to waver. In 1967 he visited the troops in Vietnam for what he insisted was strictly a pastoral visit. But when he returned, he stated that he dutifully recited the administration's line that victory was still possible. Understandably, those of us who had organized Clergy Concerned about Vietnam (later Clergy and Laity Concerned) and who had once again gotten arrested to make our protest known were immensely disheartened. Graham seemed unable to grasp the deep moral transgression being spewed out with bombs and napalm in the rice paddies and villages of a small distant country. Once again, he had missed an opportunity to bring the kind of moral and religious critique he alone could have made.

In both the civil rights movement and the opposition to the Vietnam War, many of us suspected that Graham's friendship with Johnson and Nixon, his obvious yearning to stay on intimate terms with those at the peak of power, had marred his vision. We had hoped he might do better. I continued to feel that way about Graham, even though I was gratified when he spoke out at Harvard against nuclear weapons. But when my student wrote that premature obituary, I realized the time had come to reexamine my personal judgments in the light of the larger picture of Billy Graham and his legacy. That in turn took me back to that first meeting on the ambassador's clipped lawn in New Delhi.

That scene had three elements. First, it took place at an ecumenical assembly. Second, it happened at a reception hosted by a man, John Kenneth Galbraith, who was a lifelong advocate of progressive causes, a kind of secular prophet (whose Baptist boyhood in Canada had, I am convinced, shaped his conscience). Third, it occurred in an embassy headed by a man (again, Galbraith) who devoted his diplomatic talents to being a peacemaker. These three parts of the memory coincide nicely with what comes to mind as I consider the big picture of Billy Graham as ecumenist, prophet, and peacemaker.

BILLY GRAHAM AS ECUMENIST

Graham will be appreciated in years to come for helping to bridge what once appeared to be an insurmountable chasm between evangelicals and the so-called mainline churches. This was a remarkable achievement. His background and education at the Florida Bible Institute, Bob Jones University, and Wheaton College did little to prepare him for wider ecumenical endeavors. The fundamentalist dispensational theology that informed his early education was distinctly anti-ecumenical. Part of the fundamentalist worldview held that as we approached the end of the age the churches themselves would fall into faithlessness and infidelity. They would even become, some said, weapons in the arsenal of Satan. Fundamentalists were especially wary of ecclesial institutions that tried to bring churches together, because they detected in that effort the scent of the antichrist's nefarious desire to create a superchurch that would swallow up the witness of true Christians. This produced a simple strategy in dealing with "liberal" and "modernist" churches and with the ecumenical organizations they established: Stay away from them and do not cooperate with them. Be not unequally yoked together with unbelievers.

Despite this background, Graham began very early to cast his net wider. In 1948 he even attended the founding meeting of the World Council of Churches in Amsterdam as an observer representing Youth for Christ International. But he never took much interest in organizational ecumenism. From the outset of his ministry, his attitude toward other churches and denominations was not motivated by some vague sense of tolerance. Rather, it sprang from his driving desire to reach every possible soul with the gospel message. To put it another way, he placed Christ above doctrinal or ecclesial purity: "All these people here, and all of them praising the name of Jesus Christ."

The centrality of Christology to Graham's theology helps explain a lot of things about him, and it certainly clarifies why he did not feel so closely bound to the stifling ecclesial boundaries laid down by the fundamentalism of his youthful years. It has sometimes intrigued me that another influential Christian was, at roughly the same time, also placing Christology at the center of his thinking—namely, Karl Barth, who was also present at Amsterdam. Surely, two quite different understandings of Christ were at work in these two giants of twentieth-century Protestantism. Still, the comparison is a fascinating one. Barth insisted throughout his massive systematic theology on interpreting every doctrine, including creation, redemption, eschatology, and, of course, ecclesiology, in the light of Jesus Christ. I can find no record that the Swiss sage and the North Carolina preacher ever met or corresponded. But it was the single-mindedness of their devotion to Christ that fired both of them and enabled them to break down barriers in the very different worlds they inhabited.

For Billy Graham, this christologically inspired ecumenical openness came at a stiff price. Fundamentalists saw him as a turncoat. Bob Jones cut off all contact with him. What really enraged many of his fellow evangelists was Graham's insistence on encouraging all interested churches to participate in the planning and organization of his campaigns, and these purists were especially furious that he wanted the decision cards of those who came forward in a meeting to be turned over to local churches, often pastored, so the fundamentalists charged, by pagans, modernists, and heretics. But Graham stuck to his guns and in the long run made evangelicals more mainline and the mainline more evangelical. I think he will be remembered for that.

The problem today is, of course, that the ecumenism of those early, exciting years of the World Council of Churches is now quickly becoming an anachronism. No one knows this better than the Reverend Samuel Kobiah, the present WCC General Secretary. Today the challenge is not how to help Lutherans and Baptists and Presbyterians to listen to one another, pray together, and cooperate in mission and social action. Other more serious and intractable fissures have opened up in the world church. The majority of Christians now live in the "southern world," and they are largely poor and nonwhite. They look at the gospel and at the world from a wholly different angle. The current disagreement between the African and the Euro-American branches of the Anglican Communion may be an ominous token of what is to come. Some observers even think that the question of homosexuality could split the churches today the way slavery did in the nineteenth century. In thirty years, the theological issues and social concerns that once demanded the attention of the World Council will have changed dramatically. Would Graham be able to help these diverse currents flow together or at least closer?

I am not sure he could, but there is one ecumenical issue on which Graham could indeed be helpful: the question of where the Pentecostals belong in the whole ecumenical family. Already numbering about 500 million, Pentecostals and charismatic Christians are the fastest growing segment of the Christian population. They constitute the largest non-Catholic group among the world's two billion Christians. I am entirely sure that Billy Graham, if he still had the strength, could help relationships between evangelicals, mainliners, and Pentecostals as perhaps no one else. Many evangelists and self-styled evangelical/fundamentalist leaders treat Pentecostals with a condescension bordering on contempt. This derision goes back to the beginning of the Pentecostal movement, when one fundamentalist referred to it as "the last vomit of Satan."[3] Jerry Falwell is reported to have said once that Pentecostals, with their speaking in tongues and excitability, are probably suffering from some undercooked fish they ate the previous evening.

This negative attitude is entirely missing from Billy Graham. William Martin, in his splendid biography of Graham, reports that once, during his 1955 campaign in Palamcottah, India, where 100,000 noisy and unruly people had gathered, Graham was stymied about what to do. But finally he simply prayed, "Oh God, stop the noise; quiet the people now." For whatever reason, a hush fell over the crowd. It became, Graham said, "the quietest, most reverent meeting we had in India. It was like the breath of God had fallen suddenly. You couldn't hear a sound." Then, Graham continued later, "Pentecost fell. People began to run forward and fall on their knees. Some of them began to scream to God for mercy; others were saying, 'Jesus, save me, Jesus, save me,' until about 3,000 to 4,000 people had come. . . . They were falling on their knees like flies. It was almost as if they were being slain by the Lord." Shortly after that meeting, Graham wrote, "Certainly tonight's demonstration of the Spirit is the deepest and greatest that I have ever sensed."[4]

This is obviously a sympathetic, and authentic, response to a situation Pentecostals would immediately recognize as a moment in which the preacher was, as they put it, "anointed." Billy Graham's ample vision of Christian witness reached out not only to the "ecumenicals" but also to the charismatics. It represents the kind of vision we desperately need in a Christian world still agonizing—after half a century of official ecumenism—with the painful laceration of distrust and disdain. Yes, Graham was an ecumenist, and he stood by his convictions despite the criticism.

BILLY GRAHAM AS PROPHET

Graham has said more than once that he is "a New Testament evangelist, not an Old Testament prophet."[5] But his career trajectory suggests something a little different. One of the most remarkable developments during the last fifteen years in American evangelicalism is its recovery of its earlier progressive political heritage. In this connection, it is important to remember that religiously conservative American Protestants have not always embraced the right-wing political agenda many do today. A hundred years ago when a series of pamphlets appeared called "The Fundamentals," those who supported them (and who therefore called themselves "Fundamentalists") were often populists and progressives in the political arena. After all, their nineteenth-century forebears had fought for abolition and women's rights. The "Fundamentals" were all about *religious* orthodoxy. They spelled out what their writers believed were the rock bottom beliefs threatened by liberal trends in theology. They insisted that such doctrines as the virgin birth, the verbal inerrancy of the Bible, the physical resurrection of Christ, and his imminent coming again must be staunchly defended if historical Christianity was not to be erased by what they called "modernism."

Still, the earlier impulse for societal reform did not die out completely. The best-known self-styled "Fundamentalist" of the early twentieth century was the three-time Democratic candidate for president, William Jennings Bryan. But Bryan's positions on public policy issues were similar in many ways to those of Reinhold Niebuhr a half century later. They were the complete opposite of those Pat Robertson, Jerry Falwell, and the current Christian Right contend for today. Bryan brought crowds to their feet with his stinging attacks on Wall Street and rich bankers, and he was so suspicious of militarism that he resigned from Woodrow Wilson's cabinet before World War I to protest what he saw as that president's belligerency toward Germany. Unfortunately, Bryan is remembered today mainly for his role in the Scopes "Monkey Trial" in 1925, the last year of his life. But even then, Bryan remained a progressive fundamentalist. The life and teaching of Jesus inspired his political career. He allowed that the seven days of creation mentioned in Genesis might refer to very long eons. He slyly ribbed the biblical literalists by remarking, "The Bible is about the rock of ages, not the age of rocks." His argument against the theory of evolution was not based on a literal reading of Genesis but on a moral one. He argued that the idea of "survival of the fittest" flatly contradicts the central core of Christian ethics and that it might lead to the belief that some races were more evolved than others. In this view he showed remarkable prescience. The Nazis loved evolutionary theory, which they twisted to undergird their ideology of the master race.

Some historians believe that after the ridicule poured on them during the Scopes trial, American fundamentalists retreated in humiliation and almost disappeared. They did not. During the 1930s and 1940s, Billy Graham's formative period, American fundamentalists did not disappear. They regrouped. They crafted a nationwide religious counterculture made up of thousands of independent churches, Bible institutes, summer camps, conference centers, radio ministries, and revival services. They founded their own colleges, such as Wheaton in Illinois, where Graham graduated in 1940. They advised their people to "come out and be separate." Since they were convinced that society at large was so obviously plunging toward judgment and destruction, they usually eschewed political involvement. Why patch up a ship that was doomed to sink anyway? The kind of prophetic reforms Bryan once advocated now seemed pointless to them. The best one could do was to snatch a few coals from the fire and save as many individual souls as possible.

The year Graham graduated from Wheaton also marked a major change in the American religious landscape, one in which he would play a formidable role. An influential group of Protestant religious conservatives under the leadership of the Reverend Harold Ockenga of Boston's Park Street Church formed the National Association of Evangelicals. Its purpose was to draw a sharp line not just against "modernists" but also against fundamentalists. These "new evangelicals" held some of the same religious beliefs as fundamentalists, but there were important differences. Evangelicals firmly held to the religious and moral authority of the Bible but did not consider it a dependable source for geology or history. The main point of contention with the fundamentalists, however, was that evangelicals did not want to abandon the larger society; they wanted to engage it. They longed for a rebirth of Protestant Christian influence in America, especially in what we now call "values." They went public, and the voice and face of that newly public evangelicalism was Billy Graham. If Bryan had been the most visible American purveyor of born-again Christianity in the 1920s, it was Graham who assumed that mantle in the 1950s and for the following decades.

Starting as a raw-boned fundamentalist, Graham matured and broadened and soon became much more than the icon of evangelicals. Polls showed him to be the most respected religious leader in the country. Still, as he shook off his early shell, his actions took a prophetic turn. He reaped scorn and abuse from his associates in the Christian Right by cooperating with "liberal" denominations in his many crusades. Even though he kept his distance from the civil rights movement, he insisted (after delaying the decisions for awhile) that his audiences, even in the South, should not be segregated. I myself sat with the congregation in the Harvard Memorial Church when he called for the abolition of *all* nuclear weapons, including those possessed by the United States. Despite himself, Billy Graham was something of a prophet.

The newly recovered "prophetic strand" within American evangelicalism is not uncontested. It must wrestle today with the Christan Right, whose leaders loudly proclaim their adherence to a "biblical worldview." But just how biblical is it? When a little-known Baptist preacher and self-styled fundamentalist named Jerry Falwell, with the help of conservative Republican campaign specialists, organized what he called "the Moral Majority" in the late 1970s, the core religious principles of Bryan were nowhere in sight. Rather, the movement trumpeted what Falwell and others called "traditional American values." Calling also for a curious kind of right-wing ecumenism, Falwell welcomed Catholics, Jews, and Mormons who shared his political and moral convictions into the fold. One heard little about the virgin birth, or even the inerrancy of Scripture, and almost nothing at all about Jesus or his Hebrew prophetic predecessors. Falwell's agenda was evoked by what he and his followers saw as an assault on the traditional values of American society. Some of the voices in this new and politically charged "moral fundamentalism" took the battle to the streets and, like Randall Terry, founder of Operation Rescue, were arrested for blocking abortion clinics. Now the enemy was no longer theological modernism but a series of court decisions that took prayer and Bible reading out of the schools, legalized abortion, and reached a malicious climax by supporting the rights of gay and lesbian people. It is to Billy Graham's eternal credit that he never became a part of the Christian Right and never lent his support to its agenda.

By the 1990s, Falwell's Moral Majority had faded, but it was succeeded by Pat Robertson's Christian Coalition and James Dobson's Focus on the Family. Both have explicitly political agendas, but the Hebrew prophets are nowhere in sight. However, one peculiar type of "prophecy" has continued. It is the idea of the imminent second coming of Christ, fictionalized for popular consumption by the *Left Behind* series of novels, which focus on the cataclysmic disaster we are heading for in the Middle East, a blood-soaked catastrophe that will usher in the Last Judgment. The immense popularity of these novels (they have sold some sixty million copies) stems both from a residual apocalyptic sentiment that still lingers in the American religious psyche, and from the foreboding quality of the present bewildering age. Again, it is to Graham's credit that, although his views of the second coming are undoubtedly premillenarian, he has not deployed his eschatological convictions for political purposes.

For a while the alliance Falwell forged with the most conservative wing of the Republican Party paid off, but only temporarily, for both partners. The Christian Right mobilized perhaps millions of voters for Republican candidates. In turn, Republican officeholders rewarded them with access to the highest level of the administration, including the Oval Office. But the alliance is now fraying. Republicans have not achieved the results the Christian Right expected, and may never have intended to. *Roe v. Wade* still stands. There is little chance that mandatory prayers and Bible reading will return to public schools. There is not yet, and probably will not be, a constitutional amendment banning gay marriage. Meanwhile, intemperate statements by Falwell (who attributed 9/11 to God's judgment on America for its gays and feminists) and Pat Robertson (who publicly called for the assassination of the president of Venezuela) have driven more moderate evangelicals away from the Christian Right.

How will the prophetic and progressive strands of evangelicalism fare in the years ahead? One area to watch closely in this regard is the startling emergence of the megachurches. These congregations of fifteen to twenty thousand, reminiscent of the huge crowds Graham used to draw to his crusades, are sprouting up all over the country. They are most often evangelical in style but not in substance. Their preachers generally avoid both controversial doctrinal questions and divisive political issues, but nonetheless a genuinely biblical prophetic voice seems to be arising. For example, Rick Warren, pastor of the mammoth Saddleback Church in California, recently supported a public statement against torture and has also pulled together a coalition of evangelicals to join the fight to save the environment. They call it "caring for Creation" and have urged their members to be faithful stewards of the world God has commanded us to nurture.[6] Falwell and Robertson have harshly denounced them, but they have attracted thousands of young people. They signal the rise of a new generation of evangelical leaders, one for which Billy Graham—despite his wavering on some critical issues during his long career—surely prepared the way. The future seems to be on their side. The Falwells, Robertsons, and Dobsons who once claimed to speak for American evangelicalism can no longer do so with any confidence that they will be heard.

Maybe the progressive impulse of early twentieth-century evangelicalism is making a comeback, being "born again." If so, Billy Graham must be given some credit for it. Admittedly, he was often tardy and sometimes just plain wrong in the positions he took. But he pioneered some of the social thinking of the new progressive evangelicals when it was very hard to do so. A "New Testament evangelist," Graham most certainly was, but he was also something of an "Old Testament prophet," sometimes despite himself.

BILLY GRAHAM AS PEACEMAKER

I now also find it symbolic that the event at which I met Graham for the first time took place at the lawn party of an ambassador who was a lifelong advocate of peaceful solutions, who advised Kennedy not to go into Vietnam, and who, on his deathbed in 2005, called for an end to the war in Iraq. When Galbraith died in 2005, his biographer Richard Parker writes, the casket in which he was buried carried a sticker that read "extra large." The sticker, of course, was removed before the funeral, but it was accurate in many ways. Like Billy Graham, Galbraith was more than life-size. They both loomed large on the twentieth-century landscape.

Graham eventually became an eloquent advocate of peace. His most fiercely held conviction was that nuclear weapons were inherently sinful (a conviction also brilliantly expressed in the American Roman Catholic bishops' pastoral, "Peace on Earth"). One of Graham's boldest forays into a kind of person-to-person peaceful diplomacy was his highly controversial trip to Russia during the height of the Cold War. It had become widely known weeks before he was scheduled to leave that the State Department did not want him to go. They were afraid, some people surmised, that it might "send the wrong signal." But Graham was determined. For good measure he also preached in East Germany, where he met the Communist leader Erich Honecker and told him he prayed for both sides to end the East-West confrontation and to rid themselves of nuclear weapons. When he preached in Northern Ireland, he urged reconciliation between Catholics and Protestants, which infuriated Ian Paisley so much that the radical Unionist preached a countersermon in another church while Graham was speaking. Never one to mince words, Paisley declared that "the church that has Billy Graham in the pulpit will have the curse of the Almighty upon it." Always the Christian and also a diplomat, Graham generously offered to meet Paisley for a conversation, but Paisley refused. He did not, he growled, "fellowship with those who deny the faith."[7] But Graham was not discouraged. During his long lifetime he has journeyed to count-less countries. From Brazil to Korea, from Nigeria to Hungary, from the USSR to Nagaland, and to dozens of other places he flew, preaching, meeting people, becoming for many the embodiment of the Christian gospel, and—almost inevitably—of peace.

Ecumenist, prophet, peacemaker—Billy Graham is all three. Yes, he was a "late bloomer" in some of these areas. His record is far from perfect, but then, whose is? Given the background and the era from which he came, his matu-ration over the years is nothing short of remarkable. And if we now see the return in America of an ecumenical, prophetic, and peacemaking evangelical-ism, he must certainly be counted among its progenitors.

NOTES

1. Quoted in William Martin, *A Prophet with Honor: The Billy Graham Story* (New York: William Morrow, 1991), 314.
2. Quoted in ibid., 312.
3. Quoted in Robert M. Anderson, *Vision of the Disinherited: The Making of an American Pentecostalism* (New York: Oxford University Press, 1979), 142.
4. Quoted in Martin, *Prophet with Honor*, 195.
5. See Marshall Frady, *Billy Graham: A Parable of American Righteousness* (New York: Little, Brown, 1979), 429.
6. See "Rick Warren on Evangelical Climate Initiative," http://www.pastors .com/article.asp?ArtID=9587.
7. Quoted in Martin, *Prophet with Honor*, 402.